ALEXANDER SKUTCH: AN APPRECIATION

EDITED BY HUNTER LEWIS
FOREWORD BY DANA GARDNER
WITH AN INTRODUCTION BY FRANK GRAHAM, JR.

Axios Press

Axios Press
P.O. Box 118
Mount Jackson, VA 22842
888.542.9467   press@axiosinstitute.org

Library of Congress Catalog Control Number: 2004091036

ISBN: 0-9661908-7-4

Acknowledgments

Our thanks to Ramón Mena Moya, Dana Gardner, Frank Graham, Jr., *Audubon* Magazine, the Tropical Sciences Center in Costa Rica, and the original publishers of Alexander Skutch's books: Aberdeen University Press, Nuttal Ornithological Club, University of California Press, University of Iowa Press, University of Oklahoma Press, University of Texas Press, and University Press of Florida.

CONTENTS

Ornithologist ·◆·

Philosopher ·◆·

FOREWORD

BY DANA GARDNER

For the past 28 years I have made yearly pilgrimages to Alexander Skutch's farm, Los Cusingos, to visit and do some painting in the peace and quiet of his little patch of tropical forest. This year I planned my trip to coincide with his 100th birthday. A couple of weeks before the event, however, I went down to stay with him for a few days. I am very, very glad that I did, as he passed away eight days short of his birthday. Because it was unseasonably rainy, I set up my painting table in the end *sala* where Skutch would sit and read each morning, and we kept each other company. Although Alexander had been deteriorating physically for the last couple of years, was confined to a wheel chair, and had become hard of hearing, he remained mentally alert and in very high spirits. Last year when I arrived for a visit I found him reading a book on planetary physics. This year he was rereading many of his own books that he had written years earlier. He told me he was refreshing his memory. He still received occasional visitors, and graciously welcomed them, apologizing for not being able to rise to greet them. He wished them a pleasant walk in his forest, something he had been unable to do for several years, but he enjoyed hearing about what birds they saw.

Only on the penultimate day of my stay did a nagging cough rapidly escalate to the point where he could barely talk and his breathing became erratic and labored. I sat with him that night and held his hand; I was sure he was about to die. He half opened his eyes, saw me, and struggled to tell me something. I thought I was to hear the last words of this wise old naturalist, and they turned out to be a request to have a dentist appointment made for him the next week! His tired old decrepit body was sending him a message, but he was having none of that—he was making plans for the future. I realized then that he wouldn't die quite yet. The next day was my planned departure day. He had quit coughing and had slept well, had eaten breakfast, and was once again reading. It was a gorgeous sunny morning, the first sunny morning in more than a week of overcast weather. A beautiful Turquoise Cotinga came out to sun itself in a bare tree at the edge of the yard. I left Los Cusingos in the early afternoon and planned to return for his 100th birthday party the next week, but I found out later that Alexander's health quickly deteriorated in the afternoon, and he died peacefully early that evening.

He was buried at Los Cusingos, as he wished, a few feet from the worn out, but still beautiful, old house that he built by hand some 62 years ago. Nearly 100 people showed up for the interment, including neighbors of many years, birdwatchers young and old, and a group of school children in their uniforms.

I have many fond memories of my visits with Alexander and Pamela Skutch over the years, and my best paintings were made in the tranquility of Los Cusingos. A very keen observer of the natural world, Skutch wrote 30 some books on general natural history and travel, the habits of birds, and religion and philosophy. His detailed life histories of over 300 species of tropical birds are great contributions to neotropical ornithology. He was nevertheless a very modest and humble man, and he had perhaps the simplest personal philosophy of anyone I've ever met: don't do anything that hurts other feeling creatures, and live simply and modestly so as not to tax the environment and its resources. He lived by these principles every day of his long life.

I will miss him, as will the many people who enjoyed visiting Los Cusingos and continue to enjoy reading his many books. I may still go and visit Los Cusingos, however, as it is now a sanctuary for neotropical birds run by the Tropical Science Center. Visits by tourists, birdwatchers, and researchers are encouraged. The yard and pasture by the river will be turned into a botanical garden, and Skutch's old house will be restored and turned into a museum.

INTRODUCTION

BY FRANK GRAHAM, JR.
(*AUDUBON* MAGAZINE, MARCH 1979)

Alexander Skutch lifted his machete and struck at the vines hanging like cordage across the path, and we stepped into the rain forest that covers most of his land on the slopes above the valley of El General in southern Costa Rica. We walked in single file along the path, between trees whose variety is unmatched anywhere outside the tropics. Skutch pointed to each, gave it a name, and mentioned some peculiarity that distinguished it from its look-alikes all around us. He picked out each birdcall uttered behind the congestion of leaves and identified the species. It was apparent that he lives on the same terms of easy familiarity with the plants and animals in this dim world as Henry Thoreau enjoyed in the woods around Walden Pond.

"Skutch is absolutely unique in ornithology today," Eugene Eisenmann of the American Museum of Natural History had told me before I left New York. "He's a throwback—or perhaps a logical continuation of the pioneer naturalists. He knows more about the natural history and general biology of tropical American birds than anyone else."

[Famed ornithologist and artist] Roger Tory Peterson speaks of Skutch as having done for Central American birds what Audubon did for those in North America, seeking them out and describing them to the world vividly and accurately, although in prose, rather than in paint. And Robert Ricklefs of the University of Pennsylvania writes:

> I think it is fair to say that were it not for Skutch's work and its influence on younger ornithologists, we would know next to nothing about the reproductive behavior of the tropical New World birds. Indeed, Skutch has left little of the privacy of his subjects uninvaded.

Alec Skutch's formidable reputation as a compiler of avian life histories obscures the variety of his adventures, interests, and skills.... [T]his Maryland expatriate has lived in the tropics for [most of his life], arriving there as a professional botanist and earning his living for six years by collecting plants for sale to museums. Settling down in Costa Rica, of which he is now a citizen, he has farmed,... survived falls from horses and trees, encounters with tropical snakes and diseases, and the inevitable Latin American revolution. Yet whatever the realities of danger, discomfort, or earning a living, he has relentlessly pursued his objective of uncovering the hitherto unknown habits of tropical birds.

It may be that Skutch's most ambitious, and ultimately his grandest, undertaking is the attempt to invest his lifelong experience in the natural world with spiritual significance. He has read widely in philosophy and the history of religions. As a conservationist in the most profound sense, he has looked tirelessly for a meaning behind human existence and the ties, physical and emotional, that bind us so closely to other forms of life. In dozens of articles and [numerous] books, . . . he has explored the evolutionary experience. Although dogma repels him, he ventures the conclusion that human life is not purposeless, that the moments of intense pleasure we experience in our encounters with nature may be the justification of the inconceivably long process that created a glorious natural world and put us in its midst, and that we are the organs through which the universe appreciates and tries to understand itself.

"Doubtless all animals enjoy their existence; certainly we should wish it so," Skutch wrote after returning from a "precious moment" among the wealth of living things in the rain forest. "But perhaps only to humans, on this planet, is it given to enjoy with gratitude and understanding the sources of our delight. The two poles between which the universe evolves appear to be the immensity of space and the plasticity of matter, on the one hand, and appreciative, grateful minds on the other. Perhaps the latter, whatever the form of the body that supports them, are the goal or fulfillment of the whole stupendous process, with all the strife and pain that seem inseparable from the movement that gives birth to beauty and joy. The conviction has grown upon me that this is the most fruitful interpretation of our presence here."

It is not an outlook likely to find favor with either Darwinians or egalitarians. Purists in evolutionary theory contend that natural selection has no purpose and does not necessarily lead to "higher" organisms. The process is its own justification. And, for the democratically minded, Skutch's belief that only a handful of human beings "are at any time so situated, and so endowed by nature, that they can respond to the beauty and wonder of the cosmos with the keen appreciation that it merits," must smack of elitism. But as we shall see, his attachment both to natural beauty and the extraordinary moments when the mind and senses savor it is so intense that he rebels at the prospect that they are wholly ephemeral.

What caught and held the young botanist above everything else when he went to the tropics was the splendor of its birds. For him, scientific doctrine led inevitably to esthetics: Evolution, over vast stretches of time, fashioned not only those winged creatures in their nearly infinite diversity and beauty but also the human mind which is capable in varying degrees of appreciating them.

"For a large and growing number of people, birds are the strongest bond with the living world of nature," Skutch has written. "They charm us with lovely plumage and melodious songs; our quest of them takes us to the fairest places; to find them and uncover some of their well-guarded secrets we exert ourselves greatly and live intensely. In the measure that we appreciate and understand them and are grateful for our coexistence with them, we help to bring to fruition the age long travail that made them and us. This, I am convinced, is the highest significance of our relationship with birds."

This was the man, and the natural setting, I had come thousands of miles to see. For a birdwatcher, the rain forests of Latin America and the West Indies are as El

Dorado to a sixteenth-century conquistador. The region as a whole supports a third of this planet's 8,600 species of birds, and Costa Rica alone, which is about the size of Vermont and New Hampshire combined, has 760 kinds, more than the total of all those that regularly visit or make their homes in our forty-eight contiguous states.

While nature-lovers travel around the world to see the large mammals and birds they have known from picture-books since childhood, equally as intense for me is the lure of the smaller Central American birds because of the names by which English-speaking naturalists know them. Simply to list a few of those names is to compose an elegant lyric: The White-whiskered Softwing, Blue-crowned Chlorophonia, Scarlet-thighed Dacnis (a honeycreeper), Masked Tityra, Violaceous Trogon, Three-wattled Bellbird, Scaly-throated Leaftosser, Blue-diademed Motmot, Fiery-billed Araçari, Chestnut-mandibled Toucan, Cinnamon-bellied Flower-piercer, Rose-breasted Thrush-tanager (of uncertain family), Olivaceous Piculet, Bellicose Elaenia, Tawny-winged Dendrocincla (a woodcreeper), Buff-throated Foliage-gleaner, Plain Xenops (poor thing), Slaty Castlebuilder — and my special favorite, the Oleaginous Pipromorpha. Although this last is described as "a small, olive green bird of undistinguished appearance," only a soul of lumpish tendencies would prefer its alternate name, the Ochre-bellied Flycatcher.

And now, with my incomparable guide, I was among those birds and the plants on which they live. I know I shall not experience many more such moments as those of my first walk in a tropical forest. My pleasure was doubled by the awareness that Alec Skutch shared it, that he approached the forest with the awe and enthusiasm he must have felt on his own first encounter with it.

"The Rufous Piha," he said, stopping abruptly and indicating with a nod the direction from which a piercing whistle had come. "A kind of cotinga. It's the only fairly large forest bird that has survived here in fair numbers. The local people shoot at any large target, and most of the big toucans, parrots, jacamars, falcons, woodpeckers, sunbitterns, and the like are gone."

Skutch remained motionless on the path, probing the foliage through his binoculars. "There it is," he said at last, and I followed his upward-pointing finger and picked out the piha, a ruddy-brown bird about the size of an American Robin. Skutch waited until I had had a satisfactory look and then moved on.

As he led the way into the forest, he occasionally ran his eyes over a brushy tangle before stepping through it, alert for poisonous snakes, but for the most part he searched the trees for the small birds in which the land abounds. Skutch is of medium height, slender, with a strong step.... He frequently drew the machete that was strapped to his waist and wielded it efficiently against vines and branches in our path.

"People sometimes speak of the 'jungle' in Central America," he said at one point. "But that was really a creation of William Beebe's imagination when he wrote about this part of the world. The true jungle is in Asia. This is a *forest*, where the undergrowth is not normally dense unless it has been cut over and new growth is sprouting. The tangles here are usually made up of vines and fallen trees."

Some of the vines were truly formidable, the largest of which was a woody liana called *Entada gigas*. We came across one specimen nearly fifteen inches in diameter. In its prime the liana had moved in heavy loops from one tall tree to another, smothering foliage with its twice-pinnate leaves and breaking trunks down under its enormous weight, so that now it undulated like some moss-covered serpent for hundreds of feet over the forest floor, into which its victims had long since decayed.

Trying to trace the convolutions of this enormous plant as it wandered off into the gloom, I was reminded that around me there was taking place a deadly struggle in slow motion, where plants of all kinds clambered over and strangled one another as they reached for the sun and survival. While the failures in this frozen tableau, this static violence that is the essence of the rain forest, crumbled into the leaf-litter, the winners pushed upward where their crowns fit together in places, as Skutch said, "like the tiles in a mosaic." Here and there pieces of the mosaic were missing, and columns of light broke through to be fractured by vines and foliage as they plunged to the forest floor.

In one of those miniature sunlit clearings a Morpho Butterfly, dipping and darting from the shadows on its big azure wings, surprised us into a cry of delight. As if in answer to our indiscretion in this quiet place, a small flock of Whitecrowned Parrots flew raucously overhead. (There is a band of White-faced or Capuchin Monkeys in the canopy of this forest too, but incessant shooting has made its survivors wary, and I never saw them.) My life list of birds expanded quickly as Skutch detected various chirps and trills and pointed out their sources—a

White-winged Becard, a Tawny-crowned Greenlet, a Black-hooded Antshrike, and a Dot-winged Antwren.

"That's one of the birds that ought to be named for the female," Skutch said of the antwren. "There are no dots on her wings, but she has a lovely buffy breast."

I was surprised to find the heat in the rain forest was not oppressive. Although it was July, the temperature was in the low eighties, probably cooler than it was that day in the inland forests of Maine where I live, for Skutch's land lies at an elevation of 2,500 feet. The rainy season was just getting under way in earnest in Costa Rica, and there were few birds' nests or blossoms to be seen.

But there was a discovery with almost every step we took. I stooped to examine a morpho still clinging to a creamy chrysalis that was pendant from a leaf, the wings showing a row of blue-rimmed eyespots on the underside as the butterfly held them up to dry. As if to match my discovery with one of his own, Skutch turned over a drooping palm leaf and displayed the tiny abandoned nest of a little Hermit Hummingbird, cemented there by strands of cobweb.

While the different species of trees along the path were too numerous to count, the sameness of their individual leaves in outline was bewildering, with few of the distinctive indentations and lobes found on our oaks, maples, sycamores, and other trees in the temperate zone. Even professional botanists depend chiefly on the flowers, fruits, and bark to make positive identifications in the tropics.

A prominent exception was the cecropia tree, whose palmate leaves, often a foot or two in diameter, reminded me of the horse chestnuts. The Three-toed Sloth and various monkeys eat those leaves, Skutch said, while many kinds of birds eat the green fingerlike, fruiting spikes. Of even greater interest, as he stopped to show me, are the cecropia's protein bodies—tiny white "pinheads" that cover the swollen velvety bases of the leaf stalks. Nearly every cecropia in this forest is host to colonies of Azteca ants that live inside its branches, which are hollowed out by the breakdown of the central pith, and feed on the protein grains. Some biologists believe the ants "pay" for their food and shelter by driving foliage-eating insects and browsing mammals from the tree, though Skutch is skeptical.

"The bites of these ants aren't venomous or very painful, so they don't seem to have any effect on monkeys, sloths, or other mammals," he said. "In fact, some birds, like the Vermilion-crowned Flycatcher, build their nests in the cecropia. Lineated Woodpeckers, big birds with scarlet crests, come to the tree to eat the ants. And if there isn't a large colony of ants to consume the protein bodies, I'll often see migrant wood warblers coming to feed on them—Wilson's, Tennessee, Chestnut-sided, and even Mourning Warblers that winter here. That's why I call the cecropia the most hospitable tree in tropical America."

Another distinctive tree in the forest was the chonta palm. It stood above the forest floor on prop roots, looking for all the world like a displaced red mangrove, except that its roots were studded with short spikes that inflict a painful wound on the unwary. In some places, only the prop roots remained.

"Trespassers come in here and cut the entire trunks down just to remove the 'heart of palm,' which is eaten at holidays," Skutch says. "In fact, these people have almost wiped out another species on my property, an elegant tree called the palmito, which they chop down for the same reason. There's nothing I can do to stop them."

But so great was the variety in the forest that one's spirits were renewed simply by looking off in a new direction. We turned our binoculars upward to where half a dozen brown Violet-ear Hummingbirds were feeding at the bright red, berrylike flowers of a symphonic tree. A little farther on we came to a grove of banana trees, cultivated deep in the forest to foil thieves who would otherwise carry off the entire crop. The lush plants rose on stout stems, while the translucent leaves, long and rippled, flowed outward from it in graceful curves. And just beyond the little plantation, Skutch pointed out to me a Black-throated Trogon, perched in marvelous equanimity before us on a bare limb in the shadows—my first look at a member of that family whose most illustrious member is the Quetzal.

Finally we came to the Peña Blanca, a river that has its source in the cordillera high above and rushes through the forest on its way to the valley.

"Its name means 'white cliff,'" Skutch said as we stood on a spray-dampened rock along the bank. He speaks softly, shyly, as a man who has spent a great deal of time alone, and now it was difficult to hear him over the water's roar. "For a while I thought there might be some cliffs or big rocks somewhere up above here. But I've come to the conclusion that it is just a pretty figure of speech, referring to the walls of white water thrown up when the river boils over the rocks in the rainy season."

The flow was already lively this early in the season, and I could see why it was an eternal presence to Skutch, the turbulent sound of it carrying easily up to the house through the trees a hundred yards away and sometimes prompting him to hum cheerfully in response. In places, crowns of the trees along the banks met to form arches over the torrent.

By far the most imposing of the trees on the river's edge was the sotacaballo, its enormous gnarled trunk leaning over the water like some sacred olive tree over a classical stream. Bromeliads, whose tight rosettes of leaves, in Skutch's words, "hold little aerial pools of water supporting an aquatic flora and fauna all their own," covered the sotacaballo's rough bark. So did ferns, orchids, aroids, and other epiphytes, suggesting that this tree was as "hospitable" to botanical specimens as the cecropia to animal life.

Many of the wet rocks displayed clumps of curious plants called riverweeds. One kind with its flattened leaves resembled an alga and the other a liverwort, though both bear flowers after the rainy season. They had no roots, their branches springing from fleshy cushions that clung to the rocks like the holdfasts of seaweeds. Skutch told me that when the river falls, the tiny drying seedpods often deceive botanists into believing they are the spore capsules of mosses. Eventually the pods break open, dispersing the seeds, some of which attach themselves to nearby stones where they germinate.

Although birds were few along the river at this season, we saw a Golden-naped Woodpecker and a Buff-rumped Warbler in the overhanging trees. During the winter and spring such avian tourists as the Spotted Sandpiper and Northern and Louisiana Waterthrushes patrol the Blanca; Torrent Flycatchers, tiny black-and-white birds that seem to relish the crashing spray, pluck insects from the wet rocks; and Riverside Wrens, rich chestnut above and narrowly barred with black and white below, build their globular nests on boughs over the water. Of the last, Skutch has written:

> Birds which frequent rushing mountain streams, and must make themselves heard above the incessant babble of the water, often have loud, ringing voices, sharper and more forceful than the notes of related species that dwell in more silent places. Often the clear, full notes of the Riverside Wrens carry up to the house above the roar of the river; *mil veces, mil veces* they sing, or *victory, victory*. Like many of the constantly mated tropical wrens, the male and female sing responsively.

Three kingfishers—the Green, the Ringed, and the Amazon—sometimes fly along the river and high overhead, though now there are few fish of substantial size to be found there. The same rascals who vandalize the nearby palms resort to the favorite (but destructive and illegal) local technique of fishing by dropping a bomb in the water. The fish and whatever else lives in the stream turn belly-up and float to the surface. All one needs to build a bomb for the purpose is chlorate and a roll of fuse, both of which are stocked in many country stores.

Skutch remarked in his book *A Naturalist in Costa Rica* that despite its beauty, tranquility, and endless variety, the forest after a time becomes oppressive. More than 90 percent of the lofty rain forest stands high above us, dwarfing us, reducing us to a salutary but unflattering submission:

> Scarcely anyone, no matter how much he or she loves the forest, chooses to dwell in its unbroken depth," he wrote. "We prefer to live in a clearing with a wide view and the forest nearby, where we can really see it and enter it whenever we will. For it is true that in the midst of the forest we cannot see it for the trees. Only when we stand before its edge, as on the shore of a river or in a fresh cutting, can we survey the full majesty of its towering height; only when from an eminence we look over miles and miles of billowy treetops do we begin vaguely to grasp the vastness of its sweep. To know the forest, we must study it in all aspects, as birds soaring above its roof, as earth-bound bipeds creeping slowly over its roots.

After leaving the river and walking up a steep hill, we found just such a freeing and comprehensive view at last, from the porch that runs along the front of the one-story house of wood and clay where Alec Skutch lives with his British-born wife, Pamela. We were just in time. The mornings usually are clear in the valley during July, but by noon the rain clouds begin to pile up against the massive Cordillera de Talamanca to the north and east. As we sat there, the house and lawn still in hazy sunlight, a huge rounded dome toward which we looked in the distance became veiled in a glistening mesh of rain. The downpour would soon be upon us.

Closer to us, trees of all kinds were massed in billows of foliage, many of them on the 250 acres that Skutch owns and protects. His is one of the few tracts of rain forest remaining on the valley's lower slopes, the rest having been cut and burned and the land converted to the myriad small farms where their owners raise bananas, sugar cane, corn, coffee, and other crops. Skutch's own cultivated plots of corn and bananas are tucked away in pockets of the forest, though a shortage of labor in recent years has forced him to restrict his crops to his own needs.

He calls his farm "Los Cusingos," a name with which he has never been terribly comfortable. He has recalled its origin:

> I should have preferred to call it for the jacamar, that brisk, dainty, glittering, gemlike bird that adorned my woodland and had long been a favorite with me. But this notable bird, like most of our feathered creatures, was nameless here, and none of my neighbors would pronounce the word 'jacamar' as I do. So I called the farm 'Los Cusingos,' after the Fiery-billed Araçari, a small, slender toucan, whose great, red bill makes it too conspicuous to be overlooked by even the most unobservant peasant.... It is perhaps fitting that a birdwatcher's farm be named for them. But they are shameless brigands who in the nesting season invade the shade trees around the house and pluck from the nests all the eggs and young birds they can find.

This paragraph expresses the twin themes that rule Alec Skutch's view of the natural world. His admiration for the beauty of living things has its counterpoint in pained bewilderment when confronted by one of nature's primary facts—predation. Unlike many lovers of wild nature, he does not thrill to the lion's savage charge or the falcon's swoop, because at its culmination there is only the bloody and mangled remains of a prey whose life he considers of equal value to that of the predator. Predation, as we shall see when we explore Skutch's philosophy, is, with its ugly twin, parasitism, "life's greatest evil" and the begetter of most of its others.

Meanwhile, as the early afternoon rains began to fall on Los Cusingos, the lawn and lush plantings seemed to represent the antithesis of the forest's strife. Native and exotic plants mingled in the harmony Skutch finds at the root of all beauty. A local bromeliad, long red petals crowned with a blaze of yellow, grew beneath lavender orchids that were the gift of Pamela Skutch's father, a noted collector. An African oil palm towered over the outbuildings. In the dim recesses of an old shade tree, a Scaly-breasted Hummingbird threw back its head and, with a furious pumping of its mandibles, put forth a boisterous song startling in a creature of its size. Several agoutis, long legged, dark-furred rodents as big as a hare, wandered with the domestic chickens among the shrubs.

But as we sat on the porch the center of Los Cusingos became for me the birds' feeding table, raised on a rough pole, on which Skutch leaves sliced oranges, bananas, and other fruit. Within a few minutes it seemed half of the tropics' tanagers revealed themselves, coming to the table to peck at the fruit. One by one, the Silver-throated, the Speckled, the Bluegray and the Bay-headed Tanagers appeared.

The most spectacular was the Scarlet-rumped Black Tanager, whose name supplies a rough description but leaves one unprepared for the brilliance and extent of that burst of scarlet. The female, which I thought at first to be still another species, was a beauty in her own right, sleekly elegant in brown, orange, and olive. Skutch has written at length on this species, which is among the most abundant nesters in his yard:

> The males have a pleasant although not brilliant song. Indeed, they produce more music than any other passerine bird in the neighborhood, with the possible exception of Gray's Thrush. This is the more surprising when one recalls that the multitudinous species of tanagers in tropical America are more renowned for their amazingly varied plumage than for their musical ability, and that this is a nonterritorial species. Hence I call it familiarly the "song tanager."

In winter a number of migrant birds from North America visit the feeding table. Among them are the Summer Tanager, the Northern Oriole, and the Tennessee Warbler, sometimes eight or nine of the last species crowding onto the board at a time.

Pamela Skutch, a slight, dark-haired woman some years younger than her husband, came onto the porch to call us for lunch. We followed her to the dining room at one end of the house, where the food, simple but plentiful, was already on the table. Shutters were flung wide, letting in the sound of the rain, which had increased in force. Alec Skutch will abide neither windowpanes nor screens on his house, preferring to let the wild creatures come and go as they will, though the shutters are closed at night, and as a result birds are not lured to their death by the illusory flight path promised by clear glass and insects are not trapped inside rooms.

"We often hear about how bad the insects are in the tropics, but they give us little trouble here," he said as he took his seat, and then he smiled slyly. "In fact, I've traveled all over the tropics, but the most vicious insects I've ever seen were the mosquitoes and black flies in Maine, where I spent three summers many years ago."

Our lunch, aside from canned herring, was prepared from local products—egg salad, manioc (very much like a potato, though with a stronger taste), rice, tortillas, fresh pineapple, and coffee. Alec Skutch, a vegetarian, passed up the fish, but he had no qualms about the eggs.

"The hens could not live here without the food and protection I give them, and so it's a fair exchange," he explained. "I do them no harm. Anyone who is squeamish about eating eggs only has to keep the roosters away from the hens so the eggs aren't fertilized."

His vegetarianism had provided the only serious stumbling block to his marriage. Skutch had been a friend of Pamela's father, C. H. Lankester, an Englishman who owned a large coffee plantation south of San José and was a well-known naturalist, specializing in orchids and butterflies.

"My father was skeptical about our marriage at first," Pamela recalled. "He thought Los Cusingos was too remote for a young woman. It was awfully isolated here...and the only way to get around was by horseback. But like so many Englishwomen, I was a skillful rider, and I liked the country. My father was very good about it all. He said, 'Why don't you go down there with your brother and stay a few days, then decide?'

"Well, I loved it. The only thing that bothered me was the vegetarian business, because I knew how strongly Alec felt about it. But we had a long talk, and I agreed to give up meat, but not fish. That settled it. We've been very happy together here."

Pamela Lankester had chosen to throw in her lot with a complex and remarkable man, one whose life and achievements have few parallels in our time. He was born Alexander Frank Skutch in Baltimore in 1904. His father was in the clothing business, but when Alec was about six years old, the elder Skutch bought a farm outside the city, to which he moved with his family.

"From early childhood I was attracted to the milder sorts of animals, and my father helped me to acquire all kinds of furred and feathered pets," Skutch told me. "Everything from dogs to peacocks, including a flock of Indian Runner Ducklings."

Birds were not a passion for him in those days, though as a stamp collector he was delighted by one from Guatemala that pictured a Quetzal. In fact, a birding expedition he made one day with an older boy to watch migrating warblers proved to be something of a bust. Without binoculars, young Alec saw only a blur of fleeting forms and began to wonder what all the excitement was about.

More important to his development was the strong attachment he began to feel toward all animal life. A superficial contact with Skutch—his interest in Eastern religions, his vegetarianism, his dislike of drinking, smoking, and modern sexual mores—might prompt one to classify him as "ascetic" and let it go at that. But in an essay entitled "In Defence of the Flesh," he credited the body with being as influential as the mind in helping him chart his course through life. It was his body, he remembered, that revolted against a cigarette or a glass of whiskey even when it was offered to him at home. He also attributed his compassion at least in part to his body:

> To see living flesh, in humans or any other creature, cut or lacerated sends through my own flesh a shrinking feeling that is most unpleasant, as has been true since childhood. I do not know how it may be with others, but this is one of the reasons why I cannot avoidably hurt any living thing. Certainly mind, with its capacity for insight and sympathy, plays an important part in this spontaneous reaction, which must be attributed to the whole psychophysical entity rather than to the body alone: but the latter has no negligible share in it.

A rather solitary childhood, which "made me feel different from other boys," prepared him to take a courageous step when he was sixteen years old. He announced he had become a vegetarian. At that time and place, it was like cutting all ties with the familiar.

"I felt even more apart," he wrote to me not long ago, "for I was acquainted with no other vegetarian, and no one around me seemed to sympathize with my attitude, which doubtless I was clumsy in explaining. As I grew older, I was repelled by the harsh competitiveness of the society around me, its inordinate craving for luxury, and its callous indifference to the sufferings of animals. All these things made it easier to loosen social bonds and spend my days with birds and plants in solitary places."

This is an attitude I have encountered in a number of outstanding naturalists. In essence, it is not a retreat from "real things," but an approach to a more fundamental world where the seeker, as Skutch wrote elsewhere, "has the satisfying sense of being in contact with something far older, vaster, and more stable than humanity." It was only in later years that Skutch found this path inevitably led back to [people], for "nature is greater and more wonderful when we recognize that it includes [humanity], and [humanity] greater and more understandable when we recognize that [it] belongs to nature, than either could be without the other."

Meanwhile, Skutch went on to Johns Hopkins University, where his interest in animals led him into biology. Zoology at Johns Hopkins, he quickly learned, was chiefly a preparation for medical school, "with much dissection of cats and the like," and he fled into botany where the instructors emphasized field trips. As an undergraduate, he spent his summers at the Mount Desert Island Biological Laboratory in Maine, studying the ecology of algae and other plants on Otter Cliffs.

But Skutch's thoughts were already running to a different quarter of the globe. His readings in monographs devoted to tropical botany fascinated him. "To a young student of nature in the first exhilaration of study, no John Mandeville or Marco Polo had filled his pages with more wonder stories than were to be found in these records of sober scientific investigation," he wrote later. Of all the monographs he read, none affected him more powerfully than that of A. F. W. Schimper, the plant geographer, in which he described the delicate adjustments and readjustments in that extraordinary relationship between the cecropia tree and its colonies of Azteca ants.

After his first year of graduate work in botany, the department made one of its periodic visits to Jamaica, where Skutch experienced the tropics for the first time. He approached the rain forest in those early days, as he has ever since, with awe at its wonders and with gratitude to whatever unseen force had put him in their midst. When the other members of the party returned to Johns Hopkins, Sketch went to live for two months on a banana plantation, studying the banana leaf for the United Fruit Company to earn his passage on their steamship to and from Jamaica. His studies there led to his doctoral dissertation on the anatomy of the banana leaf.

In 1928, Skutch received a fellowship that enabled him to go back to the tropics, this time to the United Fruit Company's research station near Almirante in western Panama. One day, as he sat at his microscope poring over bits of banana tissue, his attention wandered to a hummingbird—which he later identified as the Rufous-tailed—that had built her nest just outside his window. Almost nothing was known at the time about the nesting habits of tropical American birds. Drawn to these tiny iridescent creatures, Skutch finally made up his mind to devote himself to unraveling the mysteries of their lives.

On the face of it, his ambition was quixotic. He had no money and no prospects of finding support in a discipline that was not his own. On his return to Johns Hopkins, where he taught briefly, he immersed himself in Robert Ridgway's classic descriptive catalogue, *The Birds of North and Middle America*, where for species after species he came across the remark: "Nidification unknown." It became Skutch's dream to discover the nests and describe the entire drama, from courtship until the nestlings' flight, of hundreds of tropical birds.

With his meager savings, Skutch paid his way back to Central America and lived for parts of two years in Guatemala. From the beginning he was clear in his own mind what his role was to be. It was that of a naturalist, which he has defined:

> If the naturalist makes systematic observations, keeps careful records, and tries to interpret them, he or she is certainly a scientist, yet profoundly different from other scientists, even from other biologists. Many a scientist is never happier than when he or she can bring into the laboratory whatever phenomenon is being investigated, isolate it, and study it under controlled conditions. It is a triumph to summarize observations in a neat graph or a mathematical formula. This kind of scientist lives in middle-class comfort like any other professional person. To the true naturalist, the concrete experience of living things in their natural setting is at least as precious as any generalization or 'law' that may be derived from observations. To gain this experience, one must be willing to endure discomforts and privations in far places.

That was the life Skutch had laid out for himself. There was a certain amount of money to be earned at the time by collecting exotic birds for museum[s] [to] study skins, but as "collecting" meant shooting, Skutch wanted no part of such a living. There was still another means of support for which, by inclination and training, he was eminently qualified. He arranged to collect and send botanical specimens to William R. Maxon at the Smithsonian Institution, who distributed them to museums around the world, with the proceeds going to Skutch.

For more than six years he earned his living in this manner, traveling through Central America to collect plants and, in the intervals, to make observations on the birds of each district he visited. Keeping body and soul together was the least of his concerns, for as a vegetarian most of his nutritional needs were easily satisfied in the lush countryside, while he was content to sleep in any wayside shack that was available.

But there were enormous problems of ornithological and botanical observation. Field guides to the birds of most regions were nonexistent. Years later, in his book *A Bird Watcher's Adventures in Tropical America*, Skutch described the laborious struggle to sort out the hundreds of birds, many in drab, nondescript plumage, that he detected in the dense foliage:

> My method was to write in my notebook the most detailed description that I could make of any bird new to me, at the same time recording all I learned about its habits and voice. I considered myself fortunate if I could somewhat adequately describe five or six [in a day], after watching each unfamiliar kind as long as I could keep it in view.

Months, or perhaps years, later he compared his notes with the skins, plates, and descriptions in large museums and eventually put together a marvelously detailed dossier on almost every bird in Central America. Meanwhile, there were equally imposing obstacles to his plant collecting. As we have seen, tropical trees display a confusing uniformity of foliage; a leaf from one species is almost identical to those of other species nearby. The flowers, however, which are diagnostic, usually grow high in the crowns, far beyond the botanist's reach.

There was no simple solution. When Skutch picked up a new flower or fruit from the forest floor, he could never be certain from which tree in the tightly packed stand it had fallen. Moreover, most rain forest trees, in their hasty growth toward the sun, sprout few branches for most of their length. Any protuberance that would be likely to help a climbing botanist would also provide a hold for the various vines and epiphytes that sap the vigor of a young tree. Sometimes Skutch hung about places where the forest was being cleared, and when a big tree went down he would scramble over the surrounding debris and try to salvage the flowers. More often than not, those big, fragile blossoms had become hopelessly mangled in the fall.

But there are other ways to skin a cat, or pluck a blossom. Skutch knew that in the East Indies, Dutch botanists had trained monkeys to climb trees and collect the flowers.

"I met an Indian in Guatemala who was better at it than any monkey," he told me. "Coffee trees usually need varying amounts of shade, you know, but too much shade causes a fungal infection of the leaves. Plantations often hire men to climb the shade trees and prune them—a rather dangerous occupation, with occasional casualties. But this Indian who worked for a plantation said, 'I can climb any tree.' I decided to test him—and he could, even a tree with no branches below a hundred feet. He'd fling a rope over a lower tree, climb it, fling the rope over the big one, and go right on up."

In a sense, Alexander Skutch's true immortality may lie in botany. Almost all of Central America's birds had already been classified before he arrived there, and his function has been to record their life histories. But as some of the plants he sent to museums were new to science, they now bear his name. The scientific name of the aguacatillo, or "little avocado," for instance, is *Persea skutchii*. He not only collected the first specimen, but later found that it utilizes a unique and highly complex system of cross-pollination.

Time, however, has eroded some of these promises of immortality. A small tree bearing inconspicuous green flowers that Skutch found growing near San Isidro was described by two museums specialists as belonging to a new genus and named by them *Skutchia caudata*. Later, a leading authority on Central American flora pointed out that it was not even a new species!

For several years Alec Skutch made his way around that sinuous, forested isthmus, a region made all the more fascinating to a naturalist because there the plants and animals of two great continents met and mingled. Like a latter-day Audubon, he traveled on foot and by horseback, probing the fringes of civilization for what they revealed to his curiosity and admiration. "In these tiny villages and on outlying farms," he wrote, "the naturalist not too squeamish or careful of his comforts could often find accommodations of sorts, while he observed or collected." Of some concern to Skutch, as it was to all travelers in the region's small republics, was the frequency of revolutions and the attendant hazards to one's scientific or business property, or even to life itself.

His extensive travels in Latin America suggested to Skutch that the most stable of the republics was Costa Rica. In the late fall of 1935, interested by what he had heard about the remote valley of El General in the southwestern part of the country, he decided to spend some time there, collecting its plants and studying its birds. There were no roads into the valley in those days. Mountains 12,000 feet high separated it from San José and other cities to the north, and most travelers in and out of the valley hiked over the formidable Cerro de la Muerte (Mountain of Death).

Fortunately, airline service of a sort had recently begun between San José and the valley, and Skutch invested in one of his first plane rides, arriving at San José with his few personal belongings and his plant collecting equipment. The valley had been settled only in recent decades. San Isidro was a frontier town, its main street a sea of mud, its houses shacks of rough unpainted boards. The village blacksmith doubled as watch repairman. Most of the settlers lived on small homesteads scattered throughout the valley and up its slopes.

He set up temporary lodgings in an old farmhouse, northeast of San Isidro, which was built of rough-hewn timbers and thatched with long sugar cane leaves, and in which a pair of southern house wrens made their home. The forest lay only yards away, and the constant cutting and clearing of the land in the neighborhood was not without some consolation: Though the commotion and destruction were painful to him, the flowers and fruits held in the crowns of the doomed giants sometimes survived the awful crash to the forest floor and provided Skutch with highly prized specimens. Moreover, the birdlife of the valley was a revelation. Skutch wrote:

> The isolation of this heavily forested region from similar forests by the Cordillera de Talamanca to the north, by the savannahs of central Panama to the east, and by drier woodland to the northwest, has favored the evolution of a number of endemic birds, including such colorful species as the Fiery-billed Araçari, the Golden-naped Woodpecker, the Orange-collared Manakin, the Turquoise Cotinga, and the Riverside Wren. The relative isolation of the valley seems also responsible for the absence of other birds that one expects in Central America: I have never seen a resident oriole or a jay in the valley.

Skutch was not ready to admit he had found a permanent home. He worked diligently, sending out 6,000 plant specimens during the eighteen months he shared his home with the house wrens. Once, mostly for the adventure, he shipped his specimens by air to San José, but followed them by the time-honored path up and over the mountains, setting out on horseback but continuing on foot when his perspicacious steed rebelled at the exhausting climb and had to be sent back in care of a traveler headed for the valley. At the summit, Skutch divined the origin of the Mountain of Death's name and reputation. There he spent a night shivering under his blankets and heavy clothes in a resthouse that was open to the damp, penetrating winds, while children in the scantiest dresses and shirts whimpered nearby in the dark.

When Skutch left the valley in 1937, he went to live for a while in the rainy highlands of northern Costa Rica, where he at last caught up with the Quetzal whose portrait on a postage stamp had so delighted him as a boy. The Quetzal is sometimes called "the most beautiful bird in the world." Worshiped by the ancient Aztecs and Mayas as the god of the air, and in modern times designated Guatemala's national bird (though it is more abundant in Costa Rica), its plumage is a brilliant bronzy green, with rich crimson and pure white below. Already the largest of the trogon family, fourteen inches from bill to tail, the male Quetzal adds another two feet to its length with the long green plumes of its upper tail coverts.

Like most other large and showy wild creatures, the Quetzal was hunted until it became extremely rare. As late as the 1930s, ornithologists were ignorant of some of the most important details of its life history.

"I was everywhere told that the [Quetzal] nests in a hole carved in a decaying trunk," Skutch wrote: "and provided with doorways on opposite sides, so that the male, when he takes his turn at warming the eggs, can pass in through one opening and out through the other, without turning around in the cavity and damaging his long train.... Most of my informants did not claim to have seen a Quetzal's nest, and the only scientific record known to me, published many years earlier by the English ornithologist Osbert Salvin, stated that the Quetzal nests in an old woodpecker's hole with a single doorway and inferred that the duller female, who lacks the long train, incubates alone."

Skutch already had discovered the nests of seven species of Central American trogons and made known the details of their life histories. He doubted much of what was then ornithological gospel concerning the grandest of the trogons. "Observations of my own on the Quetzal would not only settle these controversial points, but crown my series of studies of the noble family of birds to which it belongs," he wrote. In the Costa Rican highlands late one afternoon, he discovered a pair of Quetzals clinging to a rotten tree which had a single entrance hole more than fifty feet above the ground.

"Quietly approaching the rotten trunk a few mornings later," he wrote, "I noticed two slender, green plumes projecting, to a length of six or eight inches, from the upper edge of the doorway and waving with every passing breeze. They resembled fronds of epiphytic ferns that were so abundant in these mountain forests. The male Quetzal was sitting on the eggs, and the two longest feathers of his train, bending upward against the rear wall of the deep cavity and then forward above his head to pass through the doorway, proclaimed his presence to every discerning passerby. My predictions, based on studies of other members of the trogon family, were already confirmed: The nest had a single entrance, and the male took his turn at incubation."

Skutch followed the activities at this and several other Quetzal nests in the area, shining new light on this magnificent bird when he published the results of his observations in *The Condor*, the journal of the Cooper Ornithological Society. His survey included an unsuccessful attempt to peek at the young in one of the nests "from the very top of a twenty-three-foot ladder, while a visiting naturalist looked on and prophesied disaster." After the young had fledged, Skutch realized how close the prophecy had come to actuality. He and his assistants pulled over the trunk to look at the nest, and it fell at once into a "formless heap of rotten wood."

Skutch felt himself drawn back again and again to the valley of El General. He lived there for a time in 1939, though disaster finally caught up with him when a fall from a horse smashed his left shoulder and put him to bed for ten days. But soon he was in the forest again, watching nesting birds through binoculars that he steadied with his right hand alone.

He was living mostly out of a knapsack at the time, a bird of passage, always moving on. He had paid a visit to his family in Baltimore in 1938, then used up most of his savings on a trip to study the birds of Ecuador. Returning to Costa Rica, he accepted a post as chief of the botanical section at the National Museum, but the lure of the forest was too intense and soon he was "on leave" to collect plants in his beloved valley. In 1940 he made his leave permanent by accepting an offer from the U.S. government to serve as botanist on a survey of potential sources of rubber along the upper Amazon and its tributaries.

For five months Skutch's headquarters was a Peruvian gunboat, which by agreement between the two countries ferried the scientists from one river to another. The duties of a botanist often restricted his observations on birds, but his first encounter with Black-fronted Nunbirds on the Río Yavarí, an Amazon tributary, convinced him that this avian family "had unusual social habits that would well repay careful study." Some years later in northeastern Costa Rica he met another species of the family, the

White-fronted Nunbird (in "somber, nunlike attire") and had the opportunity to carry out those studies.

The Amazon survey gave Alec Skutch an unforgettable experience, but also (because the Peruvian navy's hospitality had saved him almost his entire expense allotment) a permanent home. He now had enough money to buy a farm on the slopes above San Isidro. A friend put him in touch with an elderly landowner who wanted to sell 130 acres of forest.

He eventually struck a bargain with the owner, buying the land for 5,000 colones. At the time there were about six colones to a U.S. dollar. With pride and satisfaction, Skutch became the possessor of a small section of rain forest, to which he has since added 120 acres, and its complexity of living things. [With] these he determined to live in a harmonious relationship:

> I yearned intensely to dwell at peace with all creatures, destroying no living thing. I was fully aware that the perfect realization of this ideal is incompatible with the preservation of life by animals whose needs are as large and varied as ours; but I was convinced that, by trying hard, I could come much nearer its fulfillment than people commonly do. And while making this effort, I desired to do something even more difficult: to penetrate, as far as possible, to the secret springs of this multiplex phenomenon called life, to understand its significance in the whole vast drama of cosmic evolution. Here I hoped to have leisure to mature my thoughts on these baffling problems.

The house Skutch built at Los Cusingos would take on nearly equal significance for him with the world outside, because now he was able to put together a library of his own which provided the inspiration and structure for his evolving view of life. Drawing on his recollections of a plantation house he had visited in Guatemala, he designed a sturdy and comfortable shelter for himself and his books.

He and his helpers took all of the building materials from the immediate region: from nearby fields the big rocks on which the house stands above the damp ground; from a neophyte tile-maker the crude tiles for his roof; and from roadbanks the red clay which was mixed with water, "then kneaded thoroughly by a horse, who, with a boy on his back, walked round and round for an hour or more until the mess became as sticky as clay can be," and finally packed with sugarcane to form the stout walls. At a local man's suggestion, Skutch hired an ox-driver to smear the outside walls with a paste of fresh cow dung, which gave off a powerful stench for some weeks but in drying became odorless and left "a soft gray, feltlike surface that was not unattractive and was admired by a visitor ignorant of its nature." Eventually, as Skutch added to his house, he covered the inner walls with white lime and the exterior ones with a wash of light-gray cement.

We sat now at twilight in a room off the front porch, its walls lined with books, the sound of the steady rain pounding on the roof and rustling the foliage outside the open window. Edwin, the son whom Alec and Pamela Skutch adopted locally some years ago, was off to San Isidro eight miles away to play with his pop band. Alec, naturally diffident and unaccustomed to "interviews," had relaxed in the give-and-take of conversation and now talked easily and softly about his books and his work.

The library, in fact, is made up roughly of three parts: nature books and ornithological periodicals in the study, novels and various classics in one room, works on philosophy and religion in another. Very little of the frivolous finds a place on those shelves. Skutch's favorite novel remains Thackeray's *Henry Esmond*, and anything by Jane Austen delights him. Hemingway he detests. He is doubly blessed in his tropical isolation, then, having been spared the outpourings of the Beat Generation and later the antiheroes and sexual athletes of the moderns. Nor, in the political sphere, do the Marxists attract him.

"The trouble with Karl Marx," he said dryly, "was that he spent too much time in the British Museum and didn't get enough fresh air."

Writing and farming, plus an occasional grant, have provided Skutch with what most Americans would consider a wholly inadequate income. But the wants of a man who gets along nicely without the common "necessities"—a mortgage, automobiles, electricity, telephones, fine clothes, thick steaks, imported Scotch, and the like—are satisfied on considerably less than a New York sanitation worker's income. His autobiographical and philosophic books...have a small but enthusiastic audience. His professional reputation, however, rests on the articles he has written for scientific periodicals and the collections of avian life histories published by ornithological societies, which form the bedrock for a large part of the bird studies being carried on today in the tropics.

Skutch's accounts of the birds he encounters are built up with a wealth of details, useful to other scientists in themselves and furnishing endless pleasure to every reader who is interested in the natural world. The details fix certain scenes in our minds, comparable to those we retain from favorite novels:

+ A Buff-rumped Warbler at Los Cusingos, singing while it gathers nesting material, deftly holding the straws against its upper bill with the pressure of its tongue.

+ A pair of Chestnut-mandibled Toucans bathing in a lofty pool in the crotch of a tree, dipping their yellow breasts in the accumulated rainwater and energetically flapping their black wings. (Skutch has never seen any species of toucan bathe at ground level or in a stream.)

+ A Great Tinamou, flushed in the forest, darting away "like a kicked football," to drop back to earth a few seconds later in dense vegetation.

+ A Blue-chested Hummingbird, which never learned the song of its own species, picking up instead that of the Rufous-tailed Hummingbirds abundant at the time in Skutch's garden, returning to its singing station near a large rock for seven successive years to utter the aberrant phrases, its voice gradually growing weaker with age. The bird disappeared finally in the middle of its seventh nesting season, to be replaced immediately by another Blue-chested Hummer, which sang the accustomed song of its species.

Among Skutch's major contributions to the lore of bird-watchers in the north are his accounts of migrant species in their winter homes. The Myrtle, or Yellow-rumped Warblers, he reports, often consort with Fork-tailed Fly-catchers in Central America, while Tennessee Warblers spend so much of their time in the shade trees on coffee plantations that he suggests "coffee warblers" as a much more appropriate name for them. Skutch also disproved the long-held notion that North American migrants never sing in the tropics. Many of them tune up in the rain forest shortly before taking off for the north. Indeed, the Swainson's Thrush provides more melody to the woodlands of El General from March through early May than any other bird.

Skutch discovered that these migrants lead double lives, attuning their feeding and social habits to their winter surroundings. Thrushes often join mixed flocks of antbirds and other tropical species that follow swarms of army ants to feed on the insects and other small creatures driven from cover at their approach. Of the Swainson's thrush, Skutch wrote:

> The thrush hovers about the outskirts of the swarm; and I have not seen it dash into the midst of the fray to seize a fugitive, in the manner of the tropical birds more adept at this kind of hunting. What strange company for a bird hatched among northern spruce and fir trees! Who that knows this thrush only amid the severe simplicity of a northern coniferous forest could imagine it in the infinitely varied tropical silva, burdened with huge woody vines and a hundred kinds of epiphytes, where it consorts on intimate terms with such birds as manakins, woodhewers, antbirds, and ant-tanagers?

The focus of Alec Skutch's studies has been the nest and the complex series of actions that accompany the raising of young birds. Several years ago, he summed up those studies in a wide-ranging book, *Parent Birds and Their Young.* The finding of nests in the tropical rain forests, many of them well hidden or camouflaged, is an art, and Skutch is a grand master among its practitioners. Experience, intuition, climbing skills, endless patience—and luck—are some of the ingredients needed to create a successful nest-finder.

The nests are often concealed high in the trunks of trees or among almost impenetrable vegetation, built in wasps' or termites' nests, or may appear—like the royal flycatcher's—to be no more than a disordered tangle of dead vegetation. The birds themselves are often wary around the nest. Skutch spent uncounted hours during the nesting season tracking down the source of "a calm, beautiful whistle, sliding up the scale in three parts.

"For the whistle is so ventriloquial," he wrote, "that at whatever point one imagines the whistling bird to be, there one can persuade oneself is the source of the sound. It happened that the first bird of the kind that I glimpsed, unsatisfactorily, while he called was well above my head; and thus I formed the habit of peering into the trees above me for a sight of the whistler, while nearly always the retiring brown bird lurked amid the undergrowth, rarely shoulder-high. Now that I am familiar with the thrush-like manakin, have found its nests and studied its ways, and can watch it sing without much trouble, I am touched with shame when I recall how long it remained merely the mysterious, unsubstantial 'voice of the forest.'"

Having found the bird and its nest site, Skutch is then confronted with the task of setting up a blind close by and observing the goings-on hour after hour, noting the courtship displays, nest-building techniques, patterns of incubation by one sex or another, the kinds of food brought to the young, and their development in the nest. When the birds nest in tree trunks or underground burrows, great ingenuity is required to follow their progress, especially if the nesting routines are not to be disrupted and the chicks lost. Experience is required to make sense of the various acts performed by the parent bird. "An act which at first appears unique and individual," Skutch wrote, "may, upon longer acquaintance with a group of birds, prove to be more widespread than we at first suspected."

Beyond the demands of science lies another sphere, the shadowy domain that is alien to a great many scientists and that Skutch refers to as "appreciation." When he is watching a hummingbird, its form, movement, and mastery of flight are not enough. He must gorge himself on its color too, which is most often concentrated at the male's throat. Because this color is not produced by pigments, but by the reflection and diffraction of light from the angles of the bird's feathers, it may be apparent only as a dark mass to the viewer. The color, then, depends wholly on the position of the viewer and is a spectacle the wary hummingbird may not be willing to provide. Here is Skutch, scheming against the bird to evoke a sight intended solely for a potential mate:

> Often I have found it more profitable not to try to maneuver myself in front of a perching humming-bird, but to stand quietly before some flowering plant whose blossoms attract him, with the sun behind me, and wait patiently for his return. Sooner or later, unless I have worse than average luck, he will poise before a flower whose position obliges him to assume the precise angle most favorable

for displaying his splendors to me. Then, in a sudden burst of effulgence, like the light of some great revelation, what was previously black and lusterless stands unveiled in its true brilliance and glory. For it is with hummingbirds' colors as with all true revelations; they resist eager importunities and cannot be compelled.

Skutch's writings are not without controversy. "Some ethologists think he's old-fashioned and doesn't pay enough attention to the interpretation of displays and that sort of thing," says the American Museum [of Natural History]'s Eugene Eisenmann. "But they forget that Skutch is doing the basic work in an area where it has never been done before. Some of them also complain about the 'Edwardian' prose in which he publishes his observations. They seem to be saying that he has committed the sin of being literate."

Skutch himself is rather disenchanted with the professional journals, objecting to the number of manuscript copies editors demand ([photocopying] machines are harder to come by in San Isidro than on North American campuses) and the chart- and table-studded articles that are now in fashion.

"For myself, each year I incline more strongly to put confidence in those rare flashes of sympathetic understanding that seem to penetrate the outer husk of a bird and reveal the life within," he wrote some years ago, and those flashes seem to have kept recurring. "I believe that they are more likely to disclose the truth than those laborious analyses of behavior by which we attempt to discredit them. If I must incur the risk of error, I prefer to incur it with the gateways to the spirit open rather than shut."

A current topic that agitates specialists is Skutch's answer to a central problem of modern ornithology: Why do tropical birds raise broods so much smaller than those of even the most closely related species in higher latitudes?

Orthodox evolutionary theory contends that each individual animal tries to produce as many offspring as possible and pass on its genes to posterity. In evolutionary terms, the individual unconsciously struggles to supplant the less prolific strains of its own species. Ornithologists of this persuasion believe that tropical birds "want" to raise more young but cannot supply enough food to nourish the extra chicks.

Skutch, calling on his own observations, believes on the contrary that tropical birds are *capable* of raising much larger broods than they now do. He points out that if an extra chick is slipped into a nest, the parents simply work a little harder to feed the artificially enlarged brood. Among a number of other arguments, he uses the commonly known fact that in some species only the female cares for the young, yet manages to raise a brood as large as those of species where both parents bring food.

Consequently, he supports the view that tropical birds, living in a stable environment where adults face few hazards, have no need to produce a large surplus of young, as do those in higher latitudes where inclement weather, the perils of migration, and other factors take a heavy toll. He believes that evolution, over long periods of time, has enabled tropical birds to adjust the size of their broods to maintain a stable population in a stable environment. Excessive breeding, by putting a strain on available resources, is as great a defect among birds as it is among human beings.

"A standing objection to my views," Skutch told me, "is that they presuppose intergroup selection, which is anathema to many evolutionists who believe that only inter-individual selection occurs. Although it is undoubtedly true that some individuals are 'selected' to leave more progeny than other individuals, in sexually reproducing organisms they cannot do so without the cooperation of other individuals, the number increasing with each successive generation.

"So I hold that individual selection is true on the short view, but on the long view group selection prevails. After all, only groups or populations, not individuals, can evolve. To me the thesis that animals never act for 'the good of the species' (as in Richard Dawkins' recent book, *The Selfish Gene*) is logically absurd. Since genes can only persist for long periods in species, the animal whose behavior is not consistent with the welfare of its species is preparing the way for the extinction of its genes."

While critics refer to his "utopian vision of animal behavior," there is a serpent in Alec Skutch's paradise—indeed, a great many serpents, and all of them actual and deadly. He finds no room in his *ahimsa*—the Far Eastern doctrine of "live and let live"—for snakes. His colleagues in the biological sciences, many of whom would not hesitate to "collect" an animal for scientific purposes, raise their eyebrows at Skutch's practice of dispatching with gun or club any snake he encounters.

It is not difficult to find a motivation for this remorseless enmity toward snakes in a man who ordinarily insists on reverence for all life. Albert Schweitzer, it is said, killed hawks that preyed on the small birds around his hospital. There is a point at which a human being who abhors violence of any kind finally reacts to a creature which lives by preying on the things that the human loves best. Over and over, Skutch has observed the courtship, nest-building, and incubation of mated birds, grateful that he was perhaps the first scientist to record the details for that species, and then suddenly had the nestlings disappear almost before his eyes.

"By far the worst enemies of nesting birds," he wrote, "especially in tropical forests, are snakes, whose slender, sinuous bodies can reach nests far out on thin twigs and creep into cavities with narrow doorways. These are the destroyers of bird nests that I have most often caught in the act. In a Panamanian forest, two nestlings were taken successively from a nest of Crimson-backed Tanagers by two snakes of different species in less than a day. Another snake reached a colony of Yellow-rumped Caciques and, apparently hiding in plundered pouches by day, emptied nest after nest until I finally shot it in the night."

Skutch offers no apology. In his eyes, killing a snake that invades the nests of his beloved birds is as justifiable as using antibiotics on the pernicious microorganisms that might invade and destroy his own body. To him, predation and parasitism are the unfortunate results of a wrong turn taken by evolution almost at the beginning of time, when, as Earth became favorable for life, organisms sprang up in "excessive" numbers and were thrown into conflict for the means of subsistence.

Although he would not go so far as Schweitzer in repelling bird-eating hawks, he is not very comfortable with them. In lamenting the disappearance of so many of the larger birds and mammals in the forest near Los Cusingos, he remarks that of the resident hawks "only the elusive Little Barred Forest-falcon remains, and it is so destructive of small birds that I would gladly see it go, too." He feels a special affection only for the Laughing Falcon, which happens to subsist mainly on snakes.

Evolution, then, is double-edged, giving rise to insistent bloodletting among organisms of all kinds, developing ever more efficient methods for stalking and killing prey, daubing nature "red in tooth and claw," and yet out of this very conflict, as organisms develop better means for attack or defense, producing at last Earth's incredible diversity of living things.

Then evolution went a step further. It produced, out of the elements at its disposal, the human mind with its capacity "to survey the whole, in all its stupendous majesty, to find beauty throughout the natural world, and to strive to understand it all." Our esthetic side, in fact, has evolved faster than our love for truth and goodness, ahead of our cognitive and moral aspects, beyond even our social and biological adaptation.

"We have become, above all, instruments for the appreciation of beauty," Skutch wrote. "May it not be that just this capacity is our most significant contribution to the whole of which we are parts?"

Skutch has no qualms about the coherence of his conviction that evolution proceeds in a definite direction, though its advance depends upon random mutations. Chance and necessity, he points out, often cooperate to produce a result.

"Do you remember those gambling devices they used to have in country stores?" he asked me. "You dropped a coin into the top of a tall, glass-fronted box, and it struck against nails as it dropped to the bottom. You could not predict just where it would lodge, but you could be sure it would reach the bottom because it was constantly drawn down by gravitation."

"Similarly, evolution has not been directed toward the production of an animal just like humans or any other existing creature. But that it should steadily raise life to higher levels of organization and increasing awareness is a necessary consequence of the tendency of atoms to unite in patterns of ever-increasing complexity and coherence."

Is there room for religion in Skutch's esthetic view of nature? Yes, though it necessarily reflects more of eastern philosophy than the harsher creeds of the West. That evolution went awry, incorporating such an evil as predation to bring unspeakable pain to animals and pass on brutality and hatred and meanness to human beings, indicates to him that it is not directed by a beneficent power. But, like Pascal, Skutch wagers that there is something after all—that Earth's beautiful images and experiences will survive in some form, perhaps in a naturally evolving "cosmic" memory to which a human soul contributes in proportion to the purity and intensity of its appreciation, as "the light from a beacon on a hilltop goes coursing through outer space long after the fire has died."

Beyond the appreciative mind, then, lies the ideal of the custodian. Earth's ultimate possessor ought to be the race, [human] or perhaps a worthier being, that most appreciates and cherishes its beauty. Because in the end—this is a matter of faith—we may carry the memory of this treasure into eternity, we ought to live as if our souls are eternal.

"Devoted care is the very heart of religion," Skutch wrote, "that which alone gives substance to its aspirations. To become more religious is above all to care more deeply about our world."

We stood at the window in the dark, listening to the rainfall among the forest trees. Skutch spoke sadly about the disappearance of the rain forest in the valley of El General and in so much of Latin America. If tropical birds have learned to adjust their populations to available resources, human beings have not, and the present vandalism, indiscriminate shooting, and destructive agricultural techniques seem to be portents of what the next quarter-century has up its dingy sleeve.

"Once or twice lately, bright, caring young women have come through here and talked to me about their reluctance to have children and put a further burden on our planet," he said. "But I encouraged them to go ahead and have their babies....I don't think it's unreasonable to believe that appreciation, too, can be nourished by loving parents."

Before closing the sitting room for the night, he cupped his hands around a large insect that had blundered in and eased it outside. As I walked to the cabin under the huge oil palm where I was staying, I remembered something else that Alexander Skutch had written: "What could be more dramatic than to watch the released moth fly upward toward the stars, what could better prepare us for sound sleep?"

NATURALIST

THE IMPERATIVE CALL

(1979)

The Ohio River

After returning to the United States in the spring [of 1931], I went to Cornell University to continue botanical research, but it did not go well. In the tropics I had found absorbing problems that kept me working at highest pitch and resulted in half a dozen substantial scientific papers and a number of shorter articles. Now my interests were changing; laboratory research had lost its zest; I could not revive the old enthusiasm. Older botanists advised me to specialize. Although I still loved plants, I did not find one aspect of their lives so much more absorbing than another that I could focus my interest sharply upon some narrow area of the whole great field of botany. While I felt so remote from my work, it was not difficult for my friend Winslow R. Hatch, then a graduate student in botany at Johns Hopkins, to persuade me by letter to leave the laboratories and accompany him on a canoe trip down the Ohio River, which I did at the expiration of my fellowship from the National Research Council.

On August 15 we met at Harrisburg, Pennsylvania, and continued by rail to Pittsburgh. Here we took passage on the *Queen City*, a paddlewheel steamer whose somewhat tarnished elegance reminded us of Mark Twain and the great days of river travel on the Mississippi and its tributaries. For three restful days, we wound down the muddy Ohio River, between the hills of West Virginia on our left and those of Ohio on our right. Disembarking at Huntington, West Virginia, we visited Dr. W. E. Neal, a former mayor of the city, to whom Win had a letter of introduction. He took us into his home while we bought a secondhand canoe and supplies for our voyage.

The start of our canoe trip was not encouraging. Leaving the boathouse of the Huntington Boat Club at four o'clock in the afternoon, we set forth down the river under a drizzle. After paddling about eight miles, we landed on the Ohio shore to look for a campsite among the willows that everywhere fringed it. The best we could find in the dusk was a patch of rough, sloping ground halfway up the steep bank, hardly wide enough for our pup tent. Unable to find dry wood for a campfire, we ate a meager supper of crackers and apples and crept into our tent early. Sleep rarely comes readily on one's first night on the ground; and here the usual difficulty of resting tranquilly was increased by the noises of freight trains rumbling along the tracks on both sides of the river, of electric cars in the nearby town of Kenova, and of barge-pushers with loudly splashing paddle wheels passing along the channel, stirring up waves that broke noisily on the bank. During the night the sky cleared and stars shone through the willows above us. Finally, my bones became reconciled to the asperity of the ground beneath them, and I dozed off.

Rain was falling steadily when we awoke next morning, but the cheerful whistles of the Carolina Wrens in the surrounding trees assured us that the new day was not as dreary as it seemed. While we sat in our tent eating a cold breakfast of cereal, bread, and apples, a catbird peered in inquisitively but offered no encouraging song. All morning the rain continued, holding us in camp. Finally, it abated somewhat and we packed our damp equipment, to resume our voyage beneath the continuing drizzle.

An hour's paddling brought us to the second of the many locks through which we passed on this trip. The long Ohio River has been canalized, or rather converted into a series of lakes, by the construction of many dams along its course. Vessels were lowered, or raised, from one lake to another by a lock beside each dam. These locks were spacious enough to accommodate not only river steamers but the strings of big freight barges that were pushed up and down the stream.

Just when we were in the region where the screen of pungent, sulphurous smoke from the steel furnaces hung thickest, and our regret for having left the inviting hills behind us was most poignant, we noticed a break in the willows on the opposite shore. It hardly looked promising, but it offered the best escape from our present predicament.... We passed beneath a railroad bridge and a highway bridge, rounded a curve, and found three boys gathering firewood by the shore. They told us that this stream was called "The Tiger" (Tygart's Creek was evidently its correct name), and they showed us a pleasant spot in an open, streamline grove where we could camp.

Fred, the oldest boy, led me to the house of a neighbor, Harry Hunt, where provisions were available. This generous farmer would accept no money for half a dozen roasting ears and a number of excellent apples; they were, he said, a reward for my honesty in asking for what many would have taken without permission.

When we awoke next morning, a chilling mist hung over the valley and a drizzle fell. Going to the streamside for my first wash and shave since leaving Huntington four days earlier, I was delighted with the abundant tall ironweed that displayed great spreading panicles of large, deep purple flowerheads on straight stems nine feet high. After breakfast, we paddled upstream for several miles, until we came to rapids against which our most strenuous efforts were of no avail. Then, tying our canoe in a quiet cove, we pushed through the dense riverside growth of great ragweed and found ourselves in a field of corn and pumpkins, which a woman in a sunbonnet was hoeing. Nearby stood her one-story log cabin, with whitewashed walls. We seemed to have entered a world remote in space and time from the great steel mills and bustling modern industry along the great river. In this field, we made the acquaintance of the apple of Peru, an attractive if somewhat rank weed of the nightshade family. Along the field's border, tall bellflowers lifted splendid spikes of large, pale blue flowers.

Climbing a steep hillside, we came to an old apple orchard, beside which was an almost pure coppice growth of the Common Papaw, whose large leaves suggested tropical luxuriance, as well they might, as this small tree is the northernmost representative of the almost exclusively tropical custard apple family. Nearby, we found a magnificent Papaw Swallowtail Butterfly, which seemed to have drawn tropical splendor from the foliage on which it had fed while still a caterpillar. It clung amid low weeds for shelter from the strong breeze, giving us an opportunity to admire, without disturbing, its wide, pale bluish white wings boldly striped with black. A bright red dot adorned each hind wing, near the base of the long, slender "tail."

By the light of a nearly full moon, we continued downstream, paddling easily and depending chiefly on the strong flood current to carry us along. Sitting in the bow, Win kept a close watch for the large logs and rafts of brushwood that were likewise being swept forward by the stream, and directed our course to avoid a dangerous collision with them. The wooded hills that bordered this beautiful stretch of river were transformed by the soft moonlight into distant ranges of lofty mountains; the scene was even grander than it would have been by day. Only here and there, at long intervals, a light shone from the window of a lonely farmhouse by the shore. When we passed the village of Vanceburg, Kentucky, soon after ten o'clock, it seemed already to have gone to sleep.

At the base of a high bluff on the opposite shore, we nosed our canoe inward under the willow trees, whose roots were inundated by the high water, and Win landed to seek a campsite. Passing through a thicket of great ragweed, he reached a grove of small slippery elm and common locust trees high on the bank. With hardly any undergrowth, this grove, upon which we stumbled in the moonlight, proved to be one of the most pleasant campsites of our whole trip. Abundant driftwood from the spring floods provided the fuel to cook our belated supper. Then, for the first time since we embarked, two conveniently spaced trees and favoring weather invited me to stretch my hammock, in which I was soon comfortably ensconced. Win preferred to sleep on the ground.

In the morning, I awoke to catch the sun's earliest beams striking through the boughs; to gaze across the river where they were dispelling the nocturnal mists; to hear the songs of the Cardinal and the Carolina Wren and the Red-eyed Vireo and almost feel that I belonged to the feathered nation, for my sleeping body was upheld by [a hammock slung on] the same trees that supported them. Then to arise, and wash away all drowsiness by plunging into the river's clear water—but alas, too often the river was diluted mud or, what was worse, covered by a sickening, greasy scum, the unhealthy consequence of human indifference to the purity of waterways. This was the most unpleasant feature of our voyage. Years later, I traveled in a Peruvian gunboat for many hundreds of miles along the Río Marañon or Upper Amazon and its great tributaries, the Ucayali, the Huallaga, the Napo, and the Yavarí. These, too, were turbid streams, laden with silt from the high Andes; but they bore scarcely any trace of human pollution and their water supplied the ship's shower baths.

Next day, we stopped at the quiet little town of Ripley, Ohio, to buy provisions and call for mail. We had returned to the canoe and were about to push off, when some men loitering at the foot of the main street hailed us. Returning, I found the postmistress, who had walked several blocks to tell us that we had mailed a card without an address. I accompanied her back to the post office to rectify the oversight. Where could one find a more considerate postal service?

The rain that had long been threatening now came down in a deluge and continued until my teeth began to chatter and cold chills coursed along my spine. All our baggage got wet. My companion would not be satisfied with any campsite except a certain "grassy knoll" that he had noticed on our upward voyage, but this enticing spot continued until nightfall to elude us. Finally, departing from our usual practice, we stopped at a farmhouse whose lights we saw shining through the rainy night, and obtained permission to sleep in a shed.

Next morning, while tent, blankets, mosquito nets, changes of clothes, and odds and ends were spread along the shore to dry in the sunshine, I envied the chickadees who foraged among the locust trees on the bank. They, too, had weathered the deluge of the preceding evening and were now enjoying the sun's earliest rays, none the worse for their experience. Not theirs to waste hours of precious sunshine recovering from the effects of a drenching that they had doubtless already forgotten. Having acquired no wettable property, they had given no hostages to the weather.

After everything had been spread out in the sunshine, we noticed a fine yacht speeding upstream, throwing out swelling bow waves that threatened to break over our drying equipment and undo all our work. Hurriedly, we moved our things farther from the water's edge. To the passersby, this bit of shore must have resembled the bank of a Jamaican stream on a washday. As the luxurious vessel swept proudly past us, we reflected that if, instead of "wasting" our time on vagabond excursions, we applied ourselves diligently to some lucrative occupation for the next few decades, we, too, might travel the inland waterways in the grand style. But even while recovering from the effects of our recent soaking, we did not envy the people in the yacht as much as we envied the chickadees. It seemed better to be enjoying this free life before the years softened our hardihood and tamed our spirit of adventure.

In thirty days on the Ohio, we had traveled four hundred and fifty miles by canoe, not counting our side excursions up some of its tributaries. We had found and identified seventy-five species of plants new to us, although, as was to be expected, we found nothing new to science in this country already well combed by naturalists—that remained for later travels in fresher fields. And, in those days at the height of the Great Depression, our living expenses during our month on the river came to slightly less than eleven dollars for each of us.

From what we saw of this rich valley, now so thoroughly tamed and subjugated to human uses, it was hard to imagine how it had appeared to pioneer naturalists, to Wilson and Audubon, Say and Rafinesque, or to still earlier explorers who saw it in all its pristine splendor, when majestic forests, of which we saw only a few small remnants, lined the shores, wild turkeys strutted in the woodland, and tremendous flocks of passenger pigeons darkened the sky. It was sad to think that all this vast midland of North America was "developed" without much consideration for values not given by corn and wheat, cattle and tobacco. In later years, I visited valleys having a more varied flora, richer and more colorful bird life. These, too, are threatened with the same ruthless exploitation that overtook the Ohio and its tributaries. They can be saved only if a too materialistic and too rapidly increasing humanity undergoes a change of aims and values so swift and radical that it could be compared only to a mass religious conversion. Although I saw only a valley too recklessly shorn of its natural wealth, I am glad that I made this leisurely voyage through the heart of my native land, and experienced some of the kindness of its people, before finally leaving it for fresher fields.

Choosing a Vocation

When I returned to the United States after my first visit to Central America, I looked forward eagerly to learning from books more about the habits of the birds of many kinds that I had seen there. As I searched the ornithological literature, I was disappointed. I learned that many thousands of birds had been collected in tropical America, that they had all been named and classified, minutely described to the last spot of color, and measured to the last millimeter. Indeed, this business of measurement and classification had been carried so far that, when an average difference of a few millimeters in the lengths of individuals of the same species from different parts of its range could be discovered, or when a slight variation in color could be detected when two specimens were laid side by side, these so slightly differing birds had received distinguishing names. Yet in the field, the two races so designated could not always be distinguished by appearance, voice, or habits.

When I looked for what had been recorded about the habits, the mode of life, of these birds collected in such great numbers and so minutely catalogued, I found the situation quite different; the notes on habits were as scant as the necrologies of specimens were voluminous. Frank M. Chapman and Josselyn Van Tyne on Barro Colorado Island and William Beebe and his associates in British Guiana had published careful studies of the life histories of a few species. In Brazil, Carl Euler and Emilio A. Goeldi had provided less detailed accounts of the nesting of a number of widespread tropical birds. Bird collectors had recorded many incidental observations on habits and described a number of nests and eggs, not always correctly identified. But the total amount of information was slight, covering only a very small proportion of the birds of tropical America. The bare appearance of the nests and eggs of the majority of neotropical birds remained unknown to science.

The subject had begun to fascinate me in no ordinary degree. My intimate studies of the lives of a few species of tropical American birds, and fleeting glimpses of numerous others, sharpened my desire to know more about them. I thought of the thousands of kinds of lovely feathered creatures, leading their beautiful, well-ordered lives among the forests on the plains and mountains of that wild, sparsely inhabited region that I was beginning to know—leading their lives obscurely, in ways never yet watched or recorded by humans. It seemed to me, as a scientist and lover of beauty, that the most worthy cause in which I could engage, the highest endeavor to which I could dedicate my own peculiar endowment, temperament, and training, was to uncover the secrets of the lives of the tropical American birds, and to make them known to those of my fellows who are so fortunate as to be interested in these matters. It seemed, too, that by striving to understand these birds as living, breathing creatures, I could help to bring to fruition and completion all this tedious labor of description and classification of dead specimens, which, although held to be fundamental to scientific knowledge, is in itself dry and uninspiring; that I could, in some measure, justify the sacrifice to science of so many thousands of bird lives.

An even wider consideration impelled me to undertake these studies. From childhood, I have been troubled by what might be called the problem of unrealized and lost values. Those poignant verses of Gray,

Full many a flower is born to blush unseen,
And waste its sweetness on the desert air

are to my mind among the most melancholy in our language. The thought of such neglected flowers always distresses me. Their loveliness ought to be contemplated, their fragrance inhaled, by some appreciative being. Similarly, a bird's beauty ought to be enjoyed; its song heard with delight, all its habits observed with interest, not only by its feathered companions, but by ourselves, who perhaps can appreciate them more deeply.

The world in which beauty, goodness, or any other value, is wasted seems incomplete, lacking something necessary for its perfection. And who or what should appreciate all the lovely and amiable things that this world contains if not ourselves, who, of all animals, seem most highly endowed with aesthetic feeling and understanding? One might contend that our most important role on this planet, our *raison d'être*, is to complete or fulfill the world process by grateful, cherishing enjoyment of everything good and lovely that it has produced. I believed that by studying the way of life of some of the splendid feathered creatures that live obscurely in tropical forests and thickets, and sharing my discoveries with others, I could in small measure advance this great, rewarding task of bringing to fruition all the values that the natural world contains potentially and offers to us for realization.

To find financial support for such an undertaking was not easy, especially in the dark years immediately following the great financial debacle of 1929. Had I intended to collect birds in Central America, I have little doubt that I could have sold their "skins," even then, at a fair price. Had I wished to bury myself in a museum and pore over the dry and lifeless bird specimens already amassed there, it is probable that I could, with time, have found some institution to pay me a modest salary for doing so—although my special training in another branch of biology might have made it more difficult to obtain such employment. But I was already convinced of what subsequent years have amply confirmed, that few new species of birds remained to be discovered in Central America or, indeed, in any part of the world, and that the advancement of our understanding of bird life must be sought in a different direction. From these considerations, and because of my deep-rooted aversion to destroying life of any kind, I decided that I would not attempt to finance my studies of tropical birds by collecting them.

Fortunately, I was still sufficiently young and imprudent to be capable of a bold step. Although I had no income, I decided to return to Central America and continue to study the birds, devoting my small savings to the enterprise, and trusting to fortune that, somehow, I would be able to replenish my capital before it was exhausted. My father encouraged me with the dry remark that, of the many shiftless people he had known, not one had died of starvation! My decision was the more readily made because, when Professor Johnson returned to Hopkins to take over the botany course that I taught while he was on leave of absence, I would be unemployed, and any definite course of action was preferable to idle waiting. But these considerations, I am now convinced, hardly influenced the step I took. Sounding from afar, coursing with the swiftness of electric pulses over the convexity of the earth, the calls of the tropical birds fell upon my inward ear during those short, bleak winter days — and they were calls that I could not resist. Moreover, had I not already concluded that to learn about the lives of these birds was the highest endeavor of which I was capable?

A River on the Plain (Guatemala)

We gravitate to rivers like water from the surrounding hills. Their attraction does not depend wholly on the greater abundance and conspicuousness of birds and other animals along their course; even in a land devoid of animate life, we should be drawn to them, perhaps more strongly than where fields and forests are enlivened by moving creatures. Probably the secret of their attraction is that, to a high degree, they exemplify that which we too seldom realize in our own lives, the felicitous union of permanence and change.

We yearn for permanence, yet we welcome adventure and change. We wish our souls, and even the bodies that support them, to endure forever, along with those dear to us and everything we cherish. Yet spirits as restless as ours would be bored to tears in Eternity, where time does not intrude and nothing changes or perishes but everything remains unalterably the same. We crave novelty, movement, and growth; we welcome pleasant surprises, all of which belong to a world in constant flux, where things grow and decay; they are difficult to reconcile with permanence. More than most things beneath the sun, flowing streams realize this happy combination. They are never the same for two consecutive moments, a fact that Heraclitus of old recognized when he declared that you cannot step twice into the same river. Yet even if the water at the ford is always different, the river itself remains the same while the creatures that live along its course are born, grow old, and perish, as Tennyson recognized when he made the brook proclaim

> *For men may come and men may go,*
> *But I go on forever.*

This paradoxical union of permanence and change, of sameness and difference, is not the least of the river's attractions.

The Río Morjá, which wound through the banana plantations that stretched like a sea of verdure at the foot of the elevation on which the house at Alsacia stood, drew me as strongly as the mountain torrent at Lancetilla. I passed many pleasant, instructive hours with the birds that lived along it. Doubtless, back in the forested hills where it was born, the young Morjá dashed down a rocky channel as impetuously as the torrent above which the royal flycatchers nested; but before it reached the broad, flat valley where I knew it, its character changed completely. Here, in the drier months early in the year, it flowed clear and smooth over a broad channel that in many places I could cross by wading through water that did not reach my waist.

The concave bank of the curving channel was a vertical wall of deep, rich, alluvial soil that supported tall banana plants in long, unbroken ranks. Their great, wind-frayed leaves arched over the limpid water. On the convex side, bare expanses of sand or shingle sloped gently up to a dense stand of tall wild canes, which were invading the growing sand flats by means of long runners that sent up young leafy shoots. That the river was not always as gentle as I found it in February and March was attested by the freshly cut banks on the concave side, where banana plants had tumbled into the water, along with the light rails and pressed-iron ties of a washed-out tramline. As this bank receded, the exposed sand and shingle on the opposite side of the channel advanced toward it.

Stretched at ease in the rich sunshine on an exposed sandbar beside the Río Morjá, in the dry season when the water was low, I sometimes imagined myself transposed to some familiar stream twenty degrees farther north, at a later month. Clear water flowing over a stony channel speaks the same language in every climate, and sparkles with equal brilliance in the sun's rays. The willow trees along these banks look much the same as those that border some tributary of the Susquehanna or the Ohio; their light sprays of pale green foliage contrast strongly with the background of dark tropical verdure that clothes the distant mountains. The Spotted Sandpiper, still with the immaculate breast of its winter dress, and the Louisiana Waterthrush who tilter over the shore are the same who a few months later will hunt along northern watercourses. Although of wholly different lineages, these two birds of similar habitats and modes of foraging have acquired similar color patterns and mannerisms to a degree that excites my wonder. I cannot predict whether the green heron, who with infinite patience stands on the farther bank poised to spear some unwary fish, will build its nest in the thicket beyond the bend in the river, or beside some other stream two thousand miles nearer the North Pole. Nor can I tell whether the Rough-winged Swallows who course above the water will raise their young in an abandoned kingfishers' burrow in the neighboring bank or in some hole or cranny in a far northern land.

Sometimes, as I sat on the bank putting on my shoes after wading or swimming in the refreshing water that brought mountain coolness to the warm lowlands, I watched the little silvery-scaled minnows gleam and flash in the current. As each at intervals turned on its side, it reflected a silvery beam, which vanished as soon as the fish righted itself, to become almost invisible against the background of the sandy bottom with which it blended so well. Now here, now there, from a score of points, but only for an instant in each, came the bright flash from as many different minnows, just as the fireflies' sparks gleam momentarily in a hundred places above a meadow on a warm night, but rarely twice in the same spot. I wondered whether these silvery glints were the betraying signals for which hungry kingfishers waited as they perched motionless on a bough overhanging the stream, or hung above it between two misty circles of rapidly beating wings. If so, they must indeed be quick to capture their meal, for the revealing gleam of silver is more evanescent than the firefly's spark.

As the year advanced, the weather deteriorated. February and March had been dry, bright, and not disagreeably warm. May became oppressively hot and sultry. The atmosphere, polluted by smoke from innumerable fires set to clear land for planting maize, and charged with the gathering vapors of the wet season, lost the fine transparency of the early months of the *verano* or dry season. In late May, the rains began. The downpours of June swelled and muddied the once limpid current of the Río Morjá, which rose to cover the bare expanses of sand and gravel on the farther shore, where I had passed so many pleasant, rewarding hours watching the birds, and it threatened to inundate or wash out the burrows in the opposite bank. An Amazon Kingfisher and a Rough-winged Swallow, who had lost earlier broods, and the Motmot who had dug a second burrow, were the only birds who laid in these burrows after May 1; and after the middle of the month, I noticed no further attempts to raise families in them. Back in the hills, too, most of the broods that I had been watching had flown from their nests by mid-June.

For four months I had been extremely active, watching the birds most or all of every day, developing photographs and writing up notes far into the night. Amid heavy tropical vegetation, where nests are so elusive, I regarded every one that I found as a never-to-be-repeated opportunity to gain knowledge, a challenge to learn all that I could about it. Now, when the weather became so oppressive, I paid for going too hard in a climate that I found hard to bear, as had happened at Lancetilla two years earlier. Overcome with feverish lassitude, I dosed myself with quinine until my ears rang; every high-pitched sound fell upon them with preternatural sharpness; and the shrill calls of the male Great-tailed Grackles cut into my ears like a knife. But this self-prescribed treatment failed to improve my condition, so I resolved to seek a change of climate for my health's sake.

Although Alsacia Plantation had proved to be a splendid locality for my work, and never elsewhere have I learned more about birds in an equal interval, I did not depart it as regretfully as I have left many another place where I have studied nature. At first, I was so delighted with the broad prospects that spread on every side from the house perched on the hilltop, that I overlooked certain shortcomings of the immediate surroundings. As the months passed, I discovered, as John Burroughs did when he abandoned "Riverby" for "Slabsides," that scenery on the grand scale, however inspiring, cannot in the long run compensate for lack of intimacy—the unfrequented byways along which one loves to stroll; the quiet, sequestered spots that become dearer to us the longer we loiter in them. Alsacia, a plantation developed for monetary returns, provided few such spots within easy reach of the dwelling. The nearer terrain was occupied by steep, pastured hillsides, covered with tall bunch-grass, infested in the dry season by ticks and redbugs; with bushy, vine-entangled second growth, penetrable only at the price of vigorous exercise with the machete; and the bananas, noble plants indeed, but as monotonous in the endless sameness of a great plantation as a field of wheat would be to a race of lilliputians. A pleasant stream that flowed down a rocky bed in the hills behind the house had been spoiled when the tall second-growth trees on the surrounding slopes were cut and burned to make a milpa. And now, with the rising water, I could no longer wade across the Río Morjá to the exposed sandy beaches of happy memory—indeed, they were no longer exposed.

I left Alsacia early on a sunny morning after a dark and rainy night. A pearly mist filled the atmosphere, softening the outlines of the distant mountains and tempering the rays of the sun. It was a morning almost spring-like, the mild radiance of the new day lending a charm to the humblest weed. But for the overseer of the plantation and me, it narrowly escaped becoming tragic.

When we reached the main line of the railroad in the little motorcar, it was necessary to telephone to the dispatcher in Zacapa for an order to proceed down the tracks to the station. We were told to await the passing of a southbound freight train, but the dispatcher was not certain whether it had yet reached our spur. When, after waiting a reasonable interval, the train did not appear, we concluded that it had already passed and proceeded down the railroad. As we rounded a curve bordered by banana plants that shortened the outlook, a locomotive at the head of a long string of freight cars was bearing down on us! The engineer jammed on his air brakes; but before the heavy train could come to rest, we had stopped the car, pushed it into reverse, and were scuttling backward in front of the still-advancing locomotive, with only yards separating it from us. It was a narrow escape, which fortunately resulted in no accident more serious than the cancellation of Pellman's license to operate his car on the main line. Thenceforth, he was obliged to hand over the controls to his motor-boy.

A Fantastic Journey

From El Rancho, I went by motor truck to Cobán, capital of rainy Alta Verapaz, a department renowned for its coffee, its Indians who staunchly preserved their native tongue in preference to Spanish, and its varied bird life. I found the little town attractive. It was situated on a long, low, narrow ridge, so that, walking down the side streets that led out from the central plaza, I looked across green valleys to pine-clad ridges haunted by beautiful Bushy-crested Jays with golden eyes set in black heads. Such a town, unless insufferably dirty, always appeals to me. The best hotel left much to be desired; disorderly and unclean, it had a weedy patio littered with empty cans and no facilities for bathing. (I know that Cobán has now acquired a better hostelry.) I was told that the massive old church had been built early in the sixteenth century by Fray Bartolomeo de las Casas, indefatigable champion of America's oppressed Indians. I noticed many neat, substantial houses, some of which were the homes of prosperous North American and German coffee planters. Most of the larger mercantile establishments were owned by Germans; indeed, the Alta Verapaz was sometimes called "Little Germany."

The northward journey from El Rancho to Cobán had taken a day and a half. On the return trip, it took us nearly four days to cover about sixty miles by motor; that painfully slow ride remains in memory as the longest sequence of mishaps that I have ever experienced.

We set forth from Cobán at three o'clock in the afternoon. Don Antonio, the genial Galician who had come up with me from the railroad to sell brushes of North American manufacture to the housewives of Cobán, was the only other passenger in the truck. We made a brave start, for the highway as far as the Indian village of Tactic was excellent. The last few miles had been newly repaired, and the completion of the work was being celebrated that very afternoon with appropriate dedicatory ceremonies. We rode beneath verdant arches of intertwined boughs, between which the roadside was lined with leafy wood-land branches set upright in the ground. These were chiefly of pine and the starry-leafed sweet gum, the latter a noble, lofty tree common in northern Guatemala at altitudes of from four to six thousand feet and hardly to be distinguished from the *liquidambar* of the southern United States. At Tactic we found the Indians dancing to the music of the marimba, a sweet-toned xylophone played by three men together. They were dancing when we went early to bed; they still danced to the strains of the marimba when we arose at four o'clock next morn-ing to resume our journey. Indian celebrations usually continue through the night.

Between Cobán and the Motagua Valley the road crossed three major ridges between five and six thousand feet high and a number that are lower. The rough, unpaved road wound up precipitous slopes with grades so steep that we traveled many miles in lowest gear, and with turns so sharp that they could be rounded only by backing the car, sometimes more than once—a delicate and dangerous operation. The driver was assisted by a boy whose duties included placing a block behind a rear wheel whenever the car stopped on a steep slope, especially at the hazardous curves where it was necessary to go into reverse; in helping to turn the front wheels by pulling on a tire; in filling the radiator, which was continually boiling over, at the streams we forded; in putting chains on the tires and removing them several times a day, as the road changed from muddy to rocky; in loading and tying on the cargo. The young driver's assistant had plenty to do and was almost indispensable at the curves, where frequently the road sloped outward, so that if the car skidded nothing would save it from hurtling down hundreds of feet to the stream at the foot of the steep, bare declivity. I usually found some excuse for dismounting at these perilous turns, for I felt safer with my feet on the ground.

From the head of the winding valley of the Río Cobán, we climbed without mishap to the summit of the first high ridge, which supported a light growth of low, broad-leafed trees draped with long, gray streamers of "Spanish moss" or *Tillandsia*, and heavily burdened with other epiphytes. Thence we descended into an elevated valley where pine trees grew scattered over grassy slopes devoted to grazing. At the bottom of this valley, we forded a rocky stream and began a second ascent. When halfway up, our troubles began. Heavy rains had fallen; the car sank deeply into the mire; and we passengers joined the driver and his helper in filling ruts with stones brought from a distance, then jacking up the buried wheels and placing solid material beneath them. Advancing thus laboriously, we rounded the next curve, only to find that one side of the road had washed away. Luckily, we discovered some pine logs lying nearby and with them formed a makeshift bridge, then covered its approaches with brush and logs. This was a mistake, for the loose material was pushed ahead by the wheels and piled up in front, making their advance still more difficult.

After we had labored at highway-making most of the afternoon, extending our search for loose stones far up and down the next brook that flowed across the road, we were joined by two men who had been driving a two-ton load of coffee from Cobán to the railroad at El Rancho. Their truck had thrust a rear wheel through the decayed logs of a small bridge over a mere trickle of water, and they had been waiting here for two days. Ours was the first vehicle to arrive from either direction in this interval. With our new reinforcements, we finally succeeded in maneuvering our car to a firmer part of the road, when the sun was about to set.

We reloaded our truck, then walked ahead to unload the hundred-and-fifty pound sacks of coffee from the larger truck, in order to extricate it from the position where it had been resting so long. Then, by the flickering light of a fragrant pinewood torch, we jacked up the wheel that had broken through the bridge and stuck timbers beneath it. When all was ready, we watched breathlessly while the motor started. All our work was lost; the logs separated and the wheel fell again. Then, rain falling, we toiled feverishly to replace the coffee in the truck, for a wetting would spoil it. In the morning, all those heavy sacks would have to be unloaded again!

Gerardo, our driver's helper, had been sent back to a solitary farmhouse to seek something for our supper, and now he returned with a woman and a small boy, bringing tortillas, brown beans, an omelette, a mixture of chayote and egg that I found very savory, and strong black coffee already sweetened. For travelers stranded on a remote mountainside, this was a feast; but poor Don Antonio, unable to accustom himself to native food, could not enjoy it like the rest of us. After the woman and boy had carried away the empty dishes in a basket, the four of us settled down on the seats in the truck to pass the night as best we could.

From the distance came the melancholy wail of a coyote, a soul-stirring ululation that, heard for the first time in this solitude, brought moisture into my eyes. Don Luís, the owner and driver of the truck, then told us that once his car stalled on this mountain, had been surrounded by a pack of coyotes, who did not permit its lone occupant to sleep that night. I fervently wished that we would be similarly visited, for it would have been much more diverting to cast the beam of a flashlight around a circle of glowing eyes than to sit shivering in sleepless misery through much of that wet, chilly night. When finally I dozed, the car was shaken by an earthquake tremor, the only one that I have ever felt in an automobile.

It was noon the next day before we had maneuvered both cars over the rotten bridge. Then we crossed another high ridge, covered with grass and scattered agaves, with an open pine wood on its crest. At the foot of this mountain, we forded a wide stream and started across the plain to Salamá. The level valley was evidently very arid in the dry season; but now the broad roadway, defined only by deep ruts, was an almost impenetrable morass into which our wheels sank up to the hubs. To avoid getting stuck, it was imperative to move fast; we careered wildly onward, skidding and swaying from side to side, jolting and jarring, sending out to right and left wide-spreading showers of muddy water and watery mud. At the conclusion of this mad ride, which would have been a worthy subject for a ballad by the author of "John Gilpin," we crossed a river by a covered bridge and entered the town of Salamá, capital of the department of Baja Verapaz. Here a policeman recorded the license number of the car and the names of all the occupants. During the years when I traveled in Guatemala, this was the usual procedure when one entered or left every town or larger village; on a long journey, it was sometimes necessary to give one's name and destination to the police five or six times in a day.

We slept that night on mattresses of the fibrous, brown leaf sheaths of palm trees—probably the palmetto, which is abundant in the arid valleys of this region—cut into small rectangles and loosely stitched together. These mats were laid over ropes strung crisscross over a wooden bed frame, a combination none too soft. But the hardest bed could not have kept us awake after our exertions and the preceding nearly sleepless night. We were aroused at five o'clock in the morning by the clear notes of a bugle and the tattoo of a drum from the barracks across the street from our little hostelry. Soon a company of ragged soldiers filed past our window. After a meager breakfast, we set out early and unsuspecting upon a day of mishaps.

Without adventure, we crossed the plain to San Ge-
rónimo, and with much grinding of gears reached the
beautiful forest of Sweet Gum and pine on the summit
of the ridge to the south. Here a rustic shrine and some
rude crosses stood at the wayside. Throughout Spanish
America, the points where travelers have been killed are
marked with crosses, but we did not learn the details of the
tragedies that had occurred here. Our own private griefs
quite filled our minds, for now we discovered that a bolt
had been jarred out of a front spring, letting the truck's
body rest upon the axle. But this annoying accident was,
for me at least, soon compensated by a splendid view of
the upper half of the shapely cone of El Volcán de Agua,
standing out clearly fifty miles away.

At the foot of the mountain that we had just crossed,
we were delayed nearly an hour by two passengers who
started to prepare for their journey only after asking
whether we had room for them. A few miles farther on, a
valve was somehow torn from one of the rear tires. Since
we carried no spare tire, the casing was stuffed with
burlap and blankets and placed on a front wheel, while
the good tire from the front was shifted to the rear. After
this, we continued slowly onward with a rocking-horse
motion. When we stopped at a roadside farmhouse for
lunch, Don Luís discovered that a package containing six
pairs of shoes made in Cobán had been rocked out of the
car. Poor, overworked Gerardo, who was responsible for
the lading, was sent back to retrieve them. He appeared
at El Rancho two days later—without the shoes!

We galloped slowly into Morazán, a dirty, unattractive
village among arid hills, where a telegram was sent ahead

requesting that a spare tire and gasoline be sent to meet us. Here we tried in vain to buy oranges or water coconuts to assuage our thirst, for we mistrusted the local water. Finally, we succeeded in purchasing a flavorless pineapple. The padre, we were told, visited the church thrice a year, to marry, baptize the accumulated infants, perform the burial rites for people who may have been interred months earlier, and hear the parishioners confess their sins. Morazán was redeemed for me by a pair of Black-throated Orioles, resplendent in golden plumage, who were feeding nestlings in a long, woven pouch suspended from the tip of a coconut-palm frond in the central plaza. Great-tailed Grackles were also nesting here, as they nest and roost in nearly every town and village in Guatemala, from sea level up to the high western plateau.

As we rumbled slowly into the next hamlet, it appeared that the whole population had turned out into the road to stop us. A sick man, they said, wished to be carried to El Rancho, where he could take the train to the hospital in Zacapa. Don Luís at first refused him transportation, because the truck was already quite full with the passengers it had picked up during the day, and, moreover, it was bumping so much that it was not fit to carry one in his condition. Presently, the ailing man himself appeared from among the crowd, a fortnight's stubble on his wasted face, his open shirt revealing a lean and hairy chest, and began his plea by reminding us that "There is a God above, and we are all his children."

Glancing around at the mongrel crowd, the haggard women and dirty children, the dull, apathetic faces, I resented this reminder of our common brotherhood and

thought that the supplicant had made a stupid beginning. But when presently the invalid dropped into the
roadway, writhing, groaning piteously, and muttering *ai
ai ai* in an outburst of agony too intense to be feigned, our
common humanity asserted itself. I offered to give him
my seat if his neighbors would find a horse to carry me
to El Rancho. Don Antonio also relinquished his place
on the front seat. After some discussion, we resumed
our journey with the two of us standing on the running
boards of the now heavily overloaded truck.

We had not gone many miles more, through hills covered
with low, scrubby vegetation, when, ascending a grade,
the motor sputtered, gasped, and died — out of gasoline.
I feared that our invalid would expire, too, for he jumped
into the road, where he dropped down and groveled in
the dust, uttering his agonized *ai ai* and heart-rending
groans. He had borne bravely the jolting of the car, which
must have been a grueling ordeal to one in his condition,
but now he completely lost control over himself, begged
us to shoot him, and, this plea failing to move us, looked
around for a *barranco* into which he could leap and end
his agony. Full as Guatemala is of profound chasms and
ravines, none happened to be at hand in this spot.

Not finding it pleasant to watch the contortions and
hear the groans of this poor, pain-wracked creature, for
whom we could do nothing save give him the deflated
inner tube to ease his contact with the road; I suggested
to my Galician companion that we walk ahead. We were
still about ten miles from our destination. In the dusk, after
we had gone some miles, we met another truck bringing
succor to our own. Presently we were overtaken by the

returning car, in which we soon completed our journey. A good supper, a shower, then a bed with real springs, helped us to forget the hardships of the past three days. Our sick passenger survived at least long enough to board the train the following morning, after which he passed beyond our ken.

Such was travel by road into the Alta Verapaz in 1932. After so long an interval, I could hardly feel sure that I had made the fantastic journey here recorded, did I not find all the details thereof minutely set down in my journal, written upon its conclusion. Already great tri-motored air-planes were carrying passengers, cargo, and mail between Guatemala City and Cobán in forty-five minutes. Yet for thrills and adventure, travel by air is prosaic compared with the passage of the El Rancho–Cobán road, as it then was in the rainy season.

Cypress Forests and Hummingbirds

The highway leading forth from Antigua was bordered by white-plastered walls that enclosed flourishing coffee plantations, where Grevillea trees from Australia shaded the glossy-leaved coffee bushes. A roadside fountain set in one of the walls lent an antique charm to the scene. Winding up a narrow valley, above a rushing stream, the highway rose gradually to the plateau of Chimaltenango. Our cloud of dust trailed us across broad, almost treeless plains, covered with the stubble of maize and wheat, brown and barren after months of drought, frost, and wind. In the distance, the plains tilted up to meet the high, wooded ridges that dominated the

horizon. Growing along the roadside and in the hedge-
rows, Maguey plants with compact clusters of huge,
sharp-pointed, fleshy leaves imparted an exotic character
to the landscape. The highland towns through which we
passed—Chimaltenango, Zaragoza, Patzum—with their
low, crowded houses of white adobe, their narrow, dusty,
cobbled streets, were not attractive enough to invite the
dust-tortured traveler to pause.

At noon we reached Tecpán, the end of my journey by
public car. Much like the others through which we had
passed, this town is situated on a broad, mountain-rimmed
plateau at an altitude of seven thousand feet. It rests at
the foot of a long and lofty ridge, which rises steeply to
the north and stretches, gradually descending, for miles
toward the northeast; while on the west a mighty spur
sweeps like a protecting arm about the town. This apparently simple ridge is the face of an extensive mountain
complex, an intricate system of sharp ridges and deep
valleys covering many square miles. For a year I explored
these valleys and ridges, and by no means exhausted
their secrets.

In Tecpán, I was met by some of the younger Piras in
their family car. After a short run across the plain, we
turned left and began to climb steeply. Here and there
along the roadside banks grew *Wigandia kunthii*, a large,
coarsely branched shrub with broad, stiff leaves and
spreading panicles of rich purple flowers. A modest,
prostrate herb with finely divided foliage and a profusion of delicate pinkish blossoms, for which I could learn
no name more poetic than *Loeselia glandulosa*, did its best
to brighten the roadside, despite the clouds of dust that

rolled over it from every passing vehicle. As the highway zigzagged higher and higher, these pretty plants were left below, but the bushy second growth near the mountaintop was adorned with great masses of bright yellow flowers of various shrubby or arborescent composites in profuse bloom. Not far below the summit of the mountain, the private road to "Santa Elena" branched off to the right. Along this we wound for nearly a mile, through stands of young cypress trees and flowery thickets, to the two-story dwelling, which stood in a spacious, cypress-rimmed natural amphitheater in the mountainside.

On the broad stairway leading up to the front door, I was welcomed by my host, Don Axel Pira, a cultured Swede who had lived in Guatemala for a third of a century. He led me into the spacious living room, where now in the early afternoon a cheerful log fire burned in the ample corner hearth, which projected into the room and radiated heat from two sides. This fireplace was used almost every day throughout the year. The house, situated at an altitude of ninety-seven hundred feet, was the highest permanent dwelling of a white family that I had seen. At this height, nights were invariably cold. Although the outside air would warm up in the middle of sunny days, its heat did not last long enough to penetrate the thick walls and make the inside of the house comfortable without a fire.

In the evenings, the hearth was the center of interest; we would all sit within range of its generous warmth, while we read or talked over the events of the day, and the women of the family sewed. Or we would comment upon the latest news in *El Imparcial*, the daily from the capital, and propose remedies for the social and economic ills of a tortured world as earnestly as though we could do something to alleviate them, as is the pleasant but ineffectual habit of people who discuss public affairs, whether in a crowded metropolis or on a lonely and remote mountaintop.

In a bookcase against the opposite wall, I was glad to see the volumes on birds from Brehm's *Tierleben*. My host was interested in natural history and, having in his youth passed several years in Germany, read German as easily as he read Spanish and his native Swedish.

Near the house stood the sawmill. Too near the mountaintop for enough waterpower to turn the machinery, it was operated by steam generated in a wood-burning engine. The logs, chiefly cypress, were dragged from the surrounding forests attached to two-wheeled trucks drawn by four or five yokes of straining oxen. They yielded a superior lumber, light, close-grained, soft, and easily worked, but very resistant to the attacks of termites and to decay when exposed to moisture, as was convincingly attested by fallen trunks in the forest, which had remained sound while seeds had germinated upon them and grown into trees of fair size. The products of this sawmill were shipped to Guatemala City and other distant points by motor truck or oxcart, for this part of the country was wholly devoid of railroads. Indians who dwelt in huts about the sawmill did nearly all the work in the forest and the mill.

The combination of altitude and humidity at Santa Elena was unfavorable for agriculture. Beside the house was a kitchen garden, which, in the frostless months of favorable years, yielded such hardy vegetables as carrots, spinach, and radishes; but these plants grew with exasperating slowness and led a precarious existence. In the exceptionally wet year 1933, this garden was a total failure. Neither corn nor wheat was grown on the Sierra de Tecpán much above nine thousand feet; although farther west in Guatemala, as on the southern side of the Sierra Cuchumatanes, a somewhat different climate permits the cultivation of wheat, potatoes, and other vegetables as high as ten thousand feet and even more. Here oak rather than cypress appears to have been the dominant tree in the vanished forests, while on the Sierra de Tecpán I noticed few oak trees above nine thousand feet. On the slopes of Mt. Chimborazo, near the equator, barley, potatoes, quinoa, oca, Windsor beans, and melloco are grown successfully as high as twelve thousand feet. Beneath the clearer skies of central and southern Peru, cultivation extends as high as thirteen thousand feet.

I loved to wander through the cypress forests, especially on the ridges farther from the sawmill, where they grew in almost pure stand, mixed with pines and a few broadleafed trees such as the towering cornel (*Cornus disciflora*), and had not yet felt the destroying axe. In subsequent wanderings through the Guatemalan highlands, I saw no stands of cypress that approached these in magnificence. The great, fluted, columnar trunks, sometimes seven feet in diameter at shoulder height, stretched grandly upward nearly a hundred feet to the lowest branches. Their topmost twigs rose at least fifty feet higher. In the heaviest stands on the backs of the ridges, the undergrowth was too sparse to conceal the full majesty of the mighty holes, or to distract the eye that followed them upward to the lofty canopy. And the spirit, led by the eye, was exalted, until I was overcome by a feeling between reverence and exultation that vanquished the fatigue resulting from a long climb through the thin atmosphere.

More tolerant of altitudinal extremes than many plants, this tree that flourishes on high mountaintops grows well when planted at much lower altitudes. In Costa Rica, where no conifer of northern type is native, this cypress is frequently planted and does well even as low as two thousand feet.

The undergrowth in the cypress forests on the Sierra de Tecpán was largely of bamboo, which on steep slopes, where the vertical separation of the crowns permitted the influx of more light, formed dense thickets through which it was difficult to pass. Here on the cloud-bathed mountaintops, a thick garment of moss clothed the limbs of every kind of tree, and formed huge swellings, as thick as pumpkins, on the lofty boughs of the cypresses. This envelope of mosses was fertile ground for a variety of epiphytic plants, some of which were very beautiful. The most magnificent of these was *Fuchsia splendens*, a shrub with long, cable-like roots that crept over the moss-covered branches, and woody stems several yards high, from which dangled a profusion of big, bell-shaped flowers, with a deep red calyx and four green petals. Another attractive epiphyte was a false Solomon's-seal (*Smilacina salvini*), which anyone familiar with the white-flowered herb of northern woods would recognize as such. The rootstock of this air plant was a series of bulbous swellings, more than an inch thick, embedded in the mosses that covered the trunks and branches of trees. From the newest joint of this rhizome sprang a leafy shoot a foot or more long, terminated by a nodding raceme of small pink flowers. I never found this Solomon's-seal growing in the ground.

Birds were not as numerous in these dark, humid cypress forests on the crest of the Sierra as at lower altitudes, but some of the kinds that I met here were rarely or never found among the oak forests on lower slopes. Golden-crowned Kinglets hunted in lisping flocks among the somber foliage of the cypress trees, which they seldom cared to abandon. Sometimes I would see a mountain trogon, resplendent in metallic green, bright red, and white, or I would glimpse a pair of Emerald Toucanets, great-billed birds that seemed out of place in the same woods with Kinglets, Brown Creepers, Red-shafted Flickers, and Hairy Woodpeckers.

The rarest and most fantastic of the feathered inhabitants of these heights was the Horned Guan or *faisán*. One morning, while walking along the narrow back of a ridge covered with heavy, broad-leafed forest, I was startled by an explosively loud, guttural outcry. As I proceeded cautiously down the ridge, the croaking calls suddenly ceased, and in their stead came a sound like the clacking of castanets. At length, as I moved into a more open space in the forest, I beheld, clear and sharp against the morning sky, the head and neck of a Horned Guan, standing on a topmost branch of a tall, gnarled, moss-shrouded tree.

I have seen among birds few appearances so bizarre as that of the slender neck and black head with its small yellow bill, which opened and closed with a loud clacking, as though the strange fowl tried to intimidate me. With dilated pupils in bright yellow eyes, he stared fixedly at me. His bare throat was scarlet. From the crown of his head rose a tall, slender, truncate spike of bare flesh, the color of ripe strawberries. At intervals the bird, as large as a hen turkey, bent forward, stretching out and lowering his neck, and emitted more of the weird, loud grunts that had drawn my attention to him. Soon he obligingly turned around, and showed me that all the upper parts of his heavy body were black, while his fore-neck and lower parts were white. A broad, white bar crossed the middle of his long, black tail. I had difficulty naming the color of his legs, which were between salmon and pink.

I passed almost the whole of January at Santa Elena. Whenever the night was cloudless, dawn revealed a heavy frost. Sometimes, when I looked from my window on arising, the boards piled beside the sawmill, the roofs of the Indians' shacks, the bare ground, and the low herbage in the close-cropped pastures, were so white that it was easy to believe that snow had fallen in the night, and that I was in north latitude forty instead of fourteen. I have never seen snow in Central America, but I was told that it sometimes falls on the tops of the highest volcanoes, where it soon melts. One morning at Santa Elena, enough of the hoarfrost to freeze ice cream was collected. At times, sheets of ice an eighth of an inch thick formed along the edges of the rivulet that flowed through the sawmill. In exposed situations, the moist soil along the roads was frequently raised by bundles of long, needle-like crystals.

A frosty night was almost invariably followed by a bright, sunny morning with cold, bracing air. In spots shaded from the morning sunbeams, the frost crystals would frequently remain until noon, but they melted very quickly when the sun reached the zenith and poured down its heat upon them. Since frost never formed in the woodland, but only in spots exposed to radiation into the open sky, it did not anywhere persist much past midday. At intervals, clouds would roll in and veil the mountaintop for days, with occasional light rains, even in the midst of the dry season. Although this cloud-mist chilled one to the marrow, frost was absent as long as it obscured the sky.

As I lay abed those cold January nights, not quite successful in keeping warm even under several heavy Indian blankets, I thought with wonder of the hummingbirds incubating their minute eggs and brooding their naked nestlings out on the frosty mountainsides. One would hardly expect these tiny, graceful sprites to live, and far less to nest, among frosts and chilling winds. But their vitality is amazing, and where food is abundant they manage, by reducing their body temperature and metabolic processes in the manner of hibernating animals while they sleep, to keep alive through the longest and bitterest of the nights on high tropical mountains.

To hummingbirds as a family, altitude is no deterrent. As in other groups of birds, each species has a more or less restricted altitudinal range, but the hummingbird family is one of the few that are almost equally well represented from sea level up to, and even far above, tree-line, as beside bleak Andean snowfields, The bright flowers that provide a substantial part of their nourishment are, at certain seasons, far more conspicuously abundant among the light woods and open meadows of high mountains than amid the dense verdure of humid tropical lowlands; and consequently these little birds are much more in evidence, if not actually more numerous, in the cool uplands than in the thickets and heavy forests of the warn lowlands.

Now, in the early half of the dry season, many kinds of bright-flowered herbs and shrubs blossomed profusely, in defiance of nocturnal frosts. Especially abundant were the shrubby and herbaceous Salvias with scarlet or crimson blossoms rich in nectar. And because their food was more abundant than at any other season, the hummingbirds were breeding, also in contempt of the frosts. Although they had started earlier, in October or November, I still found a few of their nests as late as January.

Sometimes, in late afternoon, we climbed to the topmost point of the mountain, only a few hundred feet above the house, to watch the sun set over the Pacific.... The rocky edge of this miniature plateau, which fell off abruptly toward of Lake Atitlán, was known as "Buena Vista," as it afforded a wonderful panorama of over half of western Guatemala. I like best to remember the prospect from this promontory as I saw it on a blustery evening in late November. As we emerged from the trees onto the stony, wind-swept summit, the mists that blew over it filled the space below, and the sun, hanging low above the lake, was veiled by a pink haze. A moment later, another gust of wind dispersed the cloud, revealing the blue water of the lake far below, with the sun's orb just sinking in an orange glow behind the mountains on the farther shore.

The panorama spread before us was on the grandest scale. Toward the declining sun lay Lake Atitlán, its deep ultramarine water stretching for miles between high, precipitous shores, every irregularity of which, every salient angle on their rugged, seamed expanse, was sharply outlined in the clear evening light. To its left towered the giant cone of Volcán Atitlán, its shapely mass cut darkly into the pink and orange sky. Beside this great volcano stood Volcán San Lucas, a lesser figure with a blunted apex. On the farther shore of the lake, nearer the sun, loomed Volcán San Pedro, second only to Atitlán in majesty. Beyond and to the north, stretching toward Mexico, the high wall of the Sierra Madre met the glow of sunset in a jagged line, piercing it here and there with sharper points. Away to the southeast, in sublime isolation, stood the shapely cone of the Volcán de Agua, and the towering mass of Acatenango blending into that of Fuego. A long, level bank of white cloud, stretching afar from out of the dim east, severed the crest of each great volcano from its foot. Between the two groups of volcanoes, to the west and to the south, the coastal plain spread low and dark, with a faint line of shore beyond, and the long, level horizon of the Pacific, appearing lofty and immensely distant, curving around from Atitlán to Fuego.

Between us and the volcanoes lay a broad and comparatively level plateau, spread out at our feet in a checkerboard where dark patches represented woodland, lighter areas cultivated fields and pastures, all precisely outlined in the still evening air. Scattered here and there lay a number of small towns, whose most conspicuous features were the white mass of the church dominating the cluster of squat dwellings, and the glistening white walls and monuments of the *campo santo* or cemetery. A long, narrow line of highway stretched out toward the base of Agua. Winding through the checkered plain was a deep *barranco*, an immense gash in the earth whose scarped walls here showed green with the vegetation that clung to them, there brown in vertical streaks made by recent landslides.

Thus, for some minutes, the whole panorama would spread in clearest outline before us; then the wind, driving with mournful sighs through the moss-draped boughs of the few gaunt pines and cypresses that stood on the summit, would bear a burden of white mist that spread below us, softening all the outlines, then erasing them wholly, until we stood above a world of cloud, tinged on its western limit with the rose of sunset. The mist that filled, or at least obscured, the valley heightened our sense of its profundity and of our own loftiness—only the moss—and lichen-bedecked dead boughs of a battered cypress tree stood above us. Then the cloud, descending into the warmer air of lower regions, would dissolve again, and gradually the whole vast panorama would take form out of the mist.

Each time it was revealed, the water of Lake Atitlán was a deeper ultramarine, set among mountains of more somber purple. The warm glow of sunset intensified and spread out until it suffused the whole visible horizon of the Pacific, and its crimson and gold were interrupted only by black masses, so sharply outlined that every tree that clove the skyline was plainly visible, although many leagues away. Above us, the blue vault of the cloudless sky darkened and deepened, until the white crescent of the declining moon grew luminous, and here and there a star shone forth, while far below in Patzum lights began to twinkle. Then the chilling wind, as it drove us from the exposed summit, spread a soft blanket of cloud over all the scene, extinguishing all the earthly lights below us and leaving only the remote luminaries above, by the light of which we led our horses back to the highway, and rode homeward through forests fragrant with the scent of pine.

A Vernal Year

On the Sierra de Tecpán below Santa Elena, the Piras owned another estate, known as "Chichavac," where the vegetation was quite different and the climate more favorable for agriculture. Here, amid pines and oaks and other broad-leafed trees, lived several kinds of birds, rare or absent among the cypresses of the mountaintop, that I was eager to study. Accordingly, after I had been a month at Santa Elena, I requested permission to reside for a while in the house at Chichavac, about thirteen hundred feet lower. As it turned out, I became so absorbed in following the activities of my bird neighbors at Chichavac that I remained there for nearly eleven months, during which I made occasional longer or shorter visits to Santa Elena, about seven miles distant by the road that wound steeply up the mountain.

———·•· ❧ ·•·———

I was not sorry that few plants flowered during the final two months of the dry season, because I wished to make my botanical collection as complete as possible, yet I also desired to learn all that I could about the birds. At this period they claimed my attention so fully that I hardly had time for anything else. Before dawn, I was on my way to the woods, with my breakfast of tortillas, boiled eggs, and oranges, and a canteen full of water in my knapsack, and frequently my lunch as well, as I often passed the whole day afield. In the evening, I usually watched some bird retire for the night, as I was eager to learn how the feathered inhabitants of these heights protected themselves from the nocturnal chill. After supper, I worked at my notes until I could write no more, then went to bed with the alarm clock set for half past four or five o'clock in the morning. One advantage of studying birds in the tropics is that one need not arise so inordinately early to watch them start their day's activities, or stay out so late to see them retire, as at higher latitudes in summer. On the Sierra de Tecpán, even in June, the earliest birds did not become active until after five o'clock, Central Standard Time. In this healthful mountain climate, I could go very hard without paying for it later, as in the hot and humid lowlands.

Contrasts in a Plant Collector's Life

On my first visit to Mocá, a tall tree with pale red flowers was everywhere in blossom. After searching in vain for inflorescences that could be reached, I reluctantly felled one of the smaller of these trees, still a growth of imposing size. Collecting the five or six twiglets that I needed for specimens, I left the remainder of that fine tree to wither and rot. The thought of what I had done oppressed me. A troublesome question kept revolving in my mind too persistently to be brushed aside: Had I performed a laudable act in the service of science, or had I been guilty of vandalism? After long pondering, I found myself unable to define precisely the boundary between science and vandalism; but I suspected that some of the things done in the name of science—murderous and wasteful collecting; vivisection by tyros unfit to make the beneficial discoveries that alone might justify the suffering they cause; the removal and scattering of ancient monuments—verge dangerously upon this boundary. I resolved to walk more carefully in the future.

Independence

The great tragedy of biology is the difficulty of acquiring certain kinds of information about living things without harming them. Too often, to advance studies in such fields as physiology, anatomy, or taxonomy, the zoologist must mutilate, torture, or kill the animals that he or she professes to love. I have been content to learn what I could about birds without harming them, but others, because of professional commitments or scientific curiosity so strong that it overruled compassion, have taken a different course. To be fair to bird collectors, their effect upon populations of widespread, flourishing species is negligible, but this hardly softens their impact upon the unfortunate individuals chosen to become specimens.

Perhaps, if I had tried, I might have enlisted Chapman's support, and that of the wealthy museum which he represented, of my studies of tropical birds. But I hesitated to become dependent on a museum, lest it require me to collect the bird specimens of which museums seem never to have enough, and this I could never bring myself to do. Stubbornly independent, I knew that I must go my own way and work out my own destiny, difficult and perplexing as that sometimes was. Many years later, after Frank M. Chapman had died and a fund to support ornithological studies had been established in his name at the American Museum of Natural History, I received from it research grants that enabled me to extend my studies into new regions, but these grants were given without any obligation to collect.

A Wanderer's Harvest

We set forth on our journeys to see more of the earth's beautiful and wonderful things than we could find at home, yet we cannot avoid encountering much of its ugliness, misery, and horror. Beauty and ugliness; pleasure and pain; elation and depression; ardor and exhaustion; life and death—these are the two faces of the same coin; we might even lack names for them if they were not brought into high relief by their opposites. We undertake our travels to gather the glittering coins of beauty and joy, but too often we find them lying with their dark faces up. What could we expect? Unless we were fools, we knew before we left home that every coin has two faces.

Fortunately for our faith in life, the coin's glittering face makes, as a rule, the most lasting impression on the mind, just as the brightest object most strongly affects the photographic film. Thus our journeys frequently appear more enjoyable in retrospect than while we were in the midst of them; and memories of past delights lure us ever and again to embark upon fresh travels, and incidentally to expose ourselves once more to the old annoyances and disillusions. Nevertheless, whether they bring pleasure or pain, a naturalist's travels are a necessary education. They give breadth of vision, as long and studious sojourns, observation of the gradual growth and development and decay of organisms through the slow procession of the seasons, bring depth of understanding. To me, these sojourns have yielded more contentment and knowledge than nay wanderings, and have rewarded me more richly. I have traveled chiefly to make them possible.

I have, by inclination, been an adventurer in little things. My red-letter days have not been made by planting my banner on the summit of some forbidding peak hitherto unsealed, or by stumbling upon some ancient city lost in the forest's depths. Among them I include the day when, riding down an abrupt mountainside in northern Guatemala, I first saw a magnificent living Quetzal and heard the sweet strains of the Slate-colored Solitaire; the day years later when, after long waiting, I found my first Quetzals' nest; the day when, riding through the rain along the side of a profound Andean gorge, I saw my first glowing orange male Cock-of-the-Rock resting beside the trail. These days match in memory that on which, with my head stuck through the car window as the train speeded away from Veracruz, I beheld my first tropical snow-peak looming ahead like some whiter and more substantial cloud; and that when, the sky clearing after days of rain and mist, the snow-crowned cone of Sangay, plumed with a long streamer of smoke, stood revealed above the vast forests of the Ecuadorian Oriente.

But a place still more sacred in memory is held by the afternoon when, dragging myself from bed with a raging pain in an infected leg, I hobbled down the hill at Lancetilla to watch a nest of the Groove-billed Anis, and saw a juvenal of the first brood, hatched in July, helping to feed and protect his younger brothers and sisters hatched in September. My memorable discoveries of this sort have been as numerous as I could reasonably expect; I could not tell about all of them in this book, but most are to be found in other writings.

The most substantial harvest of these years of wanderings and sojourns off the beaten track, the reason and justification for them, is the bird lore I have garnered. I find enduring satisfaction in having built up, by long vigils and innumerable visits to nests, fairly complete pictures of the habits of several hundred kinds of birds, beautiful, shy creatures whose life stories had never been told. Moreover, it is most gratifying to recall that such insight into the lives of birds as I have won has been gained without the intentional sacrifice of a single life, without the willful destruction of a single nest. I have from the first regarded my bird-watching as a game—a serious and important game that can tax one's strength and skill to its limits, but still a game which has definite rules, and in which the odds are always in favor of the birds, where they rightly belong. And these rules prohibit the destruction of occupied nests, even, for example, cutting down a high, inaccessible nest that cannot otherwise be examined, or digging out and leaving exposed those tucked away in narrow crannies and deep burrows.

Truth and Beauty

Whatever the quality of birds' inner life may be, outwardly their lives are beautiful. Much as I have loved and sought truth, I have loved and sought beauty even more—not only sensuous beauty, but likewise moral and spiritual beauty, the beauty that ancient philosophers equated with the good. Beauty is always, in a sense, truth, although if incautious we may draw false inferences from it; but truth, in a world so full of harsh and ugly facts as this, is often the antithesis of beauty. Although one may contend that to know the truth, even about ugly and evil things, is in itself good and valuable, such knowledge can hardly avoid being tainted by its loathsome object. But to learn the truth about beautiful things, by long and patient effort to disclose their carefully guarded secrets, is one of the most satisfying of pursuits.

Birds, as I have said, are among the most beautiful of living things, and their lives, or at least those of the less fierce and ravenous kinds, are nearly always beautiful, as a whole and in their details. To learn pleasant facts about beautiful things is altogether delightful. This is what makes the study of their habits so richly rewarding, at least to one with my particular temperament. Certainly, for our survival, we need to know about many things that are dry, unpleasant, or revolting. But so many brilliant minds, supported by wealthy institutions, are dedicated to these investigations, that it can do no great harm if a few "world losers and world forsakers" devote themselves to the pursuit of the beautiful truths that enrich us spiritually even if they contribute nothing to our survival in a competitive world. Yet the study of bird life must be regarded as more than an innocent hobby; by contributing generously to our understanding of basic biological problems, it can help to make our own lives saner and more secure.

Not only did the years of wandering about which I have told in this book fill my mind with treasured memories and my notebooks with valued records, they prepared me for the undertaking on which I had set my heart: to establish a homestead in or beside unspoiled tropical forest, where I would enjoy leisure and independence to study and write about nature for decades. This was not easy to accomplish, especially by one with small resources. Until I had seen much of the tropics, and learned to deal with its people, and outgrown the spells of nostalgia that at first oppressed me, and hardened myself to isolation, and discovered in which of the many varieties of climate that tropical America offers I could live most healthfully and efficiently, and accumulated a little capital, I was not prepared to realize this dream. How it was finally accomplished, and what rewards it yielded, has been told in another book.

SELECTION FROM

A NATURALIST IN COSTA RICA

(1971)

The Call of Green Hills

A week after leaving the Quebrada de las Vueltas, I embarked at Puntarenas for Guayaquil. I was eager to see the snow-crowned volcanoes, the forests rich in palms, and, above all, the marvelously varied and colorful bird life of Ecuador. But I went at the wrong season to find many nests for study, and, before the end of the year 1939, I returned to Costa Rica to take charge of the botanical section of the Museo Nacional, as I had agreed to do before leaving the country.

It was hard to stay within the thick walls of the old museum in San José during those clear, sunny months that started off the year. All around me in the herbarium were cases full of botanical specimens, long since dry and colorless, for which I had recently become responsible. They clamored, as well as such lifeless things can, for care and rearrangement. But the weather of the early *verano*, with its cold, starry nights and warm, sun-flooded days, was like some heady wine. Try as I might, I could not imprison my thoughts within those massive walls of puddled clay, among the herbarium specimens. They persisted in floating out over the surrounding mountains whence, years before, Pittier and Tonduz and Brenes had gathered those same specimens. Through the deep-embrasured windows of the herbarium I could see nothing of those hills; only a little sunlit rectangle of courtyard where goldfish swam in a pond and a few orchids grew. But climbing the dusty, circling stairway of the old square tower at the end of the building, I could fill my eyes with the sight of the green hills that swept in a wide circle about the narrow plateau where the city stood, calling a naturalist in so many directions at once that my mind became a disordered whirl of enticing and mostly impracticable projects for exploration. In the northeast, seeming very close in the clear morning atmosphere, rose the immense bulk of Volcán Irazú, with a lofty column of smoke arising from its flat summit. Blown to the southwest by the trade wind, this eruptive material spread a fine layer of dust over the glass cases of the museum.

The call of those green hills was too strong to be resisted, especially by one who had so recently forsworn full liberty to roam them. Many a plant still unknown to science lurked among those forested mountains, so inviting in the distance, but on actual contact so rugged and forbidding, imposing such formidable obstacles to the progress of puny humans. Would it not be well to collect, now in the good weather, samples of the flora of some still unexplored nook among the mountains? A few thousand new specimens, more or less, to arrange along with the old ones during the long, wet months that would follow could make no great difference. The sympathetic director of the museum readily agreed with these arguments. I was free to take to the hills!

NATURALIST ON A TROPICAL FARM

(1980)

Los Cusingos

I wished to live simply in an unspoiled natural setting, while studying nature like a scientist, all without harming the objects of my study, or the other living things around me. This rather unusual combination of objectives was not easy to realize. For a decade, I wandered about tropical America, living for months, or sometimes for more than a year continuously, in rented or borrowed cabins, on hospitable farms, occasionally at a research station, while I intensively watched birds and collected botanical specimens to pay my way. As the years passed, and my growing mass of records became more cumbersome to transport, always with some risk of loss, I felt increasingly the need of a permanent home, where I could gather my books and notes around me, prepare my observations for publication, and continue to study nature on my own land.

When I reached this point, I thought of the Valley of El General, at the head of the Río Térraba on the Pacific slope of southern Costa Rica, where I had already spent two and a half richly rewarding years, studying birds and collecting plants in various localities. In those days, before the Inter-American Highway cut through the length of the valley, it was an isolated region, surrounded by vast, scarcely broken forests, and easily accessible only by air. Only a long, rough trail, threading the forest and passing over the high, bleak summits of the Cordillera de Talamanca, connected it with the center of the country. San Isidro de El General, now a cathedral town and bustling commercial center, was then only a small village, with a few stores that sold cheap clothing and household necessities to customers who mostly came with bare feet. From this center, unpaved roads led in all directions, between patches of the original forest and farms carved from it so recently that charred logs and stumps still cluttered the fields. No motorcar ever raised the dust on these rustic lanes. The airplane brought mail and merchandise, and a radio station provided more rapid communication with the capital, San José.

On my bay horse, Bayon, I spent days riding about the country, visiting farms that were offered to the foreigner who had come with a little capital to this valley where money was scarce and went far. Finally, in March of 1941, I found the farm that promised to fulfill my dreams. At an altitude of about twenty-five hundred feet, it stretched along the western bank of the Río Peñas Blancas, a broad mountain torrent that rushed clamorously over a bed strewn with huge boulders, bringing crystal-clear, cool water from the high, forested slopes of the Cordillera de Talamanca in the north. A steep ridge, still mostly wooded, ran almost the whole length of the farm. Between the ridge and the river lay nearly level terraces, which fell away by high, steep bluffs to the exceedingly stony but fertile benches of back soil, where in past ages the river had flowed. Three permanent streams traversed the farm, two near its northern end, the third on its western side. In the rainy season, two other rivulets also flowed through the land.

This farm belonged to Francisco Mora, known as Don Chico, a restless pioneer who alternated between seeking treasure in old Indian burials and converting wilderness into farms, which he soon sold to move on to new land. It contained about a half acre of coffee in full production, a small patch of bananas, extensive pastures, a scattering of fruit trees, and about two acres of sugarcane, with an oxdriven mill, beneath a big thatched shed, for converting the cane sap into hard, round bricks of brown sugar.

What interested me more was the forest. I was sorry to see that several acres of it had been felled and burned, so recently that prostrate trunks still smoldered. The pasture on the steep slope behind the terrace where I would build my house was littered with huge, decaying trunks. Nevertheless, a large tract of unspoiled forest remained, with trees towering up to a hundred and fifty feet, multitudes of palms with slender, soaring trunks, orchids and many other epiphytes on the trees, and beneath them many low palms, flowering shrubs, and great-leaved herbs. In this forest lived tinamous, guans, quails, trogons, hummingbirds, toucans, woodpeckers, woodcreepers, antbirds, manakins, cotingas, flycatchers, honeycreepers, tanagers, and finches, along with White-faced Monkeys, coatimundis, agoutis, forest deer, and other mammals. The woodland contained nearly everything that unexploited rain forest in this region should have, except such large animals as jaguars, pumas, ocelots, tapirs, and peccaries, which the tract was too small to support, and which I could do without. To discover the nests and follow the life histories of all the birds would keep me busy for years—after nearly forty, there are still several species for which I have failed to find a single nest.

No one who hoped to grow rich by farming would have bought such rocky, broken land, so remote, as it then was, from railroad, highway, or navigable water. But the very features that would at times have made it a farmer's despair made it attractive to a naturalist. Its diversity of habitats assured a diversity of organisms. The streams that caused transportation problems, and needed bridges, which rotted or were washed away, attracted kingfishers, winsome Torrent Flycatchers, Neotropic Cormorants, fantastic Gray Basilisk Lizards, and other creatures that enhanced the whole. When I found that Don Chico would sell his land at a price within my slender means, I bought it, fondly taking all this vast diversity of natural wealth under my protection. Now, at last, I could dwell in an unspoiled natural setting, study nature on my own land, and try to live in harmony with the teeming life around me.

Don Chico lived with his common-law wife, their small, fair-headed son, and several huge hogs, in a low, floorless, thatched cabin set at the very edge of a high, wooded bluff above the creek, a site that permitted the convenient disposal of refuse by throwing it out the back door. The contract of sale gave him the right to remain there, without the pigs, until he finished a new house on land he had acquired across the Río Peñas Blancas—a period that stretched on to a year.

I decided to build my home on a high terrace that faced the rising sun, the mountains, and the river, whose voice, softly murmurous in the dry season, thunderous in rainy October, revealed its varying phases. The river, or the creek that flowed into it almost in front of the house site, would supply water when I could not catch enough for household needs from the roof, which seldom happened except in the dry season. (Years passed before I had water piped in.) This site, near water yet far enough above the river to be in no danger from its highest floods, had evidently been favored by my predecessors long ago. Digging in the garden, I found shards of Indian pottery and a clay spindle whorl. Stones that they had probably used for crushing maize lay about. The summit of the steep ridge behind the house was their burial ground. And the huge rock with a gently sloping top that rose beside the creek nearby was incised with curious spirals, of puzzling significance, that the aborigines had carved. This enormous block of andesite was to prove most useful for drying newly harvested beans and rice in the sunshine.

The five-roomed house that I planned would be made almost wholly of locally available materials. Only the hardware and a single bag of cement came from outside the valley, necessarily by air. The stones so abundant on the lower ground and in stream beds served as bases to raise the construction above the damp ground, termites, and snakes. A man skilled in the use of the adze hewed the heavier timbers from durable hardwood trees in the

forest. Lighter timbers and boards were brought by oxcart from a small sawmill across the valley in San Isidro,
eight or nine miles away by winding roads. Since the
mill lacked a planing machine, many boards had to be
smoothed with a hand plane. Unglazed tiles for the roof
were supplied by a farmer in La Hermosa, four miles away.
By no means an expert tile maker, he made inferior tiles,
but the best I could find. Hundreds broke as the oxcart
that brought them bumped over roads rough with rocks
and roots, but with occasional shifting and patching,
the survivors of this journey have kept the house dry for
nearly forty years.

I planned my house to be economical and durable
rather than elegant. For the walls I chose *bahareque*, a
type of construction formerly widespread in Costa Rica,
as in other parts of Latin America, but now rarely used,
as it is time-consuming, requires much expensive hand
labor, and, to be secure, needs heavy timbers that have
become very costly. On both sides of the sturdy uprights,
wild canes, which grow tall along the rivers, were nailed
horizontally at intervals of a few inches. The four-inch
space between the two series of canes was filled with
clay dug from the hillside behind the house. The clay
had been kneaded with water in a shallow pit, by horses
walking around and around, until it had become very
tacky. As it dried in the walls, the clay shrank, leaving
wide fissures, which had to be filled with more clay. When
the space between the canes had been filled solidly, the
canes themselves were covered with clay, which required
several applications to fill all the cracks. Next, the walls
were thinly covered with fresh cow dung, an excellent

binder. This at first made a horrible stench, but it soon dried to a soft gray, odorless surface, which was admired by certain visitors ignorant of its origin. Finally, the inside walls were whitewashed, the outside walls coated with the sack of cement that had come in the airplane.

Work on the walls proceeded slowly, in the intervals when farm tasks abated somewhat. Not until two years after the foundation stones had been set was the house finished. Meanwhile, I made simple furniture, including tables, stools, cabinets, and open shelves for books. I also bought the larger farm, with much woodland and little cultivation, that adjoined mine to the south. After I sold part of this land, I had about two hundred and fifty acres, about half in old forest and much of the remainder in second-growth woods. I decided to preserve all the forest and plant only on land that had already been cleared.

After long cogitation, I called my farm "Los Cusingos," for the Fiery-billed Araçaris, which are found only on the Pacific side of southern Costa Rica and across the border in Panama. I was not wholly satisfied with this choice, but settled for it because certain other birds that I admired more lacked names that my neighbors knew and could pronounce. Now I am convinced it was a good choice; these agile, colorful toucans have persisted here, while other, less wary birds have disappeared.

Except for rare visitors, for nine years I lived alone. But how could I be lonely with so much varied, vibrant life around me? How could I be bored with so much to see and learn and do? When nests of the resident birds became rare, it was almost time to watch for returning migrants from the north. Most of the time I had, living nearby, a family that included a farm hand and an unmarried daughter, who came in the mornings to cook, wash, and sweep the house for me. I had cows for milk, chickens for eggs, horses for riding, and all these dependents needed much attention. I seemed never to have enough time for all the odd jobs that continually turned up: gathering fruits, mending fences and gates, repairing leaky roofs, curing sick animals, extracting fly larvae from the skins of cows. Far from finding the frequent long, rainy afternoons depressing, I welcomed them as a time for reading, writing, or carpentry.

After nine celibate years, I married Pamela, youngest daughter of Charles Herbert Lankester, a coffee planter and self-taught naturalist of wide interests. She willingly relinquished comforts to live simply on a farm still lacking many things that city people believe indispensable. Some years later, we adopted Edwin, a quiet, promising boy, already in his teens, who had grown up on the farm (his father had worked for me, intermittently, for many years) and had been left unprotected by the disruption of his family. Then, with a larger household and a growing library for which there never seemed to be enough shelves, we added a wing to the originally L-shaped house.

A NATURALIST IN COSTA RICA

(1971)

The Peña Blanca

I n my travels about tropical America, I had traversed many miles of territory where the earth was sick, shorn of her protective garment of vegetation, her streams laden with mud that betrayed her impaired health. But at Los Cusingos I had found an area where she displayed all the symptoms of exuberant vitality. Her sylvan robe, although torn here and there by the clearings of the early settlers, was still sufficiently intact to protect her most vital parts. The Peña Blanca River that formed my eastern boundary ran clear and pure. Woodland and river together invited me to come and stay, to live healthily where the earth itself was healthy.

I was not greatly distressed by the countless rocks that littered all those lower and more fertile parts of the farm where the river had once flowed. If on land the stones were mute and lifeless encumbrances, deterrent to agriculture, in the riverbed the boulders were too precious to be spared. They gave the stream its wild beauty, creating the rapids and the white foaming waters that revealed the current's vital force. They were the strings on which the rushing waters played their ceaseless tune, low and soothing when the stream was shrunken in the dry season, but when torrential rains fell on the hills, rising to a fierce insistent roaring, with overtones of deep rumbling as of distant thunder, caused by the rolling and shifting and striking together of the boulders in the channel.

The myriad rocks that littered the land and the riverbed, giving the valley its rugged charm and its living voice, made it unfit to support an opulent human culture, expressing itself in art, literature, and science. But I am not one of those who assume that the fulfillment of the evolutionary process depends on a single species of animal, that earth is solicitous of the welfare of just one of her countless kinds of children. To me it was deeply satisfying to know that here, at least, the earth, our old mother, was still in her prime of health and vigor, strong to nourish and support her brood, even if those she chiefly favored in this particular valley were other than the human kind.

Those circumstances, which are the constant accompaniment of our life, the ground and support of our being, seldom obtrude upon our consciousness save as they are altered in quality or intensity or as we are suddenly deprived of them. So it is with the air we breathe, so with those living associates most necessary to our happiness and well being; and so, as days lengthened into months and months into years, it became with the voice of the river beside which I dwelt. Although the tympana of my ears constantly vibrated to its notes, for hours together

I would remain unaware of this persistent undertone of my life. But a breeze that wafted the sound more strongly to my ears, a break in an absorbing occupation that held the mind away from its immediate environment, or the increasing volume of sound that accompanied the swelling of the stream beneath the heavy afternoon downpours—all these would revive my awareness of my cheerful companion, the river. I was always grateful for these reminders of its proximity. As I wandered in the forest, where its voice was muted by the crowded trunks and heavy foliage, it was easy to forget that it was close by. But when at length I returned to the clearing, the flood of sunshine and the river's voice united to greet me cheerfully, the voice indeed rushing forward to welcome me before I reached the brighter light.

Sometimes, as I lay in the darkness of the long nights of the rainy season, the sound of the swollen river fell upon my ears as a choir of many deep human voices hymning in solemn jubilation. But whether loud or low, whether soothing or insistent, I was happy to have that tireless voice always vibrating around me, a constant reminder that our old earth has not yet been wholly tamed and subjugated to the industrial uses of humanity.

To me, the river was more than an impersonal voice of wild nature; it was a friend and companion and comforter in distress. There were days when everything on the farm seemed to go wrong, when I imagined myself to be hated by my neighbors, scorned by my employees, and forgotten by distant friends. But no matter how gloomy my thoughts and depressed my vitality, the river could restore my drooping spirits. Its good humor was contagious; its abundant vitality communicated itself to me when I came near. As I walked beside its foaming, sparkling waters or sat on a mossy rock watching its dancing surges and listening to its vibrant voice, gloom and doubts would dissolve away, and before I was aware of the change, I would be humming a tune.

The river flowed down to us out of the rugged mountains to the north, where rose Chirripó Grande, the highest peak in the Talamancan Cordillera. Although not twenty miles away, the broken intervening terrain, the density of the trackless forests, made these summits seem far more remote. I never heard of anyone who had followed the river to its source. During my first years on the farm, I dreamed vaguely of tracing my river to its birthplace. But the expedition would have required a small party, with some to carry equipment and supplies for several days, while others cut a trail. Perhaps with a good companion, or a motive more impelling than curiosity, I would have made the journey. But every day there was so much to keep me busy on the farm itself! A naturalist who had spent the greater part of a long life in Costa Rica told me that he could never get anywhere in the country: there was always too much to engage his attention and delay his march in the first mile or two. Hence I never learned why our river is called the Peña Blanca, if there is a white cliff along its course, I have neither seen nor heard of it. From the hilltop behind our house, we can distinguish a whitish exposure of rock on a distant mountainside high above the Río San Pedro, the next fairly big stream to the east. Possibly this is the white cliff that gives our river its name. Some early settler might have seen it in the distance and, in the difficult forested terrain, become confused as to which river flowed below this conspicuous landmark.

The stretch of river that borders Los Cusingos offers no large pools for swimming. During most of the long wet season, the current is so strong that a swimmer is in danger of being dashed against one of the many rocks that encumber the channel. Moreover, the coldness of water that rushes down from chill mountain heights discourages long immersion. But in the dry season, when the stream is lower and less impetuous, there are a few pools deep and wide enough for swimming a few strokes, if one is heedful of submerged rocks that may give a painful bump. The water seems somewhat warmer then, and the sultry afternoons of February and March suggest a dip in the refreshing stream.

Although I did not often swim in the river, I washed in it regularly. As the house neared completion, we tried to dig a well behind it in order to have a convenient source of pure water not only for the kitchen but for bathing, when I came home too tired or too late in the evening to go down to the river or when the weather was unfavorable. The first well shaft that we sunk ran into a great rock at the depth of four yards. We filled it up and tried again nearby, this time going down six yards before we struck a boulder too big to be removed. So we resigned ourselves to hauling up water for the kitchen in buckets from a streamside spring some distance away and to bathing always in the river.

It was not difficult to be satisfied with such a bath, for no emperor of Rome, no opulent citizen of Sybaris, could have possessed one adorned more lavishly, yet in such exquisite taste. The walls were the greenwood trees, and especially the sotacaballo or riverwood, whose trunks were as gnarled as those of ancient olive trees, but more massive. With tough, sinewy roots tortuously inserted among the rocks that formed the shores, these aged, stubborn trees were braced to withstand the impact of the roaring flood waters and to lean far over the channel and join their crooked arms with those of neighbors on the opposite bank. The ceiling was formed by the interlacing, perpetually verdant boughs of these same spreading trees. The roof's design was no lifeless, frozen arabesque, but a living tracery capable of transforming itself with a garment of delicate blossoms. In November or December, or sometimes not until early February, the twigs and thinner branches would so indue themselves with faintly pink flowers, consisting largely of clustered stamens, that they appeared to be several times their actual thickness. Their heavy fragrance filled the air above the river and was wafted up to the house; chiefly in the late afternoon or during the night. Another change came during the dry months, when bronzy young leaves were added to the deep green of the persisting older foliage.

These were transient adornments, but at all seasons both the walls and the roof were profusely decorated with an incomparable vegetative display, for no tree of the region is more hospitable to epiphytic growths of all sorts than the Rough-barked Sotacaballo. The long catalogue of floral adornments would prove tedious to all but the taxonomic botanist. Even to convey an impression of the wealth of forms and colors in these crowded aerial gardens is an overwhelming task. There are orchids great and small, some with dainty white flowers, some with bright orange florets, and some (*Elleanthus capitatus*) with heavy heads of small, purple blossoms embedded in glistening, color-less jelly. There are ferns in almost inexhaustible variety, with wide-spreading fronds intricately compounded, with tiny, lacy fronds, with stiff, entire fronds. There are bromeliads with strap-shaped leaves arranged in tight rosettes that hold little aerial pools of water, supporting an aquatic flora and fauna all their own. There are vinelike epiphytic heaths (*Satyria elongata*) with sprays of tubular red blossoms hanging above the rushing water. There are aroids with great thick leaves and stiff spikes of red or orange fruits. Although the verdant tapestry remains much the same throughout the year, the colorful minor decorations are constantly changing. I could never foretell with what delicate blossoms the unseen attendants of my sylvan bath would adorn its walls in anticipation of my next visit. With so much to enjoy and admire, no wonder my bath was often a protracted affair.

The floor of my bath was not covered with a mosaic of colored tiles in the Roman fashion. It was composed of rocks and boulders of all sizes and shapes, with here and there a small pocket of sand between them. I had to be careful not to stub a toe or skin a knee while bathing, but the need to exercise caution helped to keep me young and agile. The irregularity of the floor provided a wide choice of pools for my ablutions. In the dry weather when the stream was low, I often chose one in midchannel, where the water was deepest. During most of the rainy season, a spot beside the shore was safest and most convenient. But sometimes in October, when the water swirled angrily and threatened to overflow the banks, prudence counseled that I stand on a massive rock and pour water over myself with a calabash, as I learned to do long ago in Mexico.

For fellow bathers, I had the kingfishers and the cormorant and the otter. Of the halcyon tribe there were three kinds: the big Ringed Kingfisher, with slate-blue upper plumage and rich chestnut breast; the middle-sized Amazon Kingfisher, clad in deep green, white, and chestnut; and the dainty, little Green Kingfisher, a duodecimo edition of the Amazon. The Ringed Kingfisher I usually saw winging its deliberate way far overhead, voicing a stentorian *kleck* in measured time. But the two smaller kinds often flew close by me while I bathed, or they plunged into some deeper pool from rock or overhanging bough at no great distance from me. Their bath, of course, was usually incidental to their fishing. But at times the kingfishers performed deliberate ablutions. Along this rock-bound river were no banks of soft, sandy loam where these birds could easily dig the tunnels for their nests, and the ornithologist could conveniently study their domestic life, as years earlier I had done along placid lowland streams in Guatemala and Honduras. At Los Cusingos, the kingfishers had to seek pockets and veins of friable soil between the impacted boulders of the higher banks, and, doubtless, many a tunnel hopefully begun by a mated pair was prematurely blocked by an intractable rock, as had happened with the well shafts we dug by my house.

In such circumstances, the kingfishers would be inclined to use a successful excavation year after year.

Another creature that I met chiefly when I went to bathe was the nutria or tropical otter. Sometimes, while undressing, I watched one of these aquatic animals playing at some distant point along the opposite shore, but it was shy and melted away when it saw me. Once, when I rose from the water just above a big rock, I found myself staring into the squat, white-whiskered face of an otter who had simultaneously risen on the opposite side of the same rock. I hesitate to affirm which of us was more startled by this sudden encounter, but the smaller animal was more mobile, and in a trice it disappeared under water. When alarmed in this fashion, the otter could swim so far beneath the surface that when next it emerged for air it was out of sight.

Sometimes, on a morning of brilliant sunshine, I would find an otter stretched at ease on the top of a great boulder in the streambed, with a broad trickle of water down the side revealing that it had just emerged all dripping from the cold river. How delightful to loll luxuriously in the warm sunshine after fishing in the chill water, to yawn, to lick one's sleek pelage, to lie full length on one's back with short legs and big paws sticking up into the air, or just to doze in the grateful warmth! Yet a creature of the wild can never afford to be quite forgetful of enemies. From time to time, eyes must be opened for a look around. Yet it is not the eyes but the nose that is most sensitive to danger. So long as the breeze drifts toward me from the river, I can stand immobile, watching the drowsy animal without arousing suspicion. But now the light, fitful wind shifts and carries human scent to those acute nostrils. The animal lifts its squat, bewhiskered head, sniffs the air, and, sensing my presence, slides off the rock to vanish in the foaming current. Only the wet spot on top and the trickle down the side reveal that he has been drowsing there.

The most winsome of all the creatures that kept me company while I bathed were the Torrent Flycatchers. These minute, chubby birdlings, whitish with dull black head, wings, and tail, are the elfin guardians of the rushing mountain streams of tropical America, from Costa Rica to Bolivia. They have no counterpart in the more northerly regions of the continent, and they promptly capture the affection of all who meet them. They seem too small and fragile to spend their days just beyond reach of the hungry surges of the most impetuous mountain torrents; yet the more boulders, the more white water, the more at home they appear to be. Like the sandpipers, waterthrushes, wagtails, dippers, and other birds of the inland watercourses, they are constantly flagging their short tails up and down. Flitting restlessly from rock to rock, they snatch some of their food from the air like other flycatchers, but much they pluck from the wet faces of the rocks, often darting down to seize some tiny larva or other creature left exposed by a receding wave, then bouncing lightly away just in time to escape the returning surge.

The male and female, who remain mated throughout the year, often stand together on some exposed rock and lift up their heads to sing a little duet of high, sharp notes. Their nest is a neat, open cup, covered on the outside with green moss and softly lined with downy feathers. As befits the nursery of a river sprite, this elegant structure is often attached to a leafy bough that reaches far out above the rushing current, and, appropriately, it may contain many wiry, brown capsule stalks of riverweeds. The male dutifully helps his mate to build, and often he comes to stand beside her on the rim of the nest while she incubates the two minute, pale buff eggs, keeping them warm in their mossy chalice so close above the cold surges of the restless mountain torrent.

Forest Trails

Fifty yards from the house, the edge of the rain forest that covers nearly half of Los Cusingos rises like a high wall. To reach this woodland, I make a detour, passing through a narrow gate in front of the house and descending by a footpath cut into the steep bank to the horses' pasture that borders the river. This long, narrow, rocky pasture is pleasantly shaded by orange, guava, avocado, rose apple, and other trees that attract many birds. To scan the treetops for rare feathered visitors, to hear the cheerful bird songs, to rub Atalanta's velvety nose or stroke Rocalpe's sleek neck, are diversions that often delay my march to the forest.

When I came here in 1941, the trees along the edges of this pasture were draped with a scandent bamboo, a species of *chusquea*, with thin, wiry stems and small, lanceolate leaves. I never noticed a flower on these bamboos until 1958, when in October and November many of them dispensile inflorescences with deep red, furry bracts, from beneath which peep tubular, yellow flowers—bizarre tropical growths unlike anything known in the temperate zones. Here I sometimes meet that rare, curious hummingbird, the White-tipped Sicklebill, whose strongly downcurved bill is just the shape for probing these strongly bent heliconia flowers. The Sicklebill's feet and legs are stouter than those of most hummingbirds; it uses them to cling beside the flowers it visits, instead of hovering on wing in typical hummingbird fashion. Here also grows a lower, more delicate heliconia, with upright inflorescences and bright yellow floral bracts prettily margined with red. Their nearly straight, yellow flowers are visited by hummingbirds with straighter bills. When the latter visit the sickle-shaped flowers of the red-bracted species, they pierce the corollas instead of probing them in the "legitimate" manner that effects pollination, as does the Sicklebill Hummingbird.

To this low-lying woodland I often come in September and October to enjoy the beauty of two shrubs of the acanthus family: *Razisea spicata*, with long, tubular, brilliantly red blossoms, and *Poikilacanthus macranthus* with equally long, lavender flowers. Both are profusely generous with their bloom. Along the low bank bordering the little-used roadway, in the deep shade, tree ferns have grown up and spread their great, intricately divided fronds high above my head.

A short walk through this old second-growth woodland brings me to the taller, more massive trees, intermingled with noble palms, of the ancient forest. Sometimes as I enter it, I repeat those fine verses of Francis Thompson:

> *This is the mansion built for me*
> *By the sweating centuries;*
> *Roofed with intertwined tree,*
> *Woofed with green for my princelier ease.*

This, too, is my garden, which nature began to prepare for me ages before I was born—a garden such as no monarch, no matter how puissant, could create for himself by royal command. Although for years my work took me almost daily into tropical rain forest, I rarely enter it without a feeling of awe, without a reverential, meditative pause, as though I passed through the portals of some magnificent temple, pervaded with delicate incense, illuminated by a dim, religious light. And is this not the fane that the mysterious Creative Energy has raised as its own monument, where in contemplative silence we come closest to it and perhaps achieve a fuller appreciation of its power and majesty, of its illimitable creativity, of the unfathomable enigmas it presents to finite human minds?

An acre of tropical rain forest supports a greater variety of living things, vegetable and animal, macroscopic and microscopic, than an equal area of the earth's surface covered by any other type of vegetation. It is even doubtful whether humanity, by concentrating the productions of all the continents and all the islands in botanic and zoological gardens, has ever succeeded in bringing so great a diversity of living organisms into a small area, as are found in the tropical forest. The spreading limbs of a single great tree may uphold a garden with a variety of shrubbery, flowers, and ferns that would be the envy of any gardener. There is even pond life in the little pools of water contained in the rosettes of the epiphytic bromeliads and in the close-set, fleshy, highly colored bracts that shield the flowers of some of the heliconias. All these creatures exist in conditions that make their study a particularly arduous pursuit because of the excellent opportunities for the concealment of all small organisms, because so much of the activity of the forest is carried on by night, and, above all, because to humans, the earth-bound, scarcely one-twentieth of the vertical depth of the forest is within easy reach.

And yet, despite its amazingly exuberant life, many people find the tropical forest monotonous. There is, indeed, a general sameness of aspect over large areas, and it has already been noticed that throughout their vast sweep, the forests of tropical America exhibit the same broad features under similar conditions of soil and rainfall. A gallery filled with the choicest paintings may soon become monotonous to one without knowledge of art or its history; and the halls of a great museum, so full of interest to one versed in the subjects they display, quickly become tedious to the mere wonder seeker. The fascination of the forest grows along with our foundation of knowledge and our skill in uncovering its well-guarded secrets.

To one who loves nature in her wild majesty, the aspect of the forest changes ceaselessly as one wanders through it. No two vistas are quite alike. Here is a fertile, sheltered dell where the trunks of the gigantic trees rise up with more than ordinary sweep and girth; here a ridge where the tall and slender columns of the palms cluster in more than usual profusion; here a ravine where tree ferns spread their broad filigree fronds in wondrous perfection; here an open glade where flowering shrubs make a display of bright color rare in the lowland forest. And just as the solitary wanderer is about to call the forest deserted and lifeless, one meets a troupe of monkeys chattering and gesticulating in the boughs above, displaying an interest in the earth-bound primate...or a band of collared peccaries...grunting away, leaving a strong scent of musk on the still air of the underwood; or a broad-winged Morpho Butterfly floating rapidly past...with flashes of azure unbelievably intense; or...a swarming legion of army ants with its motley following of small birds, so varied in form, plumage, and voice, yet all fairly tolerant of each other, as each in its own fashion snatches up the insects, spiders, and other small creatures that rush out from concealment beneath the ground litter as the devouring horde of ants approaches—the whole forming one of the most animated displays that wild nature anywhere presents.

Much of the more violent and sanguinary strife of the forest takes place under cover of darkness. It is chiefly then that tooth and claw and poison fang are at work. Rarely by day we come upon mute traces of the carnage: the hideously mangled remains of what was yesterday a beautiful creature enjoying its life, the scattered feathers, the forlornly empty nest. But unless we have keen and watchful eyes, we may wander far through the peaceful forest by day and meet few of these grim reminders of struggle and death.

Thus the tropical forest, the headquarters of terrestrial life on this planet, resembles human life, which is derived from it. We find there what we seek. If we seek beauty, it is there profusely. If we yearn for peace, it awaits us there. If, on the other hand, we gloat in strife and violence, it offers us that, too. If we search for some particular group of plants or animals, we find them, remaining oblivious of many wonderful things that are revealed to those who explore the forest with other interests. And if we enter the forest without any goals or interests, we find it a place of utter boredom. In all these ways, the forest presents an epitome of human life.

But in spite of beauty, tranquility, and endless variety, the forest at last becomes oppressive. To stay too long in unbroken forest is apt to induce a mild case of claustrophobia. After all, a human in the forest is like a mouse in a cornfield, without that animal's agility in climbing the stalks. Our ancestors eons ago lost the freedom of the forest when they abandoned the arboreal in favor of the terrestrial life. Now we are no longer able to roam through the woodland as we see the White-faced Monkeys doing and long to do ourselves; we are pinned down in the lowest stratum, and, save by an effort too exhausting to be often repeated, we cannot rise above it. Fully 95 per cent of the lofty rain forest stands above our reach. This limitation at length becomes irksome and depressing; we feel a melancholy sense of frustration. We lose our proud pose as the lords of creation and come at last to feel what we actually are, small, bewildered creatures wandering timidly amid forces immeasurably more powerful and enduring than ourselves. This reminder of what we are; is perhaps salutary, but so unflattering that we would dismiss it. When the forest has reduced us to submission, when our spirits are in a proper state to contemplate in all humility the vast, mysterious creative urge of which it is a visible expression, we hasten to escape from it.

Moreover, we need a broader outlook than we have in the midst of the forest and are most at ease when covered by a wider expanse of blue sky than we can glimpse through gaps in the high canopy of foliage. Were we birds, we might win these advantages by flying up to the treetops; but we are chained in the lowest galleries and can escape only by dragging our weight over the ground. How grateful is the wider stretch of earth and sky, the more vivid green, the freer air of the cleared lands, when we return to them after a long day amid the tree trunks; how soothing the sight of a dwelling nestling amid shrubbery and fruit trees, the scent of wood fire and perchance of cooking and roasting coffee, when we come back hungry and tired!

Scarcely anyone, no matter how much he or she loves the forest, chooses to dwell in its unbroken depth. We prefer to live in a clearing with a wide view and the forest nearby, where we can really see it and enter it whenever we will. For it is true that in the midst of the forest we cannot see it for the trees. Only when we stand before its edge, as on the shore of a river or in a fresh cutting, can we survey the full majesty of its towering height; only when from an eminence we look over miles and miles of billowy treetops do we begin vaguely to grasp the vastness of its sweep. To know the forest, we must study it in all aspects, as birds soaring above its roof, as earth-bound bipeds creeping slowly over its roots.

Farming

Since my farm was not sufficiently big and productive to afford a foreman to keep the laborers active, nor could I supervise or work with them all morning without neglecting other things that I hoped to accomplish, I solved the difficulty by going into partnership on the annual crops with my hired man. With his own labor and a little cash, he paid for half of the work, and he received half of the harvest. Since he had a major interest at stake, and it was to his advantage to produce the grain as cheaply as possible, I could be fairly certain that he kept busy in the fields without being watched. And since in addition to applying half of his own time without salary he paid half the wages of any outside labor that we employed for these crops, I had little doubt that he would look for helpers who would give us an honest day's work. Moreover, there was an advantage in having a partner genuinely concerned to see that the cornfield was not invaded by wandering cattle, a neighbor's or our own. Except one year when at harvest time the partner I then had tried a maneuver of questionable honesty, this arrangement has worked satisfactorily.

It is distasteful to me to feel that those who assist me, people or animals, are working under compulsion. If my profits have been less than they might have been, had I paid all the expenses and taken all the crop, it was agreeable to have an associate with a personal interest in the enterprise, who labored for something more than a daily wage and so worked more eagerly and cheerfully. Moreover, every successful attempt at cooperation, with living beings of whatever species, is a moral triumph. Thereby I released many precious hours for my studies. Yet even with this arrangement, there was always a great deal for me to do, both in supervising and in attending to the innumerable odd jobs that arise on any farm where there are animals and fences and gates, fruit trees and garden plots and coffee bushes—little tasks for which the hired labor never seems to suffice. On some days, when everything seemed to demand attention at once, I would wearily ask myself whether I owned the farm or the farm owned me.

When the maize had tender milky grains and the animals came out of the neighboring woodland to feast on them, my partner and I would generally disagree. He would raise the cry, "Shoot the thieving monkeys! Kill the coatimundis!" I would point out that they were here before us, and we had taken the land away from them; hence it was just that we pay a little rent to them. Or sometimes I would direct my partner to plant a few more rows for the free animals, so that there could be no complaints when they came to enjoy what had been provided for them. The chief of these maize-eaters were the squirrels, the coatimundis with long, sensitive muzzles, and the

White-faced Monkeys. When I saw what hard and taste-less fruits these animals were often reduced to eating in the dry season, I well understood their eagerness for the succulent corn, and I did not begrudge them. The only animals I have ever shot were snakes, which menace us with their venom or pillage birds' nests, and pigs. When the owners of trespassing pigs ignored repeated pleas to keep them at home, as good neighbors do, I killed the offending porkers to save our crops. This is the only legal method of getting rid of them.

If we insist on destroying every animal that touches our food plants or molests us in one way or another, there will eventually be no free creatures to give interest and charm to the country. Of course, if the depredations on our fields become too heavy, we shall be obliged to protect them somehow, or else starve; but we can well spare a little of our harvest for the birds and furry animals. Not only does a sentiment of charity or compassion or of natural justice toward those creatures whose land we have seized prompt us to allow them freely to take a small sample of its produce; there are other, more selfish reasons for adopting this course. Nearly everywhere, people spend a substan-tial part of their income on recreation and amusement. I derive entertainment, instruction, and esthetic delight from watching the free animals of the woodland. These values are cheaply bought with a few bushels of corn or some of the fruit from our trees. Few of our pleasures are at once so wholesome and so inexpensive.

Since the farm that I bought had a fair acreage of pas-ture and I like horses, I started off with the idea that I would raise them to sell. However, the first horse that I sold was so abused by the purchaser that I soon abandoned this project, and thereafter I raised only enough for the use of the farm. For many years, we kept a yoke of oxen for hauling, a few cows for milk, and chickens for eggs, never for slaughter. I tried to give all these domestic animals a happy life and regarded the work they did and the milk or eggs they furnished as but a fair return for the food and often laborious care that they received. My aim was to achieve a sort of mutually beneficial symbiosis with them.

The trouble was that the cows gave birth to too many bull calves, and the hens hatched out too many cockerels. To sell these superfluous males to people who might slaughter them was distasteful; to keep and feed them was expensive, and they often fought among themselves. While I was wrestling with this problem, a stranger approached me with an offer to buy my cows for stocking a new farm, and at the same time a neighbor sent a message that my cattle had damaged his sugarcane and he demanded compensation. The would-be purchaser had arrived at an opportune moment; I suddenly decided to sell the cows. Although it was painful to see him drive away the animals that for so many years I had attended faithfully, nursing their frequent wounds and disorders, I have never regretted their sale. Later, while we were away studying birds in other regions, most of our chickens disappeared and have not been replaced. We sell the corn that we formerly fed to the chickens and buy eggs and milk. We still have horses and our symbiosis with them has been very satisfactory; they pay for their keep with their labor rather than with products of their bodies, and we need raise no more than we want.

Although my experience with farm animals has convinced me that with thought and effort and some sacrifice of profits one may achieve a more humane and satisfying association with them than is commonly done, it would be better all around if we could live without them. Our animals fail to appreciate our intentions; they cannot understand the relation between what they receive and what they are required to give. They are often stubborn and annoying and sometimes destructive. To care for them without occasionally losing one's temper and abusing them, one needs a saint's patience; to raise them for maximum profits, one must stifle whatever finer feelings one may have. Dietetics and food processing have about reached the point where those who have access to well stocked food stores can dispense with all animal products and live in perfect health and vigor on a wholly vegetable diet, as from ancient times and in many lands people of the most refined sentiments have aspired to do. Such a course has multiple advantages: we avoid the degrading violence and the cruelty inseparable from the exploitation of animals; we increase the amount of food for direct human consumption that the areas now devoted to farming can supply; and we correspondingly reduce the inroads upon the shrinking areas of wilderness, leaving them as sanctuaries where free animals can lead their natural lives without interference by meddling humans.

Meanwhile, throughout tropical America, populations soar while the land becomes impoverished. Hungry people are forced to bring under cultivation less favorable lands that deteriorate more rapidly. If one loves humanity or the natural world, one deplores the consequences. When people live too near the margin of starvation, there is a decline in the dignity and value of human life. A chronically deficient diet is as disastrous to morals as to intellectual and esthetic development. And it is painful to see millennial forests shorn from land that can hardly yield two good crops and to witness the decimation and perhaps eventual extermination of whole species of beautiful plants and animals, which nature has taken millions of years to produce and can never replace.

Undoubtedly, some improvement can be made by giving small farmers in the tropics better varieties of maize, beans, rice, and the other crops to which they are accustomed—better, that is, for their own peculiar conditions—and showing them how to produce these crops more efficiently. But if I were to undertake, with adequate resources, a long-term program for the improvement of tropical agriculture, I would choose a radically different approach. The yearlong growing season of the more humid tropics calls for perennial plants that will keep the soil permanently covered and take advantage of the almost continuously favorable temperature and moisture. How wasteful to sow maize, which in four or five months bears its single crop and dies, when something might be growing and producing and covering the soil throughout the twelve months! How much more wasteful when, after this single sowing, the land must rest for several years more, while fresh lands and more fresh lands are requisitioned for this extravagant grass!

Annual crops are well suited to semiarid regions with a short growing season, as likewise to extratropical countries where the growing season is followed by a long period of cold that puts an end to growth; but perennial crops are appropriate for the continuously verdant tropics. It is fitting that a country like Costa Rica should export the products of perennial plants like coffee, cacao, and bananas, and import from the North flour made from annual wheat. But the international market is often glutted with these products, and a country that is primarily agricultural should not be dependent upon imported foodstuffs. I would search the world for a constellation of perennial plants that together would yield a balanced diet, and I would spare no pains to adapt them and their products to the requirements of each of the major regions of tropical America.

This, to be sure, would involve not only the introduction of new methods of agriculture, but also the development of new dietary habits among the people—a difficult transformation, for people adhere to their dietary prejudices perhaps even more tenaciously than to their religious beliefs! It would mean the passing of the tortilla, that culinary oddity peculiar to the peoples of Mexico and Central America, for which so much maize is grown and so much forest destroyed. Whenever I watch our cook making tortillas, I am amazed that so many generations of women over so great an area should have submitted to a lifetime of such drudgery, that none has had the genius to invent a more easily prepared substitute. So much boiling of maize with ashes or lime to loosen the outer pellicle of the grain, so much washing to remove the lime or ash, such laborious turning of the little hand mill that grinds the corn, such endless pat-pat-patting by the hands to shape the great stack of thin wafers that a large family will consume in a day! Each of these tortillas must receive separate attention as it is roasted and turned on the *comal*. And the product of all this labor, delicious when fresh, rapidly loses its palatability. Imagine how difficult it would be to make bread if you started with whole grains of wheat instead of prepared flour, and you will have some conception of the effort involved in preparing tortillas from the hard maize, as is commonly done on Middle American farms. The emancipation of the Middle American woman, no less than the emancipation of the Middle American soil, calls for some readily prepared substitute for the tortilla, made with the product of a perennial plant.

In the Caribbean Lowlands of Northern Costa Rica

After twenty years, at Los Cusingos, there were still birds whose nesting I had not studied. Season after season, I had searched fruitlessly for nests of the Bare-crowned Antbird, Buff-throated Woodcreeper, Smoky-brown Woodpecker, Nightingale Wren, Green Shrike-vireo, Shining Honeycreeper, and other resident birds that were not rare. Of some birds my studies were incomplete, because

I had found only one or two nests, which too often had been prematurely lost. But I had reached the point where I was certain that I could contribute more to knowledge of tropical birds by working in localities where different species occur. Accordingly, we began to spend breeding seasons in other regions. One year we worked on the Barba massif in the Costa Rican highlands; another, at Cañas Gordas near the Panamanian border. A third expedition took us to Venezuela, to study the Rufous-fronted Thornbird, which builds large, hanging nests of interlaced sticks, containing several chambers. For two seasons, we studied birds at "La Selva" in the Caribbean lowlands of northern Costa Rica. Of all the localities that we visited, this has the richest avifauna and supports some of the most impressive trees.

After several days of preparation in San José, Pamela, Edwin, and I set forth for La Selva on April 10, 1967. The bus to Puerto Viejo was scheduled to leave Heredia at nine in the morning, but the dilapidated vehicle refused to start. Two hours dragged by before it was sufficiently patched up to take to the road. The driver, in a black humor after a hectic morning, made the ancient bus sway and rattle along the narrow highway that, with innumerable sharp turns, wound between coffee plantations and pastures up to the continental divide at Los Cartagos, in the saddle between Volcán Poás and the Barba massif. When I studied Quetzals at Montaña Azul thirty years earlier, the road beyond this point was a ribbon of mud along which I painfully trudged. Now it was paved, and, as we sped downward, I tried to pick out familiar scenes. Although the years had treated harshly the attractive cottage where I had dwelt, the ugly ruin was still inhabited, by people who obviously cared nothing for appearances. The surrounding forests, once the home of the Quetzal, the Three-wattled Bellbird, and the Black Guan, had been replaced by pastures where such widespread birds as the Rufous-collared Sparrow and the Yellow-faced Grassquit flourished. Repeating the pattern typical of our modern world, the drab and commonplace had supplanted the lovely and rare.

We continued downward with the gorge of the Río Sarapiquí on our right. Amid the lush vegetation on the roadside bank, the Higuera spread huge, roundish leaves, sometimes two yards across. At an altitude of about five thousand feet, we passed an open stand of *Wercklea insignis*, a tree mallow with lavender blossoms like large hibiscus flowers. As we rounded a curve, we glimpsed the great waterfall of the Río de la Paz, a tributary of the Sarapiquí, which plunges in a slender column hundreds of feet high into a profound ravine, where a perpetually saturated atmosphere encourages the most luxuriant tropical vegetation. Aware of the state of our conveyance and our driver's temper, I was far from happy as we ground too swiftly down a narrow road that hugged the brink of sheer precipices, over which from time to time a carelessly driven car plunged irretrievably. Passing through the villages of Cariblanco and San Miguel, we at last reached the lowlands, where the straight, level highway invited a velocity that was hardly reassuring.

It took us three hours to cover the sixty miles from Heredia to Puerto Viejo, mostly over winding mountain roads. Despite our driver's perilous attempt to make up for lost time, when we reached the boat landing on the Río Sarapiquí, a short way beyond the village, the operator of the ferry told us that the boat that was to meet us at midday had come and gone but would probably return for us later. As the sultry afternoon wore on, dark storm clouds massed in the sky and distant thunder pealed, making us fear that our baggage on the shore would be drenched.

At about four o'clock, a great flock of Turkey Vultures crossed the river from east to west, sailing low beneath the menacing clouds and sometimes circling on widespread wings to gain altitude. During the next half hour, wave after wave of the big, black birds passed over us, and with them were many Swainson's Hawks. For the next month, we were to see these vultures migrating northward, sometimes in huge flocks that stretched completely across the sky at a great height and took half an hour to pass. The last migratory wave, containing several hundred birds, was noticed on May 12. In the following year, when we reached La Selva in early March, the vultures continued to pass northward from March 25 until May 7. With them were often some Swainson's Hawks, and more rarely we saw the latter traveling in a great flock composed almost wholly of their own kind, with an admixture of broad-winged hawks. Although the spring migration of Swainson's Hawks is countrywide and one of the spectacular natural phenomena of the Pacific slope of Costa Rica, I have never noticed any obviously migratory movement of Turkey Vultures on that side of the country.

The afternoon was far spent when we heard the welcome sound of an outboard motor. Soon a large dugout canoe glided around a bend in the river, turned in a graceful arc, and pushed its bow up on the muddy shore beside us. With the help of Rafael Chavarría, the caretaker and boatman at La Selva, we piled our luggage aboard and embarked for the voyage upstream. In a few minutes, we reached the confluence of the Sarapiquí and the Puerto Viejo, two rivers of almost equal size. Veering to the left, we entered the latter and continued upstream between high banks lined with sotacaballo trees, whose branches reached far out above the dark water. The current was gentle and so low that here and there Rafael had to pilot a course through shallows, but large uprooted trees, stranded in midstream, attested the force that it sometimes attained. The peaceful loveliness of the river soothed away the irritations of a frustrating day, and we felt rested when, rounding a bend, we beheld the house that we were to occupy, standing high above us on a narrow promontory between the Río Puerto Viejo and its tributary creek, the Surd. Landing in the deep shade of an ancient sotacaballo tree, in the twilight we carried our numerous pieces of baggage up the long flight of wooden steps that wound up the steep, grassy slope to the building.

La Selva was then the property of Dr. Leslie Holdridge, a forester whose original classification of life zones has been used all over the world. The two-story house was furnished as a weekend or holiday cottage, with folding canvas cots, rough tables, and kerosene stoves for cooking. When we arrived, several North American scientists were present with their families, but, after a few days, all left; through most of our sojourn, the three of us were there alone, with an occasional brief visit from a student and alternate weekends with Dr. and Mrs. Holdridge.

The rainiest parts of Costa Rica are its opposite corners, the Caribbean lowlands in the northeast and the southern part of the Pacific littoral, especially around the Golfo Dulce. In these regions the average annual rainfall exceeds one hundred and sixty inches, and the "Tropical Wet Forest" of the Holdridge classification flourishes. During our first season, our work was greatly impeded by excessive rain, which fell at any time of the day or night. In April it amounted to more than sixteen inches, and in May it was nearly twenty inches. In the following year, slightly more rain fell in these two months when nesting was at its height, but it tended to come in afternoon deluges, as on the Pacific slope; we enjoyed more clear mornings and accomplished more.

Despite the frequent rain and high humidity, the weather was rarely enervatingly sultry, as in some tropical lowlands. Often, when rain fell, it was cool enough to wear a jacket. Nights were pleasant; although we were only about four hundred feet above sea level, we nearly always slept under a blanket. Only in the early afternoon of a sunny day did we find it uncomfortably warm. Then, after a siesta, we swam in the Puerto Viejo River, which was always at a comfortable temperature. This stream, about fifty yards broad, was continually changing its level. After several rainless days, it would fall so low that, holding hands while we breasted the swift, clear current, we could walk across the nearly level bottom to the opposite shore. A day or two of steady rain might cause it to rise fifteen or twenty feet, bearing on its turbid bosom a constant procession of uprooted trees, decaying logs, branches, clusters of epiphytes torn from riverside trees, and other debris of the forest. When the river rose, the water backed far up into the tributary creeks, converting these usually shallow, clear streams into deep, muddy canals.

One afternoon, while we bathed, Edwin noticed a bird swimming along the opposite shore. Although herons, kingfishers, swallows, and other birds coursed above the river, I had never seen a bird alight on its surface, and I could not imagine what this small swimmer might be. Edwin ran up the long flight of steps for field glasses, which, focused on the distant bird, brought home the bold, black and white pattern of a Sungrebe's head and neck. The solitary bird continued to swim slowly downstream along the farther shore, where the current was slowest, now and again disappearing behind logs, piles of driftwood, or masses of foliage projecting from the high bank. Finally, it glided behind a stranded dead tree and vanished.

For the next month, we saw much of this Sungrebe and studied its habits while we bathed. It rested low in the water; its long tail hardly above the surface, and while swimming it waved its head forward and backward, like a walking pigeon. It never dived for its food but picked small objects, doubtless insects unidentifiable in the distance, from branches and foliage overhanging the stream and from decaying logs. Once it jumped almost clear of the water to pluck something from a branch above its head. It was always alone and silent. Before going to roost in the evening, it bathed, dipping its foreparts into the stream and splashing water over its back with its wings.

After wetting its upper parts, it flew up to a low branch or a stranded log and spent many minutes preening and grooming its plumage. It might enter the water for a second wetting, to be followed by more preening, before it settled down for the night.

While there was still much daylight, the Sungrebe went to roost on a long, horizontal branch that projected well out from the bank. Here it was about four feet above the water, beneath abundant sheltering foliage. Only its white underparts were visible to the watchers across the river, and this light patch gradually faded into the shadows as dusk fell. One evening, after the Sungrebe had gone to roost, an otter swam beneath it, without causing it to move. Although the bird almost certainly saw the otter, the latter apparently failed to notice the bird. Likewise, the passage of a *cayuco* with a noisy outboard motor did not frighten it away. In the morning, the Sungrebe waited until the light was fairly bright before it jumped down into the water and started to swim upstream along the bank, picking its breakfast from overhanging vegetation. It continued to sleep on the same branch until this was submerged when the river rose in mid-May.

In the evening, after our swim, we often watched the river, the birds, and the sunset from the landing at the head of the outside steps to the upper story or the grassy clearing in front of the house. Parrots, toucans, oropendolas, and Scarlet-rumped Caciques flew by, and woodcreepers called with loud, clear notes as they sought their dormitories in hollow trunks. Cattle Egrets, after foraging through the day at the heads of animals grazing in the pastures across the river, winged in small flocks toward the sunset, white against the darkening sky. It is surprising how rapidly these birds, recent immigrants from the Old World, have spread over the warmer parts of the Americas in the past two decades.

Among the many birds that flew by as the day ended was a pair of Red-lored Parrots. Over an interval of nearly a month, from mid-March until mid-April, we often saw one of these birds, doubtless the male, feed his mate. They would alight, one above the other, on an ascending dead branch at the very top of a tall tree, while the one above passed billful after billful to the one below. Before each transfer of food, the feeder alternately stretched and contracted his neck, to bring up the aliment, which the recipient took while loosely flapping her wings, especially the wing on the side toward her mate. These feedings were long-continued: one evening I counted forty-five installments; on another, forty-four; and on both occasions I had probably missed the very beginning of the process. My attention was usually drawn to the feedings by peculiar sharp notes that were evidently made by the recipient, for they continued while the donor was regurgitating food and could hardly have produced them. The feeding over, both birds called raucously in their usual fashion, then with mincing wingstrokes flew over the darkening pastures to the east. Probably the female was preparing to lay, or already incubating.

ORNITHOLOGIST

STUDIES OF TROPICAL AMERICAN BIRDS

(1972)

White-fronted Nunbird

The most memorable event of my visit to the Río Yavarí in 1940 was my first meeting with nunbirds. On the shallow-draft gunboat Amazonas of the Peruvian inland navy, our rubber survey party had voyaged over the Amazon and its great tributaries in transandean Peru from the Pongo de Manseriche in the west to the Yavarí on the frontier of Brazil. On the left bank of this southern tributary of the Amazon we went ashore to search for rubber trees at a tiny settlement which someone with a longing for cool breezes and a sense of humor had named Islandia (Iceland). While we examined a small rubber tree growing in a plantation near the forest, a little flock of blackish, starling-sized birds perched not far above our heads, twitching their tails from side to side while they uttered soft, musical murmurs. They had large, dark eyes and bright orange bills that contrasted with their dusky plumage. Although they were quite unlike any bird I had ever seen, their zygodactylous feet, with two toes directed forward and two backward, assured me that they were not passerines. Later I learned that they were Black-fronted Nunbirds, belonging to the puffbird family. My duties as botanist of the survey party did not permit further observation of these strange birds, but this brief encounter convinced me that they had unusual social habits that would well repay careful study.

Although for the next quarter-century my bird watching was done in parts of Central and South America where nunbirds do not occur, my desire to study them, born of this transitory meeting, never quite died away. My next sight of nunbirds was in March of 1965 on a short visit to La Selva, in the Sarapiquí lowlands of northern Costa Rica, where the White-fronted Nunbird is found. I was able to pass two months at La Selva during the breeding season of 1967. Although we saw much of the nunbirds, the only nest that we then found was prematurely destroyed by a predator. Returning in March of the following year we struck better weather and better luck, finding three occupied nests, two of which were successful. They amply confirmed my surmise, held for so long, that the sociable nunbirds have extraordinary habits.

Nunbirds, of which four species in the genus *Monasa* are currently recognized, are named for the somber, nun-like attire which all wear. The Costa Rican race of the White-fronted Nunbird is a fairly stout puffbird about 11 inches long. In both sexes the upper parts of the body and the wing coverts are slate-colored, the under parts lighter slaty gray. The remiges and the rounded tail, of moderate length, are nearly black. The black head is adorned with short, stiff, outstanding white feathers on the forehead, lores, and chin. Projecting from this facial ruff is a bright orange-red bill, of moderate length, that tapers from a fairly broad base to a sharp tip. (The glossy, orange or reddish bill of certain South American nunbirds has earned for them the name *pico de lacre*—lacquered bill.) The large, soft eyes are brown. The short tarsus and toes are blackish. As in a number of other puffbirds, females average larger than males in most of the conventional measurements (Ridgway, 1914), but the difference in size of the sexes is too slight to permit their separation in the field.

The White-fronted Nunbird ranges from eastern Honduras to Peru, Brazil, and Bolivia. A heat-loving bird, in Costa Rica it is confined to the Caribbean lowlands and foothills and appears rarely to ascend above 1,500 feet above sea level. Here as at La Selva, it inhabits wet forests whose dominant trees are immensely tall and heavily burdened with a vast variety of epiphytic growths. Although they usually remain well up in the trees, nunbirds on occasion descend to the ground for food, as they do to nest. More often than amid uninterrupted forest, nunbirds are noticed around the edges of, and within, openings which facilitate insect-catching. Often they venture a good way into clearings and plantations with isolated tall trees, such as cacao plantations with scattered shade.

Nunbirds travel through the treetops and across clearings in small parties of rarely more than half a dozen individuals, which are evidently family groups. These birds do not fly in a compact flock, like certain parrots, but straggle along at intervals, in the manner of toucans and certain cotingas. Often they associate loosely with other more or less social birds of the treetops. At La Selva we often watched them foraging among the shade trees of the cacao plantations with Purple-throated Fruitcrows and Scarlet-rumped Caciques, whose plumage is also predominantly dusky, and such other birds as Rufous Mourners, Cinnamon Woodpeckers, Rufous-winged Woodpeckers, Black-striped Woodcreepers, and Massena Trogons. Late on May afternoons we often found a certain cacao plantation, adjoining the forest, alive with such mixed aggregations of actively foraging birds. We never saw a nunbird behave aggressively toward any other bird, of its own or another species.

The flight of nunbirds is direct and strong but rarely long continued. Sometimes, when crossing an open space, they set their spread wings and glide. Although like other puffbirds they perch motionless while looking for food, their more social nature prompts greater activity. They tend to remain for shorter intervals in one spot, rarely puff out their plumage conspicuously, and do not give the impression of inert dullness which is responsible for a whole array of scientific and popular names denoting stupidity and sloth which have, unfortunately, been applied to this remarkable family.

FOOD

Puffbirds of all kinds rarely eat vegetable food, and the nunbirds are no exception to this rule. In many hours of watching, both while they foraged and while they fed their young, we never saw one with a berry or other fruit. They subsist almost wholly on invertebrates, with occasionally a small vertebrate, such as a tiny frog or a small lizard.

The great bulk of their food consists of insects, including many cicadas and a variety of Orthoptera, among which grasshoppers, mantids, and phasmids are prominent. Sometimes a beetle or dragonfly is taken. Many of the insects are in the larval stage. Among other invertebrates that are consumed are spiders and millipedes.

Nunbirds forage in the energy-conserving manner typical of puffbirds: they remain on some convenient branch, scanning their surroundings until their keen eyes detect some suitable prey flying in the air, creeping over the bark of a tree, or hiding amid the foliage; they make a sudden swift sally to seize their victim and carry it to a perch before they devour it. Sometimes when they dart out from a treetop to seize flying insects their mode of foraging resembles that of the related Swallow-wing. In clearings where well-spaced trees offer convenient lookouts, they catch many small creatures amid low herbage or even from the ground, ascending to a low perch to swallow each victim. The drying grass and weeds in a freshly chopped plantation or dooryard are a source of readily caught insects and spiders of which nunbirds are quick to take advantage. Often we watched them foraging in the narrow clearing, between the forest and the river, in which the house at La Selva stood. Their sharp eyes could detect a green insect amid green grass at a distance of 60 feet or so. After carrying their prey to a perch in their bills, they would often beat or rub it against the branch; but their pounding was rarely as vigorous as that to which certain flycatchers, motmots, jacamars, and other birds subject large prey, and usually they gulped down their insects with the wings still attached.

Late one morning in April I watched three nunbirds foraging with army ants (*Eciton*), near a burrow in which they were feeding nestlings. The nunbirds perched from about four to 15 feet above a broad forest pathway over which the ants were swarming. At intervals they alighted on the ground to capture some insect that the ants had stirred up, or else they plucked it from a tree trunk, or even overtook a flying fugitive. After each sally they promptly returned to a perch to watch. Repeatedly they looked at their feet, as though to make sure that no ants were crawling over them. Some of their prey was carried off toward the nest.

VOICE

Some years ago, when the only puffbirds that I knew well were a few Central American species, I wrote that "Puffbirds are among the most silent of the birds of the tropical forests of America" (Skutch, 1958b:212). Since becoming familiar with the Double-banded Puffbird in Venezuela and White-fronted Nunbirds in Costa Rica, I regret having generalized too hastily. Some puffbirds are quite vociferous and the White-fronted Nunbirds have such a varied repertoire of calls that for a while I was inclined to attribute to them any loud, unfamiliar bird note that reached my ears at La Selva. Usually, if I could trace the sound to its source, my surmise proved to be correct. Among the vocalizations of which the significance finally seemed clear are the following:

1. The flight note, a low, soft monosyllable, uttered one or more times as a nunbird takes wing.

2. The call-for-companions, a series of loud, full, "mourn-ful" notes, delivered by a lone perching bird separated from its companions, as by one who has just emerged from a long spell in the nest and does not know where its flock-mates are. One morning in April I watched a solitary bird resting on an exposed dead twig at the very top of a tall living tree. It called *how how how how*...in a soft, melancholy voice, finally rising to a crescendo *how how how how how.*

3. The approach call, so-named because it was most of-ten heard from birds approaching their burrow with food for nestlings. This call has many variations but it seems always to consist of an emphasized open-ing note followed by a series of more rapidly uttered lower notes, producing an undulatory effect, which on different occasions I described as a soft roll, a liq-uid ripple of sound, a slow trill, a soft purr, a churr, a rattle between wooden and liquid. As the nunbird begins this call, it first elevates, then depresses its tail, trogon-like. A bird hesitating to descend to its burrow with food, because it is being watched, may repeat this call over and over for many minutes together. If the food-bringer is perturbed, the trill may become lower, softer, more prolonged—a melodious wail of remonstrance. But the call is by no means confined to occasions when feeding is delayed by a human ob-server or some other potential danger; one may hear it coming from the vicinity of a nest while one stands a good way off, unseen by the nunbirds. Indeed, a nunbird preparing to take food to nestlings may give this call sparingly while still hundreds of yards from the burrow and again when it breaks its journey to rest in a tree midway of its flight. The call is heard less

often from adults feeding young already on the wing. Occasionally it is given by a solitary nunbird not bearing food; then it seems to be used as a substitute for the call-for-companions. At times this call resembles that of the barred antshrike.

4. The feeding call, a rapid series of low, sharp notes uttered by a nunbird standing at the mouth of a burrow with food for the nestlings in its bill. Often the food is delivered with no sound audible to an observer at a distance of 40 or 50 feet; but if the young delay to come for their meal, the food-bringer begins to call, the notes growing louder the longer it must wait, until they become a sharp *click click click*...

5. The begging or hunger call. As the nestlings grow older they may utter, as they come to take their meal from an adult at the burrow's mouth, a call that sounds like *tuwee tuwee*. This is especially likely to be heard when they have not been fed for some time and are very hungry. Fledglings waiting to be fed may perch on a branch and repeat these notes, in a high thin voice, for a long while. Adults soliciting food from their mate or other companions give calls, which bear more or less resemblance to this juvenile hunger call, and seem to be derived from it. Often the adult's hunger call is uttered in a soft, whining or pleading voice, but at times it becomes piercingly shrill, especially as the hungry bird flies toward a companion to take the food from its bill.

6. The chorus is the loudest and most surprising of the nunbirds' many utterances. It is given by from three to ten birds perching close together, but not in contact, in the forest or sometimes in an adjoining clearing. The choristers may be stationed anywhere from about

25 to 75 feet up, occasionally higher, on a slender horizontal branch or, very often, on a vine stretched horizontally between two trees in the midst of the forest. Frequently they rest in a row, at intervals of a few inches and all facing the same way; but if numerous they may form two rows on neighboring branches or vines, and sometimes one or two perch singly, slightly apart from the others. Even when in a row, all do not invariably face in the same direction. One of these performances may last, with short intermissions, for 15 or 20 minutes, during which the birds from time to time change their perches and their grouping.

Perhaps "chorus" is too grandiose a term to apply to these performances, which in reality are no more than bouts of simultaneous shouting, with little rhythm and no melody. Tilting their heads upward, the dusky participants call all together in loud, ringing, almost soprano voices, with such vehemence that their whole bodies shake, making as much noise as a flock of chachalacas. Some relax their wings, or spread and close their tails, as they pour forth their high-pitched notes through their bright orange-red bills. At times one nods its head emphatically downward, as though in approval, or to encourage its companions to proceed with the "music." The chorus swells louder or wanes, as more or fewer birds join in, but for many minutes there are only the briefest intervals of silence. The shouting nunbirds appear to enjoy the chorus immensely; but if they are susceptible to sore throats, I imagine that they are so-afflicted when, after perhaps a quarter hour of almost continuous vocal effort, they fall silent and fly off through the forest in small groups or singly.

We heard these choruses through most of our sojourn at La Selva, from late March until early June, that is, from the outset of the nunbirds' nesting season until most, if not all, of their young had fledged. Probably they are by no means confined to this season. The choruses were especially frequent from mid-April until late May, when the young were growing rapidly in the nest or were already on the wing. We heard them most often late in the morning and around midday, sometimes in the early afternoon.

The nunbirds' choruses are not quite like anything else that I have heard in the avian world. In a way, they remind one of the social singing of certain gregarious birds, such as siskins, goldfinches, and Evening Grosbeaks, numbers of which sing simultaneously as they rest in a tree. But there is no coordination in the singing of such birds, each of which pours forth his medley as the spirit moves him, whereas the nunbirds' chorus is obviously a coordinated performance. In this it resembles the duetting or antiphonal singing of many constantly mated tropical birds, especially wrens, although it lacks the exquisite melody and the precise synchronization of many of these duets. Nevertheless, its function may well be the same, to strengthen the bond between the members of a family; only in this case the family consists not merely of a pair but of the three, four, or possibly more individuals who cooperate in caring for a nest.

This interpretation is supported by an observation that I made at the end of April. Hearing a chorus near the house, I entered the forest to seek the choristers. The sound moved from place to place, and presently five adults alighted almost above me on a slender, horizontal vine, 25 or 30 feet up. One held a large insect in its bill. Here they raised their voices again, and at the conclusion of this bout of calling, one, who had perched somewhat apart from the others, flew westward alone. Then the bird who held the insect flew eastward, followed by the three others in single file — an impressive sight. They alighted in a tree where these four nunbirds habitually paused before delivering food to the well-grown nestlings in a nearby burrow.

Two days later, in the early afternoon, there was another long continued chorus, just within the edge of the forest near this same nest. Seven or eight nunbirds were present, and they joined in various shifting groupings, sometimes three, four, or five perching and calling close together, sometimes a single bird resting somewhat apart and remaining silent. I noticed no antagonism, but one alighted rudely almost on top of another, making it move. One nunbird called for a while with an insect in its bill but finally swallowed its food and continued. After about a quarter of an hour, when the excitement had almost died away, one bird gave the whining hunger call and another, who had been resting nearby, tried to mount her; but she flew away.

On 23 April I watched a chorus with eight participants, who at first perched close together on slender horizontal boughs, about 25 feet up in the forest. After a while they separated into two groups of four, lined up on branches about 20 feet apart, and continued to shout as before. After about 15 minutes the assembly dispersed, the birds flying off in different directions, leaving only two who remained to preen. This choral gathering occurred between a nest with young attended by four grown birds and another nest, where also at least four birds were in attendance, which had been destroyed by some predator about ten days earlier. Evidently these two groups or families composed the assembly. Possibly it had territorial relevance, although it was much nearer the nest with young than the nest, which had been plundered. However, I have found no evidence of territoriality in nunbirds—nor, indeed, in any other bird that roams through the upper levels of tropical forest.

These are a few examples of the nunbirds' choruses that we witnessed. They vary considerably in circumstances while conforming to the same general pattern: the simultaneous shouting of birds perching close together, typically in a row with approximately equal intervals of a few inches between them. Although their biological function is not wholly clear, one carries away the impression that nunbirds indulge in them so frequently because they enjoy shouting together.

In Bolivia, Niethammer (1953:299) found four or more Black-fronted Nunbirds singing in chorus. He believed that they were sometimes stimulated to perform by hearing the shouting bouts of the Speckled Chachalaca.

SUNNING

Late on a morning in May, when the sunshine was pouring down hotly into the clearing behind the house, three adult nunbirds flew down to lie on the lawn, where the grass had grown rather long. The one that I could see best had both wings widely extended. The birds snuggled down in the grass, preening and scratching in the brilliant sunshine. They were not shy and permitted me to watch them a few yards away. Soon they flew up into the forest trees that bordered the clearing.

Nunbirds scratch their heads by raising a foot outside a closed wing rather than over and inside a drooped wing, as most passerine birds do. The nunbirds' "direct" mode of scratching appears to be general among piciform birds. I did not see them bathe.

FEEDING OF ADULTS

When, after a morning in the forest, I returned to the house toward noon on 17 March, I was told that nunbirds had for some time been feeding young in the clearing. However, I could detect no sign of immaturity in any of the four individuals who composed the group. Late on the following morning the nunbirds again foraged among the scattered trees in front of the house. One of them repeated the hunger call much of the time, and this bird was fed thrice in 20 minutes by two others. Probably three members of the party were supplying food to the fourth but I could not keep them separate long enough to prove this. Doubtless one of the feeders was the recipient's mate, engaging in "nuptial feeding." But since it is improbable that the begging nunbird, evidently a female, was mated to two or three others, the term seems inapplicable to the whole activity. Sometimes the feeders brought the insect to her; at other times, she flew up to a companion who had returned to a perch after making a capture and, without alighting, snatched the object from its bill—just as dependent juveniles do. She also caught many insects for herself, quite expertly. Many of the small creatures devoured by this party were caught amid low herbage, to which the birds descended from low boughs or even a projecting root of an overturned tree. With these nunbirds were a Rufous Mourner and a pair of Great Kiskadees who perched quite near them and from time to time flew down to catch insects or spiders from the grass, exactly as the nunbirds did.

At the time when we witnessed this feeding, a female who nested in the forest near the house was evidently laying, or preparing to do so. Through the rest of March and the first week of April, we continued from time to time to hear the whining food call from one member of the flock that frequented the clearing, but it was fed more seldom than at first. After this the eggs hatched and the attendants, busy supplying the nestlings, rarely solicited food from each other and were never seen to receive any.

In late April and early May begging calls again sounded with some frequency among the trees near the house. Not only did the family nesting nearby forage here, but likewise another group whose nest was about 800 feet distant. This nest was destroyed in mid-April and I surmised that these renewed calls for food by an adult signified that she would lay again. But no replacement nest was ever found.

NEST

Three days after our arrival at La Selva on 10 April 1967, Dr. Dennis Paulson told me that he had found a nunbirds' nest. While studying dragonflies in a small grassy swamp he had seen three nunbirds flying across the open space from the neighboring cacao plantation, with food in their bills. Following them into the forest beyond the swamp, he soon found their burrow in a moderate slope beneath tall trees. Since the afternoon was already far advanced, we decided to visit the nest on the following morning. The next day dawned with rain and we waited until it abated before we set forth. To our dismay, as we approached the site of the burrow a heap of freshly dug earth greeted our vision. Some animal had dug out the first nest of the White-fronted Nunbird ever, to my knowledge, to be found by a naturalist, before even it could be properly described. Later I searched for a replacement nest on the surrounding slopes, but in vain. We found no other nest in 1967, although by late April fledglings were being fed in our study area.

In the following year we arrived earlier and began hunting nunbirds' nests in the second week of March, but the first was not discovered until 1 April, when it already contained naked nestlings. Another nest, also with nestlings at most a few days old, was found on 9 April, and the third, with older nestlings, was discovered on 21 April. These three burrows were revealed to us by the calls and movements of the attendant birds, which make the discovery of a nest relatively easy to the initiated, if one comes within hearing of the approach calls of nunbirds feeding nestlings. Of no other forest bird did we locate as many as three occupied breeding nests during our two seasons at La Selva. But it is most difficult to detect the narrow hole in the leaf-strewn forest floor, amid tangled undergrowth, without guidance from the nunbirds themselves. If while incubating they enter and leave the burrow only twice a day, as White-whiskered Soft-wings do (Skutch, 1958b), they are not likely to reveal its location during this period. Unfortunately, we found no nest until after the eggs had hatched. The burrow, which we chiefly studied, was only about 50 feet from a path along which we passed dozens of times while incubation was in progress. Indeed, I had searched repeatedly for a nunbirds' nest on the opposite side of the path, where the slope of the land was greater, as the only nests that I had hitherto seen were in such slopes.

The four burrows (including that prematurely destroyed in 1967) were in heavy forest, but only a short distance from a clearing or plantation in which nunbirds gather much of their food. They were in moderate slopes (up to about 30 degrees) or nearly level ground, and they descended at a slight angle from their mouth in the leaf-strewn forest floor. The first of the burrows found in 1968 was in a 30-degree slope on which many small palms, with cane-like clustered stems, grew beneath tall trees. It was situated below one of the clusters, and a large mossy log lay close in front of it. About 40 inches long and almost straight, the burrow descended into the ground with an inclination of about 20 degrees. Near its mouth the tunnel was three inches high and 3¾ inches wide, and it varied little in diameter until it expanded into the brood chamber at its inner and lower end. The bottom of this chamber was lined with many pieces of dead leaf.

The second burrow opened only 10 feet from the edge of a high, wooded bank beside the Río Puerto Viejo. Inland from the bluff the land inclined slightly downward, but the burrow entered the ground at a point where a small irregularity of the surface increased the slope. The mouth faced inland, away from the river. This burrow, which had only a slight downward inclination, was 55 inches long and nearly straight; but the enlargement at its inner end was offset to one side, making it impossible to see, by looking in at the front while the tunnel was illuminated by a small electric bulb, what it contained.

The third burrow was in gently and uniformly sloping ground (less than ten degrees) in a little clear space amid the tangled undergrowth of heavy forest. It inclined slightly downward from the mouth and was at least 55 inches long, as I learned by probing with a slender stick. The outer part of the entrance tube was nearly straight, but toward the end it curved enough to cut off the view of the chamber where the nestlings rested. Near the mouth the tunnel was three inches in horizontal diameter, which varied little in the visible portion.

Since the tubular tunnel intersected the surface of the ground at a very acute angle, the opening of this third burrow was greatly elongated. An untidy collar of mostly coarse, decaying sticks, mixed with petioles and dead leaves, surrounded and reduced the oblique aperture, making it less conspicuous. Sticks that were evidently placed there by the nunbirds were up to 22 inches long, and some of the shorter ones were ½ inch thick; but the larger sticks were decayed and very light when dry. This collar was broadest and thickest above the elongated mouth of the tunnel, which it covered for a distance of five inches inward from the definitive opening, with a roof about two inches thick. On the sides and in front, the pile of sticks was thinner. The other two burrows, which intersected the surface of the ground at greater angles and accordingly had less elongated mouths, had thinner, less obvious collars, or scarcely any. At none of these burrows could the accumulation of sticks and trash compare with that over a burrow of the Black Nunbird found in Venezuela by Cherrie (1916:322). This burrow, 1.5 m. long, descended from heavily wooded, level ground at an angle of about 45 degrees from the horizontal. Over its mouth had been heaped half a bushel of rotten, coarse, dead twigs. From the edge of this pile a rounded tunnel ran along the ground to the mouth of the burrow proper.

In a number of points the nest of the White-fronted Nunbird resembles that of the White-whiskered Softwing, which inhabits the same forests but is much more widely distributed in Central America. Both are burrows in nearly level or moderately sloping ground, but those of the nunbird are two or three times as long as those of the softwing. Both of these puffbirds surround the aperture of their tunnels with a collar of twigs and petioles, and both line the brood chamber with dead leaves. Another similarity is that in neither case is any freshly excavated earth evident in front of the burrows at the time they are used for breeding, and the same was true of the burrow of the Black Nunbird found by Cherrie. We can only surmise why this is so. Do these puffbirds carry to a distance the earth they remove from their tunnels, as Prong-billed Barbets and certain other birds carry away the chips from the holes they carve in trees, and Yellow-eyed Juncos carry away in their bills the much smaller amount of earth they scratch out of the depression in the ground in which they build their nests (Austin, in Bent et al., 1968:1129)? Do they, like certain motmots, dig their burrows half a year or more before they will lay in them, so that the earth thrown out in front, washed away or impacted by rain, mixed or covered with vegetable debris, is no longer evident when nesting begins (Skutch, 1945, 1964-c)? Do they not dig burrows for themselves, but depend upon holes they find ready made, perhaps altering them just enough to meet their needs? In many years of residence among forests in which White-whiskered Soft-wings nest I have failed to solve the riddle of their burrows. In at least one instance the same burrow was occupied in successive years; and in the measure that such reuse is general among Ground-nesting Puffbirds, the chances of discovering the origin of the burrows are correspondingly reduced.

Another unanswered question is whether nunbirds ever nest in burrows in vertical banks, as kingfishers, motmots, jacamars, and many other birds often do. On 22 March I saw a nunbird fly up and hover in front of a hole in a high, nearly vertical earthen bank of a meandering stream that flowed between the forest and a cacao plantation. After looking into the hole the bird turned away without alighting at its mouth. It did this again and again, then flew out of sight. Soon this or another nunbird came and the performance was repeated. After another absence, these flights up to the entrance, without landing there, were resumed. At least two nunbirds, of a group of four that a little while before had chorused in the vicinity, were doing this. Between flights to the hole, they perched low and voiced soft, soprano notes. The mouth of this cavity in the bank was much wider than high, and far larger than it needed to be for a nunbird to pass through. If it had been made by birds, perhaps kingfishers or motmots, it had been considerably altered since they finished it. When examined a few days after the nunbirds showed such great interest in it, there was no indication, in the form of scratches on the bottom, that they had entered the cavity. Unfortunately, after this episode I lost much time seeking nunbirds' nests in banks, where none was ever found.

NESTLINGS

Doubtless the White-fronted Nunbirds' eggs are pure white, as are those of the Black Nunbird (Cherrie, 1916:322), and indeed all puffbirds (and all members of the order piciformes), as far as we know. As to their number, the only indication I have is that provided by the short burrow discovered on 1 April, which contained three recently hatched nestlings.

Appearance and development.—When I first saw these nestlings, by looking into the burrow with a flashlight, they were a few days old and dark feather rudiments were visible beneath their pink skin. They were devoid of down. Their eyes were closed and when they gaped widely I saw that the interior of their mouths was flesh-colored. So long as they remained in the chamber at the inner end of their burrow these nestlings were inaccessible to me; but on one occasion I was able to take one in hand. Nine days after we found this burrow, when the nestlings were probably about 12 days old, I was looking into it when an attendant alighted close behind me and trilled softly. Immediately the young started to run up the inclined tunnel and I easily caught the one that reached the mouth first. Its dark gray contour feathers were expanding quite generally, except on the crown, but much bare skin was still exposed. The flight feathers on wings and tail were still ensheathed. The nestling's eyes could open about halfway, but it seemed mostly to keep them closed. Its bill was light horn-colored. On its heels were prominent callous pads, smooth as in jacamars and motmots, rather than tuberculate as in kingfishers, or spiked as in nestlings, which grow up in holes in trees or termitaries. When I replaced the young nunbird in the mouth of its burrow it promptly turned around and ran down to rejoin its mates at the lower end.

This was the only time that a nestling was so incautious as to permit itself to be caught by me. Usually they did not come to the burrow's mouth unless an attendant was already standing there with food, and after taking it they promptly retreated into the depths of the tunnel. Looking past the parent, I sometimes enjoyed a fleeting glimpse of a nestling as it took its meal.

When I found the long burrow at the top of the bluff on 9 April, the nestlings, whom I could see only when they came to take food, were still small and pink, evidently not more than two or three days old. The last nestling left this burrow on the morning of 7 May, when it was at least 29 days old, and probably a day or two older. Thus the nestling period of the White-fronted Nunbird is about one half longer than that of the smaller White-whiskered Soft-wing, which is only 20 days.

Brooding.—When I first looked into the short burrow on 1 April my electric light disclosed a well-grown bird in dusky plumage. Its head, with the revealing orange-red bill, was hidden; since it had not flown when we approached rather noisily, and remained while I examined the nest, even touching it with the end of the measuring stick, I supposed that it was a well-feathered nestling. When next I peered into the nest, however, only three naked nestlings were present. The feathered bird that I had first seen was a brooding parent, steadfastly remaining at its post in the face of our intrusion. I was reminded of the Double-banded Puffbird who remained bravely covering her single fresh egg while Cherrie (1916:321) cut and hacked at the termitary in which the nest chamber had been excavated.

On 5 April when we watched this nunbirds' nest all morning, the naked nestlings were left alone from 06:40, when the parent who had brooded through the night left them, until 11:29 when an adult entered to brood.

On 11 April we watched this nest from dawn to dusk. The parent who was brooding at daybreak left the burrow at 06:15, and for the remainder of the day the partly feathered nestlings were alone. As night approached no adult entered the burrow to brood. As later events proved, this was a most fortunate omission.

After brooding ceased in the burrow at the top of the bluff, I noticed at dawn that leaves from the floor of the chamber had been raised to form a low wall or screen, reaching halfway to the roof, in front of the nestlings, such as I was able to examine more satisfactorily in the case of short burrows of the White-whiskered Soft-wing (Skutch, 1958b:222-224).

Feeding.—At dawn on 9 April I stood at the top of the riverside bluff watching a burrow of the Broad-billed Motmot. Presently a nunbird's approach call drew my attention to one of these birds perching in a neighboring tree with a small walking-stick insect dangling from its bill. Acting upon this hint, I soon found the nunbirds' burrow a few yards from where I stood. Meanwhile, two other nunbirds had alighted near the one with the insect. Suddenly a large dead branch directly above the three broke off and fell, but they darted away just in time to avoid being struck. They promptly returned to the same small tree, where they were joined by three more nunbirds, making six adults in all perching close together. Evidently some of these birds belonged to another family but I noticed no antagonism between them. While I examined and measured the nest, most of the birds flew off; but soon two returned with food, making three that waited with offerings for the naked nestlings. After I withdrew to watch from a distance, two flew down to feed the nestlings, but the third finally carried away its insect.

Many hours of watching at this burrow throughout the month that the young remained in it convinced us that four grown birds were feeding the nestlings. This was apparently the group of four that we had earlier seen giving insects to one of its members in the neighboring clearing. Frequently we saw the four together near the nest, and often three were carrying food simultaneously; but it was more difficult to assure ourselves that all four were attending the young. At the short burrow in the hillside four nunbirds were also bringing food. At the third nest found in 1968, with an unknown number of nestlings already well grown, at least three nunbirds were bringing food. It will be recalled that, in the preceding year, Paulson was led to the discovery of the ill-fated first nest by seeing three birds approach it with insects in their bills.

Aside from the tattered tails of some, which helped us to recognize them as individuals, there were no obvious differences between the three or four attendants of a nest. All appeared equally mature. One might suppose that these nunbirds were nesting communally like anis (*Crotophaga*), two pairs sharing a burrow. However, the only nest at which the number of eggs or young could be ascertained, without digging out and probably ruining the burrow, contained only three nestlings of about equal size and age, which seemed to be the offspring of one female rather than two. I believe that each burrow belonged to a single pair and the extra attendants were helpers, probably yearlings who would not themselves reproduce until a later nesting season, as in White-tipped Brown Jays and Banded-backed Wrens (Skutch, 1960a), apparently also Collared Araçaris (Skutch, 1958a), and certain other birds (Skutch, 1961b). To demonstrate beyond doubt the relationship of the several attendants of a nest would necessitate the banding of nestlings and following them through the succeeding year or more. Such a study would encounter great difficulties because it is so hard to find burrows and to reach the nestlings without breaking up the nests, and because the short legs of nunbirds are mostly hidden beneath them while they perch, which would make it difficult to see the bands.

While attending nestlings, nunbirds are far more tolerant of a human observer than are many other birds of lowland forests, especially those whose nests are low. We watched them while sitting or standing 30 or 40 feet from the burrow's mouth, with little or no concealment by the vegetation. At the short burrow at least some of the attendants would deliver food while we stood only four or five yards away. Some of the nunbirds hesitated longer than others to approach the nest in our presence; but this was not wholly a disadvantage, for while they delayed others might arrive with food, and such piling up of attendants helped us to learn how many there were.

We never saw a nunbird approach the nest with more than a single item of food, usually held in the tip of its vivid bill. Usually this was of substantial size, especially after the nestlings were some days old. Insects, which provided the bulk of the nestlings' diet, were nearly always delivered with their wings still attached; there was little or no beating or rubbing to detach them after the attendant arrived in sight of the burrow. Very frequently the nestlings received cicadas, which were also a major item in the diet of young Broad-billed Motmots in neighboring burrows. Orthoptera, some of which were green and quite large, were frequently brought. Other items that we recognized were beetles, spiders, caterpillars, rarely a small frog or lizard, only once a large and conspicuous butterfly or moth, once apparently a *Peripatus*. Once, to my amazement, an attendant gave to a half-grown nestling a large, green caterpillar covered with branched stinging spines, such as a person cannot touch without being punished with the most acute pain. I had doubts about the wholesomeness of such food, but when I looked into the burrow three hours after it had been swallowed, none of the nestlings appeared to be unwell. The Squirrel Cuckoo sometimes eats such stinging caterpillars and feeds them to its little ones.

Flying up with food for the nestlings, often from a neighboring clearing, the attendant nunbird never went directly to the burrow but always alighted in a nearby tree, usually from 15 to 30 feet up. Here, flagging its tail up and down, it gave the rippling or churring approach call, already described. As a rule, this call was repeated over and over for about two or three minutes; rarely it was given only once or twice or even omitted. Some of the more timid or distrustful attendants would continue to call for far longer, occasionally as much as half an hour, and perhaps finally fly away with the food undelivered. This delay, spent in calling, doubtless gives the nunbird an opportunity to scrutinize the surrounding forest and assure itself that none of its hereditary enemies (among which humans are probably not included) is lurking in sight. Finally assured, the attendant flies down and alights at the burrow's mouth. Usually it delays a good fraction of a minute (possibly repeating the feeding call in a voice too low to be audible to us a dozen yards away), before a nestling comes to the entrance and takes the food from it. If the delay is prolonged the sharp notes of the feeding call are heard, and they become louder, more insistent, the longer the attendant must wait. A few seconds after delivering the meal the attendant rises into the trees, to fly away promptly, or to wait for the companions who have accompanied it to the nest to deliver what they have brought and fly off with it. On only one occasion did we see two attendants stand at the burrow's mouth with food at the same time, but one of them flew up again without having delivered it. Only when it intended to brood, which was seldom, did an adult enter the burrow with food.

Even the youngest nestlings that we found, still blind and naked, took their meals at the burrow's mouth, as do White-whiskered Softwings from a very early age. They ran up the tunnel bobbing their sightless heads and waving their rudimentary wings. In the case of the longer burrows of the nunbird, the round trip from the chamber to the mouth and back again was eight or nine feet, a long pedestrian journey for a tiny mite that crawled out from beneath a brooding parent and then pushed back into its sheltering warmth. Apparently the nestlings do not ordinarily respond to the approach call, which seems loud enough to reach them even at the end of a burrow four or five feet long, no matter how often this call is repeated. If they did they should be waiting at the burrow's mouth when the attendant descends to it, but nearly always the feeder must wait on the ground for a nestling, and sometimes it must entice it outward with a loud feeding call.

Nearly always a single nestling appears in the doorway to take the food, then backs out of sight as soon as it has seized the object. More rarely two nestlings come to the doorway, although only one can be fed. This is especially likely to happen with very young nestlings. Doubtless, as they grow older they learn that it is useless to go to the doorway behind a nest-mate. Older nestlings sometimes give the begging call, *tuwee, tuwee*, as they take their meals. Except when coming for food, nestlings of all ages remain discreetly out of sight in the depths of their long burrows, and they are rarely heard.

Exceptional behavior is exhibited by nestlings who appear to be very hungry. On 8 April rain fell almost continuously throughout the day and there was no gleam of sunshine. One of the nunbirds who foraged in front of the house perched with drooping wings and a badly frayed tail, begging for food in a whimpering voice—the very image of dejection. I feared that the nestlings would suffer, but on the following morning those in the short burrow on the hillside were very much alive. They sat looking outward, repeating soft little *peeps*, while I peered in at them with a flashlight. Soon an attendant bearing a cicada alighted about four yards from the burrow and repeated the approach call. Hearing this, at least two nestlings moved up to the entrance and stood there, exposed and uttering sharp, insistent notes for a minute or so before the attendant flew down and fed one of them. After the adult flew away the nestlings delayed in the doorway for another minute. Even on 10 April, after a day of abundant feeding, these nestlings were noisier than those in deeper tunnels, and one ran into my hands at the burrow's mouth, as already told. The behavior of these nestlings, noisily exposing themselves at the surface of the ground, seemed most imprudent, and perhaps was the reason why disaster overtook them a few days later.

Although there was much daylight in the forest by 05:30, the attendants brought little food, and sometimes none at all, before 07:00, and on some days it was 08:00 before they fed actively. The nestlings received rather infrequent but substantial meals. On 2 April, when the three nestlings in the short burrow were about four days old, they were fed only four times in the three hours between 08:25 and 11:25, during much of which interval rain fell hard. On 5 April these same three nestlings received 12 meals in the six hours from 05:40 to 11:40. On this morning rain fell until about 9:00, after which the sky cleared. On 11 April, when these three nestlings were becoming feathered, they were fed 30 times in the course of the first rainless day that the month brought forth, from 05:40 to 18:00. Twenty of the meals were brought in the forenoon and 10 in the afternoon, only four of them after 14:00. On 10 April an unknown number of naked nestlings in the burrow beside the bluff were fed 11 times in the six hours from 05:40 to 11:40, on a morning with intermittent showers. Some of the attendants of this nest were more timid than any of those at the short burrow, and carried away food that they had brought for the nestlings.

Behavior of attendants who lost nestlings.—I returned to the short burrow late on the morning of 12 April to be greeted by a gaping hole with a pile of freshly dug earth in front of it. Some powerful animal, probably a tayra (*Tayra barbara*) had plundered the nunbirds' nest. The three nestlings had vanished without a trace. Fortunately, for the first time they had passed the night alone, and no adult had been with them to share their fate. From the brood chamber I raked out a handful of fragments of dead leaves, amid which many small white larvae wriggled. Although attendant nunbirds do not remove droppings from their nest—indeed, seem never to enter it after brooding ceases—I noticed little waste matter. Probably the larvae had helped to disintegrate it.

While I examined the ruined burrow, four attendants arrived with food. One soon vanished but three perched in neighboring trees for a long while, holding their intended contributions and repeating soft approach calls. After I withdrew a short distance, they went, one by one, to stand in front of the gaping hole and call the vanished nestlings with sharp feeding notes. One did this while I stood only a dozen feet away. A melancholy spectacle! Finally, the nunbirds flew off toward the neighboring clearing, each holding the food that it could not deliver.

On the following morning, 13 April, no nunbird came near the pillaged nest while I watched from 08:30 to 09:30. As I was leaving I heard the approach call from a bird in the distance and hurried back to my observation post. The nunbird continued to call in the trees above me and after a while I managed to see it. It held a large cicada in its bill, while it repeated over and over its soft, liquid trill. Finally, after about 20 minutes, the bird descended to the ground with the cicada. Standing on the mound of freshly dug earth in front of the hole that the pillager had made, it gave the feeding call, at first in normal tones but soon rising to almost frantic intensity as the nunbird continued to call the missing nestlings. Evidently attracted by these insistent notes, a second nunbird arrived with food. This bird soon left and presently the other followed, still bearing the cicada.

Thus food was brought for the nestlings at least 24 hours after they had vanished. I have known a number of birds of other species to continue to bring food for hours or days after their nestlings were taken by predators. A pair of Golden-naped Woodpeckers did so for six days.

As in the case of the nest, which had met a similar fate in the preceding year, I searched vainly for a replacement nest. This seems generally to be the way with birds of the tropical forest. If they replace a lost nest the new one is so far from the site of the old one that there is no indication that it belongs to the same pair.

YOUNG AFTER LEAVING THE NEST

On 5 May, when the young in the nest by the bluff were well feathered, a great horde of army ants (*Eciton*) swarmed over and around the mouth of the burrow, while Bicolored Antbirds, Ocellated Antthrushes, Black-faced Antthrushes, Barred Woodcreepers, and Broad-billed Motmots picked up insects and other small creatures that fled from the marauders. In the hour during which the ants were present the adult nunbirds did not appear, but I heard the nestlings' hunger call, *tuwee, tuwee*, issue from the depths of the burrow. I should have been more concerned for the young nunbirds' safety had I not, years before, watched a swarm of smaller army ants (*Labidus*) flow over the mouth of a White-whiskered Soft-wings' burrow without harming the feathered nestlings (Skutch, 1958b:229). In neither case did I notice ants entering the burrow; indeed, I have never known army ants to harm birds of any kind or age, although this is far from true of other kinds of ants, especially fire ants (*Solenopsis*).

As I had expected, the young nunbirds suffered no harm and two days later, on 7 May, the last of the brood left the nest, at the age of about 30 days. At noon on this date, guided by approach calls, I discovered adults taking food to a fledgling perching high in a forest tree about 100 feet from the burrow. On the following day, also, the attendants were carrying food into the high treetops, where they gave approach and feeding calls. After a few days the family disappeared from the vicinity, without our having seen much of the young. Sticks set upright in the burrow's mouth after the last fledgling flew indicated that it had not been reentered by 3 June, when we left La Selva. Similar observations were made at the third nest of 1968, which the young vacated about the end of April. nunbirds do not, like certain jacamars, barbets, toucans, and woodpeckers, return to sleep in their nests; and if there is a second brood in the same burrow (which I doubt), it is started more than a month after the departure of the first.

In 1967, when we found no successful nest, we saw much more of juvenile nunbirds than we did in 1968, when two successful nests were studied. In the former year, fledglings were first seen on 28 April, about the date the young in the most advanced nest found in 1968 would have flown, had they survived. There were three of these fledglings who sat on high branches of shade trees in a cacao plantation, calling *tuwee, tuwee* in thin voices. Near them were at least four adults. The young birds, although nearly full grown, were readily distinguished from the adults by their darker body plumage, their orange-buffy (rather than white) foreheads and chins, and their whitish or light horn-colored (rather than orange-red) bills.

During the next month, or until the end of May, nunbirds continued to feed juveniles, often about the edges of the clearing in which the house stood or in neighboring cacao and banana plantations, where it was easier to watch them than in the forest. The food was usually transferred in a spectacular manner. After catching an insect, or sometimes a small lizard or frog, the adult would beat it against a branch, then hold it in its bill until a juvenile flew up and snatched it away, without alighting. Once a young bird flew a hundred feet to grab food from an adult's bill in this fashion. In coming to the attendant for food, rather than waiting for it to be brought to them, the young were, in a way, continuing the habit they had formed as tender nestlings when they came to the mouth of the burrow for their meals. They were also gaining skill for snatching insects from foliage or bark, without alighting, as they would do when older. More rarely a young nunbird would alight beside the adult to take its food, or the adult would fly up to the juvenile and deliver it. If the young were slow in coming for something that an adult had caught for them, the latter would repeat the rolling approach call until the food was taken. A young bird who received a walking-stick insect some six or eight inches long seemed embarrassed by this big meal. After a while the bird started to swallow it little by little, but a quarter of an hour elapsed before the last of the insect disappeared into its mouth.

One would suppose that young birds with such excellent control of flight as this method of taking food demanded would be quite capable of feeding themselves, but their attendants were very indulgent. Moreover, the juveniles' power of flight seemed to develop more rapidly than their knowledge of what was good to eat. Once I watched one of them, after taking food on the wing from an adult, pluck a piece of curled bark which it soon dropped from its bill. Sometimes they tried to take food from unrelated birds. As already recorded, nunbirds often associate loosely with Purple-throated Fruitcrows, black birds of about the same size. One morning in the cacao plantation, I saw a male fruitcrow catch a large green insect, which required a good deal of beating against a branch and mandibulation to make it swallowable. While the fruitcrow was engaged in this operation a young nunbird flew up beside him, as though to take the insect. The fruitcrow promptly flew to another branch, to which the nunbird pursued him, making him retreat once more with his insect, which at his next stop he gulped down.

At the end of May, when some juvenile nunbirds had been on the wing for a month or more, I looked for them to participate in the choruses that then were frequent, but I never detected a pale-billed bird in these gatherings. Not until early June did I see one catch an insect for itself.

SUMMARY

White-fronted Nunbirds inhabit wet primary forests at low altitudes. In small parties of rarely more than half a dozen individuals, they straggle through the woodland canopy, whence they often make foraging excursions into neighboring clearings with scattered trees. These nunbirds were seen to take only animal food, chiefly insects, with an admixture of spiders, millipedes, and an occasional small frog or lizard.

Nunbirds are voluble, uttering a variety of expressive vocalizations, of which six are described. Loudest and most surprising is the "chorus," a bout of simultaneous shouting by from three to ten individuals who perch close together at middle heights in the forest and may perform almost continuously for 15 or 20 minutes.

At about the time that eggs are laid one member of the flock, evidently the breeding female, is fed by several others.

Nunbirds nest in a burrow 40 to 55 inches long, in sloping or nearly level ground in heavy forest. At the inner end is a chamber lined with dead leaves and around the entrance the birds arrange a low collar of twigs and leaves.

One nest held three nestlings, three others an unknown number of young, in late March, April, and May. Hatched blind and quite naked, the nestlings have prominent callous pads on their heel joints.

In each of four nests, the nestlings were attended by three or four nunbirds, all outwardly similar. In one case, four grown birds fed three young, apparently the progeny of a single female. The extra attendants were evidently nonbreeding helpers.

Unless it intended to brood, the attendant never entered the burrow with food. Even while still blind and naked the nestlings ran up the tunnel to receive their meal at its mouth, which in the longer burrows entailed a round trip of about eight or nine feet. Three nestlings becoming feathered were fed 30 times in a day. The attendants never came with more than a single insect or other small creature, held prominently in the bill.

The attendants were never seen to remove waste from the burrow, where maggots soon battened in the bed of dead leaves.

In two burrows the nestlings were destroyed by animals that dug them out. For at least 24 hours after a brood was lost the attendants continued to alight with food in front of the gaping hole and call the nestlings.

After leaving the burrow at the age of about 30 days, the young rose high into the trees. Soon they were taking food in a spectacular fashion, flying up from a distance to snatch it from an attendant's bill while on the wing. This gave practice in the nunbird's habitual manner of foraging.

After the departure of the young, neither they nor the adults returned to sleep in the burrow. Apparently, only one brood is raised.

HELPERS AT BIRDS' NESTS

(1999)

The Significance
of Interspecific Helping

The foregoing ... contain[s] many instances of birds of one species feeding ... or otherwise attending young of different species. To these may be added a few [more] examples.... In Alaska, a pair of Arctic Loons (*Gavia arctica*) adopted five ducklings of the Spectacled Eider (*Somateria fischeri*), hatched near the loons' nest on a small islet in a lake. The loons fed their fosterlings from their bills, as ducks do not, and carried them on their backs while they swam. The ducklings responded appropriately to the warning calls of their foster parents. A Screech Owl (*Otus asio*) and a pair of Northern Flickers nested in holes in the same tree. After the owl's eggs were destroyed, she was found on five consecutive days brooding the young flickers, while the latter, always uninjured, were regularly fed by their parents. The owl even brought a small bird to the young woodpeckers! In Mexico, a young White-eared Hummingbird (*Hylocharis leucotis*) was fed by a green Violet-ear Hummingbird (*Colibri thalassinus*), a bird much heavier than a White-ear.

One of the first points that emerges from a survey of interspecific helping is the great disparity between the helpers and the helped in many of these episodes. Often they belong to different avian orders, with different diets or methods of feeding their young, as in the cases of the loons and the Eider Ducklings, the owl and the nestling flickers, the Common Starling and Northern House Wren that also fed flickers, and the Mountain Chickadees who brought food to the Williamson's Sapsuckers. A bird that nests in the open may carry food to young in a box or hole, as the Gray Catbird did to Northern House Wrens, or a hole-nesting bird may attend young in an open nest, as exemplified by the Blue Tit who fed nestling European Robins and the Eastern Bluebird who gave food to young Northern Mockingbirds. Likewise, birds may place food into nestling or fledgling mouths that differ in color from those of their own young. A Dark-eyed Junco, whose nestlings have red mouths, fed Yellow-mouthed Bewick's Wrens, and a Red-legged Honeycreeper, also with red-mouthed nestlings, gave food to a fledgling Yellow-green Vireo that exposed a yellow gape. Or the mouth colors of helper and helped may be reversed, as when a Tropical Gnatcatcher, whose nestlings' mouths are yellow, attended the red-mouthed nestlings of Golden-masked Tanagers, and an Eastern Kingbird fed Baltimore Orioles. Strangest of all was the case of the Northern Cardinal who fed seven goldfish at the edge of their pond.

With few exceptions, all the instances of interspecific helpers that have come to my attention have been reported from the North Temperate Zone, in Western Europe, the United States, and Canada. My only examples from the tropics are the green Violet-ear who fed the White-eared Hummingbird and three that I have myself found, the Tropical Gnatcatcher and the Golden-masked Tanager, the male Red-legged Honeycreeper and the fledgling Scarlet-rumped Tanager, and the female Red-legged Honeycreeper and the fledgling Yellow-green Vireo. In contrast to this sparse harvest of only two species of in-terspecific helpers, I have watched intraspecific helping, habitual or occasional, in twenty-three species of birds in tropical America.

Why this great difference in the relative frequency of the two categories of helpers at low and at high latitudes? In the first place, intraspecific helpers, especially coopera-tive breeders, are, for reasons that will be given in [a later] chapter, actually far more numerous in the tropics and subtropics than farther north. But the paucity of records of interspecific helpers in tropical countries appears to be due largely to the fewness of those who are likely to observe and report them. Everywhere, interspecific helpers are more likely to attract the attention of people only casually interested in birds than are intraspecific helpers. To learn how many birds of the same kind are visiting a nest often requires concentrated watching of banded or otherwise individually distinguishable birds. But to notice, in the garden or outside the window, birds of different species bringing food to the same nest is so unusual that it arouses the curiosity of anyone even mildly interested in nature, who may report the occurrence to some professional or amateur ornithologist or to the biology department of the nearest university. Thereby, many of these occasions are carefully documented and finally published in an ornithological journal, the local birders' newsletter, or the daily press.

The records of interspecific helpers are so scattered that I cannot claim to have found more than a small fraction of them. I have none from South Africa, Australia, or New Zealand, where I doubt not that interspecific helpers have often been discovered. In the tropics, especially tropical America, people likely to notice and report unusual events in the bird world are much fewer and, until recently, most have been ornithologists from northern countries, often collecting or concentrating on particular studies and not likely to notice interspecific helpers.

Although, for the foregoing reasons, I believe that published records tend to exaggerate the frequency of interspecific helpers relative to intraspecific helpers, the former are certainly not negligibly rare. When I reflect upon the number and great diversity of helper-helped combinations... [already discussed], the many reported cases that have undoubtedly escaped me, and the infinitesimal proportion of all bird nests that have been seen by humans, I suspect that almost every species has occasionally helped, and been helped by, every other species not too different in size and habits with which it has been associated over a large area for many years.

Although juveniles and older non-breeding birds often help at nests of their own species, I have found only one mention of a juvenile interspecific helper among free birds— a young house sparrow who fed nestling tree swallows, as reported by Marilyn Shy. In aviaries, however, juveniles supplied with abundant food frequently offer some of it to birds of different species with whom they are closely associated. Examples include a Black-shouldered Kite who adopted and reared a nestling buzzard, a six-week-old Eastern Bluebird who helped feed fifteen nestlings of several species, and the Japanese White-eyes who fostered nestling House Finches and House Sparrows.

Except in captivity, interspecific helpers are nearly always breeding adults. Male birds, and sometimes incubating females, are often so impatient to feed their expected nestlings that they bring food to the nest and present it to eggs far from hatching—the phenomenon that I have called anticipatory food bringing. If the female happens to be sitting when her mate arrives with food, she may or may not accept it, but often it is clearly not intended for her. Or a male bird may satisfy his premature impulse to feed by attending young in a neighboring nest, which among territorial birds will more often belong to a different than to the same species. Male Scarlet Tanagers of two different pairs fed nestling Chipping Sparrows while their mates incubated. Similarly, a male Northern House Wren fed a brood of Northern Flickers in a hole near that in which his mate incubated, a male Dark-eyed Junco fed nestling Bewick's Wrens, and a male Eastern Bluebird attended nestling Northern House Wrens. More rarely, both members of a pair with eggs feed a neighbor's nestlings, as happened when male and female song sparrows nourished a brood of American Robins. After their own young hatch, parents eager to begin feeding turn their attention to their offspring but may continue to bring more or less food to neighboring young.

Frequently, interspecific helpers are breeding adults who have lost their own brood or reared their young without exhausting their impulse to feed dependents. Included in this category are a male Northern Cardinal who, after losing his own nest, satisfied his thwarted parental instinct by feeding four fledgling American Robins; a male Brown Towhee whose first brood no longer needed care joined a pair of Northern Cardinals in feeding three fledglings of the latter; an Eastern Phoebe whose first brood was becoming independent transferred her attention to a brood of Tree Swallows; after rearing two of her own young, a female Eurasian Blackbird continued for two or three weeks to offer food to any bird who came near. Temporary thwarting of the impulse to feed offspring may divert this impulse to receptive young of a different species, as when a female American Redstart, whose young were being photographed in the hands of children, presented the contents of her bill to a neighboring brood of American Robins.

Sometimes parent birds become interspecific helpers by accident. When the collapse of a thin partition in a rotting trunk dropped a Mountain Chickadees' nest into a cavity occupied by nestling Williamson's Sapsuckers, the chickadees fed the young woodpeckers. As a parent Gray Wagtail (*Motacilla cinerea*) flew over a brood of young thrushes, they opened their mouths, whereupon the wagtail faltered in flight, turned, alighted, and gave all its food to them. A male Chaffinch, attracted by the persistent calling of newly fledged Hawfinches, fed them six times. A pair of Black-and-white Warblers fed a recently fledged ovenbird who had apparently become separated from its parents. When two birds of rather similar habits have young of about the same age in nests close together, each is sometimes diverted to its neighbor's brood. Thus, a male Rufous-sided Towhee frequently fed nestling field sparrows, and the parents of the latter reciprocated by bringing food to the nestling towhees — a case of reciprocal altruism.

Recently the question of altruism in animals has been much discussed. If we regard altruism as a moral quality, dependent upon the state of mind or intention of the altruist, then we must withhold judgment, for the minds of animals are closed to us. If, on the other hand, we assess altruism solely by overt behavior, then interspecific helpers are undeniably altruists, for neither they nor their descendants derive any benefit from it. Their only reward is the satisfaction of their instincts or impulses — as is often true of our own uncalculating altruism.

The relations between helper and helped range all the way from harmony to mutual antagonism. Harmony prevailed between a helpful Northern Cardinal and parent American Robins, between the helpful Brown Towhee and a pair of cardinals, between a Northern House Wren and parent Black-headed Grosbeaks, and between a Winter Wren and the Townsend's Solitaires at whose nest it assisted. Among helpers antagonistic to the parents were a Gray Catbird at a Northern House Wren nest, one of the latter at a Northern Flicker nest, and a Tropical Gnatcatcher at a Golden-masked Tanager nest. Such antagonism sometimes increases as days pass and the helper develops a more proprietary interest in the nest where it assists. In other cases, the parents repel their uninvited assistant, as Worm-eating Warblers did to a helpful Black-and-white Warbler, and Tree Swallows did to a well-disposed Eastern Phoebe. Finally, helper and helped may be mutually hostile, each trying to keep the other away, as when a Common Starling fed nestling Purple Martins.

The Rufous-sided Towhee–Field Sparrow association mentioned above is an example of mutual interspecific helpers. Others are provided by birds of different species who share a nest. In a nest in which both laid, a Yellow-billed Cuckoo and a Mourning Dove incubated side by side. Another Mourning Dove shared with an American Robin a nest with two eggs laid by each, both of whom incubated and attended the nestlings. A robin and a House Finch took charge of a nest in which both had laid. A pair of Northern Cardinals and a pair of Song Sparrows tried to rear their broods in the same nest. These attempts to nest communally are likely to be partly successful only when the participants are more similar than doves and cuckoos or doves and thrushes; and at best only the young of the larger species are likely to survive until they fledge.

A survey of interspecific helping with all its strange combinations impresses one with the strength of birds' impulses to place food in other mouths, which overrides the limits of species, family, and order, disregards the appearance of the nestling or the color of the mouth into which the food is thrust, is not inhibited by a quite different nest site, persists in the face of strong opposition by the recipients' parents, and may occasionally impel a bird to neglect its own eggs while it feeds young of a different species. The impulsion to feed is one of the strongest in all the behavioral repertory of altricial, semialtricial, and subprecocial birds, because the perpetuation of their species depends upon depositing sufficient nourishment in the mouths of their young. It is one of the first components of parental behavior to become manifest in fledglings or even nestlings (although sometimes they make gestures of nest building at an equally callow age); it persists in birds unable to breed; it prompts bereaved parents to bring food to their nests for days after they have lost their nestlings; it may be redirected to social companions well able to nourish themselves; it enters into the courtship of many birds; applied to the bird's mate instead of the young, it helps form her eggs and sustain her while she incubates.

Even nest parasites that have lost most or all other parental behavior may retain the impulse to feed: the Shining Cuckoos (*Chrysococcyx*) of Africa have repeatedly been seen to feed nestlings or fledglings of their own species raised by foster parents, as well as to give food to their mates; and, more rarely, Brown-headed Cowbirds have been reported to feed young cowbirds. Finally, the impulse to feed may find expression in fantastic situations, as when a captive common raven passed food through the bars of its cage to a free black vulture, a Northern Cardinal fed goldfish in a pond, and a Jackdaw, regarding Dr. Konrad Lorenz as his mate, pushed food into the distinguished ethologist's mouth and even his ear!

The variety of nestlings and fledglings, and indeed animals of other kinds, which birds occasionally feed is proof that this behavior is not precisely adjusted to the features of the birds' own offspring. Apparently, instances of interspecific helping, although numerous in the aggregate, are too infrequent to diminish appreciably the reproduction of any species, and, accordingly, natural selection has failed to produce a finer adjustment. However, in another context, that of nest parasites and their hosts, greater discrimination by parent birds could save many species a huge drain on their reproductive output—a drain that has threatened the extermination of such rare species as the Kirtland's Warbler (*Dendroica kirtlandii*).

The parasitic female's chief problem seems to be to have her eggs accepted by the prospective foster parent, who may throw them out, cover them with nest materials, or abandon the violated nest. If the parasite's dupe accepts and hatches the alien eggs, it apparently never fails to feed the fosterlings, no matter how greatly they differ in size and appearance from its own young. Eggs of numerous old world cuckoos (although not of new world cowbirds) frequently match those of the host closely in color and size, but mimicry of the host's young by the parasite's young is rare. It occurs in the parasitic Whydahs, whose gaping nestlings expose the same curiously patterned mouths as their closely related Weaver-finch (*Estrildidae*) hosts; in the Koel (*Eudynamys scolopacea*) and Great Crested Cuckoo (*Clamator glandarius*), whose black fledglings resemble those of their black corvine hosts; and in the Screaming Cowbird of South America, whose young are confusingly similar to their foster parent, the non-parasitic Bay-winged Cowbird. Evolution's failure to give frequent hosts of nest parasites the protection from parasitism that finer discrimination of the objects of their parental care might bring them is another indication of the irrepressible strength of their impulse to feed and to brood. If mating were not more strictly controlled than feeding, by more numerous and salient specific characters, avian hybrids would be more common than we find them.

Interspecific helping is evidence that birds' parental behavior occasionally escapes the strict genetic control, which, if sufficiently strengthened by evolution, might confine their ministrations to their own offspring. The behavior, such as feeding young of a different species, is innate, but the context in which it occurs is obviously not narrowly limited by heredity, except in a few species such as the Sooty Tern (*Sterna fuscata*), which, if given eggs of the Brown Noddy (*Anous stolidus*) to hatch, will throw from the nest or kill the nestlings so similar to its own. The bird who attends alien nestlings appears to enjoy a measure of freedom, of self-determination or spontaneity — as it also does when it selects the situation of its nest amid a variety of potential natural sites. Release from the strict determination of activity by the genes is a most important component of freedom, especially our own: we owe almost everything that civilization has achieved, intellectual and moral as well as material, to our ability to think and act in ways not programmed in our genes. Interspecific helping reveals that at least some birds are sometimes free to innovate behavior, even to act capriciously, in ways that might have important consequences for their descendants.

Because interspecific helping is too sporadic to influence to a measurable degree the reproductive potential or the demography of any species, its significance has been largely neglected by students of the evolution and ecology of cooperative breeding. As far as we know, no avian species has been less successful in maintaining its numerical strength, because some of its members occasionally spend some of their time and energy helping other species. Nevertheless, by revealing the great strength of birds' impulse to feed as well as their freedom to act in ways not strictly determined by their heredity, the study of interspecific helping may contribute to our understanding of the more advanced forms of intraspecific helping.

Although, evolutionists stoutly maintain, genetically controlled behavioral ways tends to maximize the number of an individual's own genes in its descendants, the same need not be true of behavior that escapes strict genetic control. Birds are occasionally free to behave in ways that they find satisfying, regardless of any effects upon reproduction. They may remain in their natal territory in a subordinate role, instead of hazardously emigrating to rear broods of their own, because they enjoy companionship and feel more secure in the home of their childhood. They may return to that home after failure to establish themselves elsewhere. They may build covered nests for more comfortable sleeping even if this takes time and energy that might be applied to reproduction. If the innovation jeopardizes the perpetuation of the species, it will be suppressed by natural selection. But if it is compatible with the continued prosperity of the species, it may persist in innovative individuals until it is supported by the process variously known as organic selection or genetic assimilation, whereby behavior that is at first individual and spontaneous is finally supported by mutations that establish it firmly in the heredity of the species.

To recognize that this is one of the ways in which co-operative breeding might arise is to attribute to the birds' choices, to their minds, far-reaching consequences in the evolution of avian behavior. Evolution can promote the development of an organ or function only if that organ or that function influences the course of evolution. The eyes of birds, for example, have been perfected because visual acuity has so powerfully influenced the evolution of birds. It is not otherwise with mind, which can modify behavior by discrimination, choice, and intelligence. If mind did not influence the course of evolution, as it obviously has done in our own species, it would never have developed beyond its first rudiments. Although birds' minds are much simpler than ours, they are neither negligible nor devoid of flexibility. The phenomenon of interspecific helping is evidence that birds enjoy a measure of freedom from strict control by their genes, and the exercise of this freedom may in the long run lead to advanced cooperative breeding.

Characteristics of Cooperative Breeders

In the foregoing...we broadly surveyed the incidence and activities of nest helpers and cooperative breeders among the families of birds [W]e shall [now] consider some of the widespread features of these cooperative birds. We shall concentrate our attention upon advanced cooperative breeders, whose young remain with their parents at least into the nesting season following that in which they hatched and are integrated into fairly stable social groups. Sometimes it is difficult to draw the line between advanced cooperative breeders and those somewhat less than advanced; but species that have only occasional helpers are excluded from the present discussion, as are those, such as Long-tailed Tits, whose helpers are chiefly breeding adults who have lost their young. Those with helpers of different species [have already been] considered....

Where do we find advanced cooperative breeders? Since long-distance migration or wide wandering in the inclement season causes the disintegration of families, except those of certain larger birds, such as swans and geese, cooperative breeding occurs mainly in the tropics and subtropics, where birds are continuously resident. Nomadism appears to be less disruptive of families than long-distance migration, and in Australia a substantial minority of cooperative breeders are nomadic. The Acorn Woodpecker, one of the cooperative breeders that ranges farthest from the equator, up to northwestern Oregon at 45 degrees north latitude, can remain on its territory throughout the cold months thanks to its abundant stores of acorns and the snug holes in which it sleeps.

The number of cooperative breeders that have been carefully studied amid the dry, open woodlands, savannas, and arid scrub of Africa, Australia, and other regions with light vegetation might lead one to conclude that these are the habitats most favorable to this lifestyle. It would be truer to say that these are the habitats most favorable for studying cooperative breeding. Nests are relatively easy to find and to watch and, as in many of the drier parts of Africa, living accommodations are available to visiting scientists and it is easy to move about in a Land

Rover. Cooperative breeders are found in almost every terrestrial and freshwater habitat in Earth's warmer regions that will support them, from arid deserts, such as the Kalahari and the Arabian, to the wettest rain forests. In two breeding seasons at what is now a field station of the Organization for Tropical Studies at La Selva, in the rain forest of the Caribbean lowlands of northern Costa Rica, we found seven species of cooperative breeders, three of which were not previously known to have this habit. But despite much searching, we discovered only one to three nests of each of these species, and the risk of losing these precious nests by too-frequent or too-close approaches limited what we could learn about them. Certainly many more cooperative breeders remain to be discovered in the rich avifaunas of tropical rain forests.

Just as cooperative breeders are not confined to any single habitat, so they are not restricted to a particular diet. Insectivores (in the broad sense) are in the majority, doubtless because insectivorous birds tend to be sedentary and strongly territorial, whereas many tropical frugivorous and nectarivorous birds wander widely as, now here, now there, a tree or shrub blossoms or ripens its fruits. Frugivorous and nectarivorous birds tend to the opposite extreme from cooperative breeding: to nesting by solitary females unassisted by males, who vie for their attention in leks or courtship assemblies, as in manakins, birds of paradise, and hummingbirds. But cooperative breeders include the largely frugivorous barbets, Collared Araçari, and Purple-throated Fruitcrow, the mainly vegetarian Acorn Woodpecker and Purple Gallinule, seed-eating weavers, and omnivorous jays.

Most cooperative breeders reside throughout the year on defended territories. They may be either facultative or obligate. The latter, which include the White-winged Chough, Yellow-billed Shrike, and Gray-breasted Jay, appear rarely if ever to nest successfully as unaided pairs. Among the former, which are far more numerous, many, often most, pairs lack helpers, frequently because they are birds who are breeding for the first time or who have lost all their progeny of earlier years, with the result that they have none to assist them. In addition to unaided pairs, cooperative breeders live in groups of three to about ten or twelve individuals, with extremes of twenty reported for the White-winged Chough, Jungle Babbler, and Gray-breasted Jay, twenty-five for the Yellow-billed Shrike, twenty-six for the San Blas Jay, and thirty-five for the Chestnut-bellied Starling. Some of these very large groups contain several breeding pairs. The huge nests of sociable weavers may have as many as five hundred inhabitants, who cooperate in maintaining the superstructure, while other modes of cooperation are confined to much smaller subgroups or families. In certain cooperative species, including the Southern Ground Hornbill, some individuals, mostly females, remain alone or with a companion or two of the same sex during the breeding season.

Advanced cooperative breeders tend to lack colorful plumage; often they are black, brown, or gray. Notable exceptions are the handsome Purple Gallinule, Green Jay, Tufted Jay, Golden-breasted Starling, and Superb Starling. Whether dull or brilliant, the sexes tend to be alike; even the male and female Red-cockaded Woodpecker are difficult to distinguish in the field, although the sexes of most woodpeckers are readily separated by their head patterns. Outstanding exceptions to this rule are the Blue Wrens of Australia, among which the elegance of the males contrasts strikingly with the plainness of the females. Apparently, subdued coloration and the absence of conspicuous sexual differences help reduce sexual jealousy among closely associated adults.

In contrast to the similarity of fully adult individuals of the two sexes, younger birds tend to retain for a long while features that distinguish them from their elders. These lingering signs of immaturity often involve the colors of bills, eyes, or bare facial skin. The black bills of fledgling Green Wood-hoopoes take a year or more to become red, as in adults. Bills of cooperatively breeding jays darken from yellow to black as the birds mature, a change that may take more than a year and that proceeds irregularly, producing variously pied patterns, which facilitate the recognition of individuals. Until about six years old, Southern Ground Hornbills are distinguished by the colors of their eyes and the bare skin of their faces and throats. The irises of White-winged Choughs, brown at first, take about four years to become wholly red. Similarly, Gray-crowned Babblers' eyes brighten from dark brown to yellow in about two and a half years. Birds, whose plumage may change when they molt, appear to recognize their companions mainly by their heads. The maintenance of group cohesion and harmony appears to depend upon a subtle balance of likeness and difference, equality and subordination; small rather than striking differences in the appearance of a group's members seem to make this balance easier to preserve.

A group of cooperative breeders usually consists of a single breeding pair with one or more auxiliaries who are usually their offspring from an earlier year, often with one or more immigrants from other groups. Birds of the immediately preceding season, yearlings, often predominate among the helpers, but older individuals are frequent. Group members are usually, perhaps always, arranged in a hierarchy or rank order; however, this may not be obvious, because a peck order—such as develops among domestic chickens and certain other birds—is absent, and aggressive interactions may be rare. They are seldom so rough as the bill wrestling with wing blows by which older Laughing Kookaburras keep younger ones in their place. To learn the hierarchical order among gentler birds, investigators sometimes intensify competition to an unnatural level by offering a concentrated source of food, such as peanuts in a can.

In a typical rank order, the breeding male takes precedence over all other individuals in his group, who rank below him in descending order of their ages, the youngest at the bottom. The breeding female heads individuals of her sex, also ranked according to their ages. The breeding female may be subordinate not only to her mate but likewise to helpers subordinate to him. The persisting signs of immaturity that we have just noticed may help preserve this order. In most cooperative breeders, the hierarchy is not a system of exploitation or bullying but a gently maintained order of precedence that promotes concord and facilitates cooperation. It is hardly different from the situation in many harmonious human families, in which unmarried sons and daughters live with their parents and help maintain the household, and the father, or in matriarchal societies the mother, is head of the family and chief decision maker, and the children exercise authority in the order of their ages, experience, and strength of character.

In many cooperative breeders males outnumber females, often by as much as 1.5 to 1 or even 3 to 1. Exceptional are Pukekos, Laughing Kookaburras, White-winged Choughs, Gray-crowned Babblers, and Yellow-billed Shrikes, whose groups contain approximately equal numbers of the two sexes. Since males and females tend to be equally represented among fledglings, why do the former predominate in the adult population? The reason is that in most cooperative breeders females emigrate more often than males, who much more frequently remain in their natal groups. Wanderers confront more perils, and suffer higher mortality, than birds who stay on the familiar home territory, with the result that the sex more inclined to emigrate becomes less numerous. Another cause of the higher mortality of females is the fact that the sex, which incubates, especially at night, suffers higher predation than other group members.

An exception to the greater tendency of females to emigrate is found in the White-browed Sparrow-weaver, in which males wander abroad more often, and a lost reproductive female is replaced by a member of the same group. In other species, the oldest surviving male of the group usually inherits the rank of a lost breeding male, while the female breeder is more often replaced from outside. Sometimes both sexes emigrate, in parties of two to four of the same sex, who together seek another group or try to form a new group, in which they have better prospects of rising to the top. If they succeed, the oldest will become the breeder, and his or her companions will serve as helpers.

Among social mammals, females commonly stay in their natal group, while young males seek their fortunes elsewhere. Why female birds leave home more often than males is obscure. It can hardly be because they are subordinate to males, because this will be true in whatever group they enter. If they find a group that has lost its reproductive female, they may attain breeding status sooner than they would in their natal group; but apparently they are more likely to perish than to become breeders, resulting in the unbalanced sex ratio that we have noticed. Instead of remaining in comparative safety at home, females seem to sacrifice themselves to avoid inbreeding and to spread their group's genes more widely through the population, with possible benefit to their species. However, in some species they rarely go much farther than neighboring groups, and if their quest of a vacancy that they can fill proves futile, they may return after absences of days or weeks and be accepted by their erstwhile companions, as has been recorded of Florida Scrub Jays, Straight-crested Helmet-shrikes, White-browed Sparrow-weavers, and Black Tits and is probably generally true. Cooperative breeders are home-loving birds.

Most cooperative groups dwell in harmony, with rarely a serious dispute or aggressive behavior. Fledglings and juveniles of Jungle Babblers, Arabian Babblers, and probably others are often quarrelsome or unruly, but as they mature they learn better manners. Puerto Rican Todies, whose helpers have not been associated with them since the preceding breeding season but appear after their nesting is well advanced, first repel but later accept these volunteers. Instead of preserving an individual distance while they perch, many cooperative breeders are contact birds, who rest by day and sleep by night pressed against each other. Those that breed in open nests roost at night in a compact row on the branch of a tree or shrub or sometimes even more closely massed together, some on the backs of others. Species that raise their families in a roofed nest or a cavity of some sort commonly sleep together in the same or a similar closed space, so that even if they do not perch in contact by day, they must be packed together at night, in layers if they are numerous. Those that possess such dormitories usually lead their fledglings to sleep in them with their elders — a habit not confined to cooperative breeders.

Exceptional is the White-browed Sparrow-weaver, in which group members build special dormitories for the fledglings, while adults sleep alone in separate lodges. Also unexpected is the behavior of Red-cockaded Woodpeckers, who leave their fledglings outside while each adult seeks its own particular hole for sleeping. This is the way of some other woodpeckers, including the Red-crowned (*Melanerpes rubricapillus*), in which helpers have not been found; but Golden-naped Woodpeckers, who have only rare, mostly inefficient juvenile helpers, lodge in a hole with their young until the following breeding season.

Among both birds and mammals, mutual grooming or preening ranks high among the ties that bind social animals together. While they rest in intimate contact, cooperatively breeding birds frequently preen each other. Allopreening, as this is called, occurs among Pukekos, Tasmanian Native Hens, Anis, Green Wood-hoopoes, Southern Ground Hornbills, Purple-throated Fruit-crows, White-bearded Flycatchers, Green Jays, Yucatan Jays, Apostlebirds, Sittellas, Banded-backed Wrens, Babblers, Blue Wrens, Wood-swallows, White-eyes, and others. It appears to be rare in sociable weavers, absent in Gray-breasted Jays, and unrecorded in some other cooperative breeders. Allopreening is certainly not peculiar to cooperative breeders, but in other birds it tends to be restricted to members of a pair, especially just before and during the breeding season.

Somewhat less frequent is exchanging food or feeding fully self-supporting companions, other than a female preparing to lay or engaged in incubating or brooding; but it occurs in Pukekos, Harris' Hawks, Pied Kingfishers, Yucatan Jays, Black Tits, Babblers, Wood-swallows, and Northwestern Crows. Although the attitude of the recipient, often with fluttering wings and begging cries, is often interpreted as a gesture of submission to the donor, it is probably no more than the persistence of the fledgling's habit of receiving its meals in this fashion. Northwestern Crows, Black-faced Wood-swallows, White-breasted Wood-swallows, and Laughing Kookaburras (and even several big birds that are not cooperative breeders) have substantially prolonged the life of an injured companion, unable to forage, by frequent gifts of food. From all these activities emerges a picture of groups of birds who, far from living in a state of tension and rivalry, dwell in relaxed friendship.

In a number of cooperative breeders, group members join in choruses or displays or both simultaneously. Among the nonpasserines, choruses tend to be loud and stirring rather than melodious. Such are the performances of White-fronted Nunbirds perching in a row high in a tropical rain forest, the far-carrying dawn chorus of Southern Ground Hornbills, and the startling outbursts for which the Laughing Kookaburra is named. At daybreak, Noisy Miners sing together for many minutes. Among the notable displays are the flag waving and rally of Green Wood-hoopoes and the huddles of Gray-crowned Babblers, all accompanied by much sound. Confrontations of two groups of cooperative breeders at their common boundary generally excite far more displaying than fighting. San Blas Jays and Gray-breasted Jays are reluctant to cross territorial boundaries.

Cooperative breeders defend their companions as well as their nests and fledglings. When a Gray-crowned Babbler is caught by a predator or held in a human hand, all babblers within hearing, including members of neighboring groups, rush toward it and join in a simultaneous distraction display. White-winged Choughs crowd around and defend a companion attacked by an aggressive Black-backed Magpie. White-breasted Wood-swallows vigorously attack predatory animals, flying or flightless. Collared Araçaris pursued a hawk that had caught a fledgling. Finally, cooperative breeders, young and old, are sometimes playful. The social frolics of Southern Ground Hornbills, Apostle-birds, Common Babblers, and Brown Jays are described elsewhere.

Most groups of cooperative breeders have a single breeding pair, composed of the ranking male and female, and a single nest at any one time. Occasionally, Acorn Woodpeckers, White-winged Choughs, and some populations of Gray-crowned Babblers nest communally, with two or rarely more females laying their eggs in the same nest. In promiscuous groups of Pukekos, two or three females frequently share a nest. Two or more pairs of monogamous Anis often occupy the same nest and raise their young together. Instead of laying several sets of eggs in one nest, other cooperative breeders build a number of contemporaneous nests in their territory, each belonging to a breeding pair. Large groups of Common Babblers sometimes had two nests at the same time, but the second always failed. A group of Yucatan Jays may have two or three breeding pairs, Gray-breasted Jays up to six, and southern San Blas Jays six to ten, all with as many separate nests. A large group of Chestnut-bellied Starlings has from two to six nests at one time. A group of Guira Cuckoos may have several nests, or several females may lay in the same nest.

All this looks much like colonial nesting, in colonies defended against other colonies by all members. However, when a cooperatively breeding group has several simultaneous or temporally overlapping nests, usually all of them are attended by many or all members of the group, including those with nests of their own, so that they are no less communal breeders with mutual helpers than the anis, to which this designation has long been applied. By reciprocally feeding each other's young, Wood-swallows also become mutual helpers.

Several groups of Gray-capped Social Weavers occupy different parts of the same tree, forming a colony of groups, which they defend from intrusions by members of other colonies. Pied Kingfishers sometimes dig their burrows in loose colonies in inviting banks. Aerial flycatchers, including swifts, swallows, and bee-eaters, often nest in colonies. Since it is hardly possible to delimit territories high in the air whence most of their food is procured, their territories, if they may be said to have them, are little more than their nest sites. The nonmigratory Red-throated and White-fronted Bee-eaters are advanced cooperative breeders. Despite the various ways in which migratory house martins help their neighbors, they can hardly be admitted to this category because their families do not remain intact from one season to the next, and who helps whom appears to be largely a matter of fortuitous contacts. The same appears to be true of those other long-distance migrants, Barn Swallows and Chimney Swifts.

The number of helpers at a nest is always somewhat less than the number of birds in a breeding group because the parents are, by definition, not helpers (except among communal breeders), and other group members, especially juveniles, may not aid. From the single helper at some nests of nearly all cooperative breeders, their number ranges up to a recorded maximum of twelve at nests of southern San Blas Jays, thirteen at nests of Gray-breasted Jays and Chestnut-bellied Starlings, and fourteen at nests of Bushy-crested Jays. These communal breeders with a number of contemporaneous nests in a territory tend to have more helpers at each nest than do species with only a single breeding pair; but once ten attended a nest of

Green Wood-hoopoes, and nine have been identified at nests of Common Babblers and Sociable Weavers.

When their parents raise two or more broods in a season, juveniles, and even birds hardly past the fledgling stage, often serve as helpers. These young assistants may begin at a surprisingly early age—twenty-five or thirty days in Sociable Weavers, forty-eight days in Smooth-billed Anis, sixty days in Splendid Wrens, sixty-nine days in Purple Gallinules, seventy days in Brown Tree-creepers—and quite frequently when about three months old. In many cooperative breeders that seldom or never raise second broods, the majority of the auxiliaries are yearlings, hatched in the immediately preceding breeding season. From this peak the number of assistants declines as individuals emigrate, graduate to the position of breeders in their own group, or die. Two-year-old helpers are present in many species; and among Florida Scrub Jays, White-winged Choughs, Yellow-billed Shrikes, and Splendid Wrens, individuals five or six years old remain among the auxiliaries. The fact that a bird serves as a helper is no proof that it is sexually immature or that it is not old enough to breed if it could become a dominant member of a group. Laughing Kookaburras, Red-throated Bee-eaters, Chimney Swifts, Acorn Woodpeckers, Superb Blue Wrens, and probably many others are sexually mature when about one year old but at this age often serve as non-breeding auxiliaries.

The activities (other than self-maintenance) in which helpers engage are, in the order of increasing frequency, incubating and brooding nestlings, nest building, feeding the incubating parent on or off the nest, feeding the young and cleaning their nest, and defending eggs and young—which is the order in which male birds of all kinds serve at their mates' nests. Helpers have been found incubating among Chimney Swifts, Puerto Rican Todies, Laughing Kookaburras, Red-throated Bee-eaters, Red-cockaded Woodpeckers, Acorn Woodpeckers, White-winged Choughs, and Common Babblers, in all of which the male parent shares incubation with his mate. Nearly always a bird who incubates performs the very similar activity of brooding. In species of which the breeding male does not incubate, helpers rarely do. As a rule, when juveniles participate in an activity, they are less diligent and efficient than yearlings and older birds. But in nest defense, especially against human intruders, youngsters often protest more vehemently and take greater risks than older birds, probably because youth tends to be reckless and imprudent.

Despite the number of attendants, some cooperative breeders nest with poor success, but they compensate for low fecundity by living long. Southern Ground Hornbills produced an average of one fledgling per group every 6.3 years. Their average life span was calculated to be about twenty-eight years. The much smaller Acorn Woodpeck-ers raised to the age of nest leaving only 0.2 or 0.3 young per adult per year, which is one fledgling for every five or every three adults in the population. Adult males, the more numerous sex, had an estimated life span of thirteen years, females one of about ten years. White-winged choughs, who produced only 1.14 fledglings per nest, took four or more years to become adult, which suggests that they live a long while. Another bird whose delayed maturity indicates longevity is the Yellow-billed Shrike. After studying this bird for six years, Llewellyn Grimes had not learned at what age it is ready to breed; two six-year-old female auxiliaries had not yet nested. At the other extreme, little Sociable Weavers acquire adult plumage when about four months old, breed early, nest with very poor success, and appear rarely to survive for more than three years. They compensate for their high losses of eggs and young and their short life expectancy by nesting three or four times in years when frequent showers help keep the desert green.

Benefits and Evolution of Cooperative Breeding

A pattern of life so widespread as cooperative breeding, adopted by so many species of birds of different families in such diverse habitats throughout Earth's warmer regions, must certainly give some substantial benefits to its participants. What are the benefits and who are the beneficiaries? This question may be divided into two: what does cooperative breeding contribute to the welfare of individuals, and how does it affect the reproduction and stability of the species?

Let us look first at the young birds who serve as helpers. Instead of the hard lot of all those inexperienced juveniles who are cast upon their own resources in a perilous world soon after they can feed themselves, the young of cooperative breeders remain with their parents on the home territory, guided by adults and shielded by them from many dangers. Although, like most young birds, they are innately equipped to support themselves, their inherited capacities can be strengthened and improved by experience. From their elders they become familiar with the most productive spots for foraging and the safest refuges from danger; by participating in mobbing, they learn to recognize enemies. As in the flocks of mixed species that wander through the woodlands, so in cooperative groups many keen eyes and alert ears bring prompt warning of the approach of a predator that might pounce unperceived upon a solitary individual.

By sleeping with companions in a snug dormitory or even by pressing close to them on an open perch, the young bird conserves heat and energy on cool nights. Its associates may preen and remove vermin from parts of its plumage inaccessible to its own bill. The individual bird doubtless feels safer in a group than by itself; that it actually is safer is attested by the fact that the sex which stays at home, usually the male, survives much better than the sex that more often emigrates — leading to the unbalanced sex ratios that we have noticed in many cooperative breeders. Male Galapagos Hawks prolong their lives by becoming members of nesting trios or quartets instead of remaining in the floating non-breeding population.

Moreover, by helping with its parents' subsequent broods, the young bird acquires experience that will increase its efficiency when it in turn undertakes to rear a family.... [We have previously seen] how Yellow-tailed Thornbills and Brown Jays became more proficient builders of nests or feeders of young by assisting their elders. We have a growing body of evidence, chiefly from birds that are not cooperative breeders, that experienced birds breed more successfully than novices. The educative experience might be gained more cheaply by assisting at another's nest than by trying inexpertly at one's own. A helper often becomes a breeder by inheriting the rank of its deceased father or mother or by joining some other group. In the former situation, the nestlings that it has fed, now grown, may reward it by serving at its nest.

For the parents, the gains from cooperative breeding are equally great. The auxiliaries commonly help defend the territory, which may become larger or of better quality thanks to their assistance. Often they help build a nest, especially a dormitory where the whole family sleeps warm and dry. Some helpers take turns at incubation, thereby giving the parents more time for self-maintenance, or they feed the incubating parent. Usually they contribute substantially to feeding nestlings and fledglings, lightening a burden, which for unaided parents with large broods can be debilitating. Some of the results of such relief were noticed . . . earlier. . . .

In double-brooded species, such as the Laughing Kookaburra and the Superb Blue Wren, parents with helpers are much more likely to have the energy to nest again in the same season, and to do so successfully, than are unaided parents. While the parents are engaged with the later nest, their assistants care for the fledglings of the first brood. Common Babbler parents with three or more helpers could molt—a process costly in terms of vital resources—while they had nestlings, as those with fewer assistants rarely did. Breeding female White-browed Sparrow-weavers survived best in large groups, as did subordinate parents at the communal nests of Groove-billed Anis, where the dominant male alone undertook the dangerous duty of nocturnal incubation. Another advantage of having helpers is that the young could be more rapidly fed after a prolonged interval of enforced neglect while a predator was in view, as frequently happened to groups of White-browed Sparrow-weavers and Gray-capped Social Weavers. James Councilman concluded that scarcity of food made helpers necessary to feed young Gray-crowned Babblers and abundant predators made them needed to defend the nest.

Some students of cooperative breeding have surmised that helpers are manipulated or exploited by the parents; others, that they are spongers who impose upon their parents. Neither is probable: if auxiliaries feel that they are overworked or harshly treated, they are free to leave; if the parents find their helpers burdensome or annoying, they are able to expel them from the territory. Others ask whether helpers are altruistic or selfish. If by "altruistic" we mean benefiting others with no reward beyond the satisfaction that this beneficence brings, and by "selfish" we mean exploiting or manipulating others for one's own gain, neither of these attributes is applicable to avian auxiliaries. Helpers are neither more nor less altruistic or selfish than the boy who, unpaid, aids his father in the chores of a farm or the girl who lightens her mother's tasks. Each gives and receives benefits without calculating the amount. Just as a wholesome child helps its parents without remembering that it may inherit from them, so the helpful bird aids its elders unaware that it may rise to breeding status on the parental territory, however much this possibility may have influenced the evolution of cooperative breeding; to believe otherwise is to ascribe longer foresight to young birds than to human children. The relationship of breeding adults and their auxiliaries in cooperative breeding systems is just what the term implies: cooperation or mutualism. Sharing of efforts and rewards binds individuals into a coherent society; pure altruism is often a unilateral relationship that emphasizes the inequality of individuals; slaves are compulsory altruists.

When evolutionists or sociobiologists ask whether nest helpers are altruists, they usually give to this term a special meaning, closely associated with the concept of fitness. When we hear of "the survival of the fittest," we assume that the fittest are the strongest, healthiest, most capable animals, best able to find food and escape enemies. The modern evolutionist has a single measure of fitness: the number of progeny an organism produces in its lifetime. At first sight, this appears an arbitrary restriction of the word's meaning; but we may reflect that in a state of nature, the strongest, healthiest, most capable animals are the ones most likely to beget the greatest number of equally capable offspring. An altruist, in the special meaning of the term, is an individual that sacrifices its own fitness—the number of its progeny—while augmenting the fitness of another.

Whether helpers are altruists in this special sense is a question difficult to answer. Possibly those who serve as auxiliaries for a single breeding season are not; although they contribute to the fitness of the parents whom they assist, they may be preparing themselves to breed so much more efficiently, with less risk to themselves, that they compensate for the loss of one season when they might be attending their own nests. However, to give a definite answer to this question, we would need to weigh the probability of winning a territory and a mate by emigrating against the probability of inheriting the territory on which they serve. The relatively few birds who continue as helpers for three, four, or five years do indeed appear to be altruists; but if the probability of finding a territory and a mate is very slight, perhaps they do the best they can for themselves. I would leave the question of whether intraspecific helpers are altruists in this special sense to mathematical sociobiologists, with their assumptions and complicated calculations, and continue to regard these auxiliaries simply as collaborators in the business of perpetuating their species and their way of living. Most obviously altruistic are the interspecific helpers.

This brings us to one of the theories of the evolution of cooperative breeding, which ascribes it to habitat saturation. Some avian species have an optimum habitat, where breeding is possible, adjoining or at no great distance from a marginal habitat, where individuals can survive but insufficient amounts of food, cover, or nest sites prevent reproduction. Excess individuals overflow into the marginal habitat, awaiting an opportunity to enter the optimum habitat and breed if and when vacancies occur. They provide a standby population that may help replenish a breeding population somehow depleted. But for some birds in some regions, marginal habitat is sparse or lacking because of the absence of an ecological gradient, or intermediate zone, between areas where breeding is possible and those where individuals can hardly survive.

Young birds who cannot find an opening in the optimum habitat must either remain on the parental territory or perish. Not surprisingly, they prefer the first of these alternatives. Some who try fruitlessly to raise their status elsewhere return to their natal group.

The theory briefly outlined implies that cooperative breeders are successful species that fill their habitat to its carrying capacity. It does not ascribe their success to the presence of helpers but, at least, since these species continue to saturate their habitat, the auxiliaries are no detriment. Like the marginal populations of other birds, the helpers are a reserve to replenish losses among the breeding adults or to take advantage of such opportunities for range expansion as might arise. Moreover, they are a superior reserve, for they already have experience in nest attendance, which a marginal population of non-breeders lacks. Cooperative breeding is rightly viewed as a flexible method of population regulation. Ornithologists in Australia, where cooperative breeders are numerous, view this system as especially appropriate for the unpredictable climate of their mostly arid continent. In drier years when food is hard to find, the helpers may be needed for provisioning the young; when more generous rainfall creates more favorable conditions, the auxiliaries may help rear second or third broods or, already experienced, occupy newly tenable areas.

Theorizing that habitat saturation promotes cooperative breeding seems to apply to birds like Acorn Woodpeckers in California, if not over their more extensive tropical range. Their special requirements of acorns, trees for storing them, and trees for drilling sap wells in the bark are not everywhere to be found. The theory does not appear applicable to the Banded-backed Wren, one of the most adaptable birds that I know, at home in open woods of pine and oak high in the altitudinal temperate zone, at the edge of tropical rain forests, and in shady seaside gardens. Nor does it seem to fit the Brown Jay, an aggressive bird which for many avian generations has been occupying new territory as the Caribbean rain forests of Middle America, the interior of which it avoids, have receded before clearings with scattered trees, where it thrives. Evidently, diverse roads lead to cooperative breeding.

An avian species that has filled all available space, as the habitat saturation theory implies, and that is, moreover, long-lived might advantageously restrain its reproduction, thereby reducing the expenditure of valuable resources to rear progeny whose prospects of survival are slight. Here we meet the knotty problem of the regulation of reproduction, a subject beset with paradoxes, contradictions, and disagreements among biologists. An influential school, of which David Lack was a leading protagonist, holds that every organism, birds included, must rear as many sound progeny as it can because, if it does not, its lineage will be submerged by more prolific members of its species. This seems difficult to reconcile with a dominant trend in the evolution of animals, which for ages has been to produce fewer offspring and take better care of them, as is evident when one compares the great number of eggs laid and neglected by fish and amphibians with the small broods or litters, often of only one or two, produced and carefully nurtured by birds and the more advanced mammals.

Moreover, excessive reproduction may be self-defeating. For many animals—even for birds in evergreen tropical rain forests—seasons of more abundant food, when they breed, alternate with seasons of less abundance, when reproduction is suspended. If animals overload their habitat in the favorable season, many will succumb in the leaner months that follow, but before dying they will have consumed food that might have kept others alive until the following season of greater abundance, so that species which produce more than a certain optimum number of offspring may enter the next breeding season with smaller populations than they might have had if they had not reared so many young. This optimum rate of reproduction might be defined as that which can be exceeded only at the price of a mortality that will cancel all its gains—which, indeed, might have disastrous consequences in the form of widespread disease or starvation. Although maximum reproduction might give natural selection more material on which to operate, the price, in wasted resources and lives prematurely extinguished, is very high.

Birds avoid excessive reproduction by various means. In the humid tropics, where annual mortality is low, many species lay only two eggs in their nests; some lay only one. Some birds devote to the time-consuming construction of elaborate nests energy that they might apply to rearing larger broods. Males of many species remain totally aloof from nests while they indulge in visual and vocal displays to attract females, thereby halving the labor force available for rearing the young. Many birds both terrestrial and marine delay breeding for several years after they have grown to adult size, in sharp contrast to what happens in many mammals. Whether or not some of these birds could increase their reproductive output as evolutionary orthodoxy requires, by laying more eggs, building simpler nests, or breeding at an earlier age, is a question endlessly debated by ornithologists.

Among the birds that delay breeding are the helpers in cooperative breeding associations. In most of the foregoing accounts, we noticed that pairs with helpers produce more fledglings per nest, or rear more of their young to independence, than do simple pairs of the same species; if they did not, they would confirm the doubts of those who question whether helpers really help. In some species, perhaps most, the auxiliaries' contribution to breeding success is greater between nest leaving and independence than between egg laying and fledging; but since the latter period is easier to quantify, and nesting success is usually expressed as the percentage of nests or of eggs that yield fledglings, how much the helpers increase the survival of the young after they leave the nest is not revealed even by some of the most prolonged studies. Although in general helpers increase the success of nests and the survival of mobile young, exceptions are not lacking. Among the Pukekos studied in New Zealand by John Craig, simple pairs raised two or three times as many young per family, and three to six times as many per adult, as larger groups did. Many factors contribute to breeding success: the simple pairs may have been more experienced birds or may have occupied areas with more abundant food or fewer predators. Sandra Vehrencamp's study of Groove-billed Anis in Costa Rica showed that the advantage of having more nest attendants was greater in some habitats than in others.

Does cooperative breeding realize the maximum reproductive potential of the birds engaged in it? This is an important question because if it does not, these birds do not rear as many young as they might do if all nested as simple pairs, and cooperative breeding might be included among the means that birds use to adjust their populations to their resources. This would accord well with the theory that relates this breeding system to habitat saturation, but it would clash with the theory of maximum reproduction. To answer this question, we must examine the output of young per individual attendant rather than per nest or per group.

From his pioneer study of Superb Blue Wrens in eastern Australia, Ian Rowley concluded that groups with helpers annually produced 1.9 fledglings per adult, whereas simple pairs raised only 1.2. However, after a more prolonged investigation of splendid wrens in western Australia, the same author wrote: "Whether fledglings or yearlings are considered, the seasonal production by simple pairs does not differ from that of groups with helpers." More frequently, groups with helpers rear more young per nest or per season than unaided pairs, but the latter produce more young per adult, as in the Harris' Hawk, Galapagos Hawk, Red-throated Bee-eater, and Puerto Rican Tody. In other species, including the Groove-billed Ani, Acorn Woodpecker, Florida Scrub Jay, White-winged Chough, Jungle Babbler, and Common Babbler, the number of young per adult rises with one or a few helpers but remains constant or falls after they exceed a certain number—the parents have more auxiliaries than they need for efficient reproduction. Although the evidence is not wholly consistent, it points to the conclusion that cooperatively breeding birds do not raise as many fledglings as they might if they nested as simple pairs or with fewer assistants, but they compensate for reduced fecundity by the better survival of fledged young and the greater life expectancy of adults, which may be due, among other reasons, to the fact that cooperative breeding lightens the burden of parenthood.

In this book our chief interest has rested in how cooperative breeding affects the welfare of the helpful birds themselves, giving them safer, longer, apparently more satisfying lives. Evolutionary biologists have been mainly interested in what happens to the genes that control the birds' heredity, of which the birds themselves are unaware. Adult birds who devote their time to rearing others' offspring instead of multiplying their own genes in their own progeny perplex evolutionists, because they are difficult to reconcile with current evolutionary theory. To overcome the difficulty, biologists have recourse to the concept of kin selection. A large proportion of helpers, but by no means all, assist their own parents to rear younger brothers and sisters. Siblings have many genes in common. Since the chromosomes that bear the genes are transmitted to offspring much as cards in shuffled decks are dealt to players, in extreme, improbable cases siblings might have identical sets of genes (without reference to identical twins, which are not known to occur in birds), or all their genes might be different. On the average, siblings should share half their genes, which is often expressed by saying that their relatedness is one-half. Cousins and more distant relations have correspondingly fewer identical genes.

Accordingly, the helper who attends its younger brothers and sisters, or even its cousins, helps multiply many genes just like its own, including those that make it a cooperative breeder. Indeed, if a nest with auxiliaries is likely to be much more productive than the nest of an unaided pair, the helper may contribute more to the multiplication of its genes by attending it as a nonbreeder than by breeding in a solitary pair. And when its chances of acquiring a territory and a mate, even of surviving, apart from its natal group are slight, it will certainly transmit to posterity more genes identical with its own by helping at home than by venturing abroad. Its inclusive fitness (the number of genes identical with its own that it helps transmit to future generations through its brothers and sisters or more distant relatives, as well as through its own children if it has any) may be high even if its individual fitness is low or zero.

Kin selection fits cooperative breeding into the general evolutionary structure that biologists have so painstakingly erected, but it is not the whole story. It hardly accounts for the many intraspecific helpers who come from other groups and who may not be related to the parents whom they assist; all that is needed for a bird to become a helper is its acceptance by a group, as Jerram Brown's membership hypothesis recognizes. This tells us how cooperative breeding can persist even in the many species which each year have a substantial proportion of pairs nesting without auxiliaries, but it hardly even suggests how cooperative breeding arises. For this I offer the following theory, based upon two widespread avian traits.

Birds cling to the known and shrink from the unknown. If one has been long in a cage, it may be in no hurry to escape, even when the door is open. As I have repeatedly seen, juveniles resist expulsion from the family territory where they grew up or exclusion from the family dormitory. Migratory birds appear to be an exception, for without external compulsion they undertake long, perilous journeys. I suspect that migrants, especially those that travel by night, fly in the mental state of somnambulists, who, it is said, walk safely in their sleep where they would fear to tread while awake. I doubt that the small nocturnal migrant is aware of the marvelous navigational feat that it accomplishes when it alternates each year between two pinpoints on the map, perhaps thousands of miles apart—a feat that a trained human navigator accomplishes with charts and a whole panel of instruments. I believe that the bird is guided subconsciously by a wonderful innate mechanism, perfected by countless generations of natural selection and hardly understood by ornithologists. The nocturnal migrant does not hesitate or resist separation from its natal spot because it does not know what it is about to do. Moreover, if it fails to migrate it will probably starve or freeze in the inclement season.

The situation is different with the small, non-migratory bird of warm lands. Its parents, having reared it to independence, try to expel it from their territory, so that they can breed again without interference and with less revealing movement around their nest. The juvenile, attached to the only place that it knows, tries to stay. If it belongs to a species that rather fully occupies its optimum habitat and has little marginal habitat, so that to leave home may be suicidal, it will cling more stubbornly to its birthplace, not because it anticipates what will befall it if it leaves, but because natural selection will have strengthened its innate determination to remain. The same selection pressure will have mitigated the parents' drive to expel their self-supporting progeny. Even a juvenile of a species not so limited by habitat will often resist exile into the unknown. If it clings tenaciously enough to its birthplace, or if the parents are indulgent, it may be permitted to stay. Then, closely associated with its siblings of the following brood and fairly competent at foraging, it will be driven by the bird's strong impulse to place food into begging nestling mouths . . . to feed its younger brothers and sisters. It will become a juvenile or a yearling helper.

After remaining on the parental territory for a year or more, the young bird may spontaneously leave; but now it is more experienced, better able to take care of itself, than a juvenile barely self-supporting. Often it emigrates with siblings of the same sex, and frequently it goes no farther than a neighboring territory which it already knows and in which it has detected a vacancy. Its departure from the home territory is much less hazardous than that of a juvenile unfamiliar with the wider world; and if it fails to find another domicile, it can return home and be accepted.

For this situation to become stable and hereditary, two changes are necessary. The parents' impulse to drive away their young must weaken. The young helper must remain subordinate to its parent of the same sex, and it must remain sexually quiescent even if it becomes reproductively mature, lest disruptive conflicts arise. It will be recalled that waywardness of the young female Southern House Wren...led to prolonged fighting and the final expulsion of the too-precocious helper. If the continued presence of grown young in the parental domain increases the survival of nestlings, fledglings, helpers, or the parents themselves, the necessary modifications will probably evolve. Persisting traces of immaturity—as in the colors of bills, eyes, or facial skin... —will help maintain the group's rank order by indicating the status of its younger members.

...[We have seen] abundant evidence that birds frequently behave in ways not strictly determined by their heredity, although everything that an animal does must have an innate foundation. The first step in the evolution of a cooperative breeding system may well be a young bird's spontaneous refusal to leave its natal territory. If such home-loving youngsters frequently remain and contribute to the welfare of their own close relations, kin selection should promote the process of genetic assimilation whereby, through supporting mutations, beneficial behavior that was originally individual and spontaneous becomes inherent and widespread in the species. By such alterations, the group of parents and their grown-up offspring becomes a stable, harmoniously cooperating association.

By their reluctance to abandon their natal spot and their readiness to respond to any gaping nestling mouth, birds seem preadapted for cooperative breeding, which has evolved independently in many families in the most varied habitats. Since the behavioral traits at the root of cooperative breeding are widespread in birds, we may ask why this system is not more common than we find it. One reason appears to be that the increased activity at a nest may draw the attention of predators. Antbirds (*Formicariidae*), eminently adapted to life in the lower levels of predator-ridden tropical American forests, build inconspicuous nests and minimize their visits to them by taking long incubation sessions and bringing their two nestlings infrequent, large meals. Since so many nests are prematurely lost, small broods appear more appropriate for this situation than large ones attended by more birds and more expensive to replace. A greater number of attendants may be able to repulse certain less aggressive predators that the unaided parents could not successfully confront, but their presence might not substantially increase the security of a nest whose safety depends chiefly upon remaining undetected.

In other cases, the territory might not yield enough food to support adults additional to the parents, who without aid must exert themselves strenuously to provision their young. Although helpers usually increase the yield of nestlings per nest, they do not always augment the number per individual adult, and some species may need the greater reproductive potential that early breeding by unaided parents might give them. This is especially true of birds that suffer high mortality on long migrations, which, moreover, disrupt the family bonds that are the basis of cooperative breeding. For a variety of reasons, many avian species may not be able to afford the luxury of cooperative breeding, even if it would be more congenial to them.

Communal nesting, in which two or more females lay in a nest attended by all of them and frequently also by their mate or mates, is sometimes practiced by species with nonbreeding helpers, including Anis, Acorn Woodpeckers, Pukekos, White-winged Choughs, and Gray-crowned Babblers. Incubation and brooding by three or more parents taking turns greatly reduce the burdens and the risks incurred by each participant, all of which would seem to make this breeding system attractive to birds. Why is it not more widely practiced? The difficulty of synchronizing laying by the several females weighs against it. The nestlings of the female who lays last will usually hatch last, be smaller, and fail to receive their due share of food in a crowded nest; some or all may starve. To avoid this, the last female Ani or Acorn Woodpecker removes earlier eggs before she starts to lay. The other females continue to deposit eggs to compensate for their losses but may end with smaller sets than the last female. This results in more synchronized hatching and a more equitable production of fledglings by the associated females, but it is a crude, wasteful method of overcoming the difficulty. Often, too, more eggs than can be properly incubated are laid in a communal nest, and the activity there makes it too conspicuous. Moreover, females tend to be less tolerant of female coworkers than males are tolerant of males. For all these reasons, only a fraction of nests are communal even in species that most often practice this system.

The other variety of communal nesting, with several pairs occupying as many separate nests in a group's territory and all or most reciprocally helping each other feed the young, as in Chestnut-bellied Starlings and several species of jays, is also infrequent but for different reasons. Its rarity suggests that special, little-understood conditions are necessary for this system to originate and to prosper.

The retention of young by their parents is not the only road to cooperative breeding. Sometimes adults unite in a nesting association, as when two male Galapagos Hawks or Harris' Hawks mate with a single female and join in attending her nest. Disparity in the numbers of the sexes is likely to promote such arrangements.

For cooperative breeding to arise and persist in any avian species, it need not produce more, or as many, fledged young per nest or per adult as nesting by unaided pairs might yield, but by prolonging the average life span of all cooperating individuals, it should be at least as successful in maintaining a flourishing population as the alternative of earlier breeding by individuals in simple pairs that is still an option of many cooperatively breeding species.

Our attention is first drawn to a pattern of life exhibited by only a minority of avian species — and hardly known half a century ago — by noticing that more than two birds are bringing food to a nest or otherwise attending it. Then, if we are professional ornithologists, we try to demonstrate, by prolonged study and by gathering a mass of numerical data that this rather exceptional breeding system is compatible with individual selection, or kin selection, or group selection, or whatever interpretation of evolution the investigator favors. We should be more open to the possibility that the three modes of selection operate together. Many of the birds in cooperatively breeding groups are, or become, parents, often after serving for a while as helpers. According to their competence and that of their assistants, as well as their success in escaping the hazards that afflict all nesting birds, they produce more or fewer progeny. Many of the individuals also help rear siblings, again with varying degrees of productivity. Moreover, groups differ in the number of progeny that they rear and the number that emigrate to spread their genes among neighboring groups. Accordingly, at each of these levels—the individual, the sibling, and the comprehensive group—we find the differential survival and reproduction that natural selection implies. It is obvious that individual selection, kin selection, and group selection are simultaneously involved in cooperative breeding.

Prolix discussions as to which of these modes of selection is predominant tend to divert our attention from the wider significance of this life-style, the enduring family bonds, the enhanced cooperation, the rise of life to higher levels of social integration and harmony. Group members do not exchange food, preen one another, build dormitories and sleep in contact, join in group displays, and engage in similar intimacies because the non-breeders among them help the breeding pair raise the latest brood; on the contrary, they become helpers because they are already so closely associated with the parents and their nest. The intimate association throughout the year is primary, helping at the nest for a fraction of the year one of its consequences—just as exposure to nestlings may induce unrelated birds of the same species, or even those of different species, to attend them.

Unfortunately, the widely used designation "cooperative breeding" tends to distort the situation by emphasizing one aspect of a far more comprehensive association. "Family unity" would more adequately describe this development, the highest expression of family life among birds, if not among vertebrate animals except, perhaps, the most harmoniously integrated and cooperative of human families. Although "cooperative breeding" is inadequate as a designation of the most closely integrated groups, it is useful because it covers a wider spectrum, including species in which occasional helpers are less intimately associated with the parents.

Family unity is of varying degrees and takes diverse forms even among closely related species. Golden-naped Woodpeckers sleep with their parents in the family dormitory until nearly a year old; but as juveniles Golden-napes contribute little or nothing to the care of a second brood, and they are not known to help as yearlings. By contrast, a Red-cockaded Woodpecker will not share a hole with another individual past the nestling stage, even when holes, which take a long while to carve, are so scarce that members of its family must roost clinging to the outside of a trunk or fly afar to surreptitiously enter a vacant cavity in the territory of a different family. Social integration and the benefits it brings to individuals may amply compensate for a concomitant reduction of fecundity, especially when the reproduction of the cooperative breeders is adequate to maintain the species in a flourishing state, and additional young would have poor prospects of surviving.

In contemporary evolutionary theory, animals are viewed as little more than machines for producing the maximum number of offspring, regardless of the quality of their lives. This may be true of more primitive organisms, but more advanced animals may resist the tyranny of reproduction and numbers while they seek a more gratifying existence. Birds are not feeling less mechanisms for the multiplication of their genes but sentient creatures concerned for their own safety and comfort. I surmise that many birds breed cooperatively because they value the feeling of security that comrades give, enjoy companionship, and find this a satisfying way of life. These, of course, are values that are not amenable to scientific investigation or to mathematical treatment by evolutionary biologists, but we cannot for that reason dismiss them as fanciful or unimportant. To the philosopher or indeed to anyone seeking to fathom life's meaning, they are of paramount interest.

If, despite its crude gambling methods and many miscarriages, evolution did not raise at least some of its creations to higher levels of awareness and enjoyment, it would be a prolonged, complicated, harsh futility, an endless sequence of transformations producing nothing of worth; and it could make no slightest difference to any creature whether it continued or ceased to exist. All of which reminds us once more of the pathetic limitations of our sciences, which leave almost totally unexplored beyond the narrow human realm the psychic aspect of the Universe, for this aspect, which is probably coextensive with the material aspect and appears to be intensified as beings rise in the scale of creation, gives to existence all the value that we can discover in it.

PHILOSOPHER

HARMONY AND CONFLICT
IN THE LIVING WORLD

(2000)

Biodiversity or Biocompatibility?

Many years ago, I established a homestead beside a large tract of tropical rainforest, in a region still wild. Around my new dwelling, I planted fruit trees and shrubs with colorful flowers, to provide nectar or berries for birds, and daily placed bananas for them on a board in a tree. Soon many, from the adjoining woodland as well as those of open country, nested around my house. With the troublesome exception of the nest-stealing Piratic Flycatcher, all dwelt peaceably together, singing their songs and rearing their young. But predators, chiefly snakes, small mammals, and an occasional raptor, invaded the garden to capture the adults or plunder their nests.

What should I do about this distressing situation? I believed that I owed protection to the birds that I encouraged to nest near me. After much thought, I adopted the principle of harmonious association. I would do all that

I could to protect the creatures that dwelt harmoniously together, taking measures to remove those that disrupted this concord. For the adjoining forest, I preferred the principle of *laissez faire,* or refraining from meddling with nature. Although the situation there, where predators abounded, was not ideal, it appeared too big and complex to be controlled by me, or by anyone.

Today, half a century later, humans have increased so greatly, and made their presence felt so widely, that the situation nearly everywhere is becoming more like that in farmlands and gardens than in wild, undisturbed woodland. During the same interval, the conservation movement has grown much stronger, notably in tropical countries where it was weak. Other than that all true conservationists try to preserve some part of nature, and beyond general agreement that the protection of habitats is indispensable, a wide diversity of preferences is evident among conservationists. Some are more concerned about forests, others about wetlands or oceans. Some are interested mainly in a special group of animals—birds or bats or amphibians. Some try to protect or increase raptorial birds, while others deplore the decline of birds on which raptors prey. These divergent aims sometimes clash, with the consequent waste of effort and of the inadequate funds available for the protection of nature. We must clarify our aims; we need a comprehensive goal for conservation.

As a guiding principle for conservation, the following alternatives are worth considering. We should endeavor to promote: (1) maximum diversity, or number of species; (2) the maximum sustainable number of individual organisms; (3) those elements of the natural world that contribute most to human prosperity and happiness or are the least threat to these ends. Let us examine them in this order.

"Biodiversity," a neologism, has become the rallying cry of conservationists. That we could not survive without biodiversity, and a great deal of it, is a truth too obvious to naturalists to need elaboration. We need plants to produce food; insects, birds, and other creatures to pollinate their flowers; fungi and microorganisms to decompose dead tissues and return their fertilizing components to the soil; and much else. Recent explorations of the canopy of tropical forests have revealed that the number of extant species is much greater than we had supposed only a few decades ago and may run into millions.

Biodiversity has certainly become excessive, and is responsible for a major part of the sufferings of animals, including humans. In addition to all the predators that strike down living victims and too often begin to tear them apart before they die, an immense diversity of parasites torture, debilitate, and kill their hosts. Since most multi-cellular animals appear to be infected by several kinds of parasites, internal and external, many of which are restricted to a single species or closely related group, it is probable that parasites far exceed, in number of species and individuals, all other metazoa, or multi-cellular animals. Moreover, they can weaken and kill plants or ravage whole forests. Undoubtedly, a great reduction of biodiversity, probably 50 percent or more, would make life much more pleasant not only for humans but for many other creatures.

Although we hear much about biodiversity, I am not aware of any widely accepted statement of its desirable limits. Should we promote the absolute maximum, which would include all parasites, pathogens, and predators, or should we be more discriminating? I doubt that any advocate of biodiversity would oppose the extermination of organisms responsible for human diseases, or of the blood-sucking insects that spread diseases and can make life miserable for many kinds of mammals. In regard to larger predators, the situation is confused. Many friends of animals would welcome the great reduction, if not extinction, of venomous and nest-robbing snakes, voracious alligators, the fiercer raptors, or the most dangerous sharks. If conservationists could agree on the desirable limits of biodiversity, cooperation and efficiency might increase.

Instead of promoting biodiversity absolutely or within certain well-defined limits, we might choose the alternative of making our goal the maximum number of individuals, of all kinds or of certain specified kinds, within the capacity of Earth to support them indefinitely in a flourishing state. The contrast between the first and second alternatives presents an interesting analogy to that between two opposing principles of human government. Totalitarians hold that individuals exist for the wealth, power, and glory of the state, which certain philosophers, such as Hegel, have viewed as having a collective spirit or soul, above that of its inhabitants, and which can demand their sacrifice for the exaltation of the whole. Liberal democrats believe that the state, devoid of a collective spirit, exists for the welfare of individuals, who alone enjoy and suffer.

Similarly, advocates of unlimited biodiversity might view the global community of animals and plants, or perhaps the planet itself, with all its living cargo, as a superorganism, Gaia, which thrives most grandly the more species of all kinds, as well as individuals, it supports. Opposing this view, we might remember that we lack evidence of consciousness, or the capacity to suffer and enjoy, except in individual organisms. Accordingly, a liberal, compassionate conservation movement should be concerned with the welfare of individual animals rather than the entire biological community regarded as a mystic whole, and of individuals rather than of species. Some humanitarian philosophers, like Tom Regan (1983), maintain that every member of a thriving species has no less claim to our forbearance than have the few surviving individuals of a vanishing species. Thus, we may recognize a holistic or "totalitarian" approach to conservation, and an individualistic or "liberal" attitude.

A third alternative arises: widespread is the belief that we should protect the natural world, not for its own sake, but for its importance to humankind. Vegetable and animal species favorable to human interests should receive preferential treatment; others, useless or harmful to humans, might be neglected or extirpated. If we adopt this view, we should remember that organisms that do not directly contribute to human welfare are often necessary for the ecological health of the biotic community in which useful species thrive; as, for example, Mycorrhizal fungi, that envelop the finer roots of forest trees and help them absorb nutrients from the soil, are of no direct use to people but contribute to the maintenance of forests where timber trees thrive. Moreover, we should not forget that nature is rich in aesthetic and intellectual as well as economic values, which unfortunately sometimes conflict. A land that yields a maximum of food, fibers, and other salable products might become so monotonous and uninteresting, so poor in aesthetic appeal, that our spirits might droop while we contemplate it. Narrow concentration on the welfare of humankind might in the long run be injurious to humans.

The task of preserving the natural world from destructive exploitation by an ever-growing mass of humans is so vast and many-sided that no individual, and probably no private organization or governmental agency, can effectively undertake all of it. Efficiency is promoted by specialization. It is fortunate that certain individuals or societies devote their efforts to protecting a small part of the natural community—rainforests, wetlands, dolphins, pandas, or whatever—without, I hope, forgetting that their specialty is only part of a much greater endeavor, that of saving the planet from utter spoliation; for unless we preserve the whole in a flourishing state, we cannot save the parts.

As an approach to conservation less daunting than biodiversity of indefinite compass, I suggest that we devote our efforts to biocompatibility, or compatible biodiversity, the harmonious association of diverse species. To start a program for biocompatibility, we should choose a large community of diverse creatures that coexist without destructive strife, or better, with mutual support, and then add whatever other organisms might be compatible with this nuclear group. An appropriate association is that of flowering plants, their pollinators, and the dispersers of their seeds. Such a community of reciprocally helpful plants and animals includes plants of many families and growth forms, from herbs and vines to towering trees; among their pollinators are bees, butterflies, moths, beetles, dipterous flies, and (in the New World) hummingbirds and certain tanagers; the disseminators of their seeds are a multitude of frugivorous birds, bats, and flightless mammals, including the widespread, terrestrial agoutis of tropical America. The plants attract the pollinators by their colors and fragrance, and reward them with nectar and excess pollen. With eagerly sought fruits and arillate seeds, they recompense the animals that digest only the soft pulp and spread viable seeds far and wide.

To injure the organism with which it exchanges benefits would not advantage any member of this association; only exceptionally do some break the unwritten "contract" by stealing nectar from flowers without pollinating them, as hummingbirds and bees occasionally do. Frugivorous birds rarely harm one another; the only exceptions to this rule in tropical American forests known to me are the Great-billed Toucans, who swallow fruits and disseminate seeds too big for the smaller birds in this guild, but they too often plunder the nests of lesser birds. Bees occasionally raid neighboring hives of different species, stubbornly fighting the residents and, if victorious, carrying off their stores of nectar and pollen. Like most things in this perplexing world, the plant-pollinator-disperser association is not perfect, but it is nevertheless one of evolution's most admirable achievements, contributing immensely to nature's harmony and productivity, and, especially by flowers, birds, and butterflies, to its beauty. Moreover, directly or indirectly, the association provides nourishment for a large proportion of terrestrial life.

To learn how many species belong to the plant-pollinator-disperser association in any given area might require a prolonged study by a team of botanists, entomologists, ornithologists, and mammalogists, which to my knowledge has never anywhere been made. I surmise that in a tract of temperate zone woodland the association would include hundreds of species. In a similar area of tropical rainforest, where wind pollination is much rarer than in the temperate zones and more winged pollinators are needed, the number might run into thousands. Around this nucleus cluster other species that are neither pollinators nor dispersers. Among them are many insectivorous birds and other creatures that coexist harmoniously with the dispersers, and are indeed indispensable to them, for without the former, insects might devour all the foliage and kill the plants that yield the fruits and nectar.

Less closely allied to the plant-pollinator–disperser association, but living harmoniously with it, are many other animals; in tropical American forests, tinamous, guans, quails, pigeons, and, among raptors, the Laughing Falcon, that subsists almost wholly upon snakes. Parrots that digest seeds instead of the pulp that surrounds them may slightly reduce the reproduction of trees but neither injures them nor harms other birds. Among mammals, armadillos, anteaters, sloths, many primates, and others also belong to the compatible community. Not to be excluded are the indispensable but more obscure multitudes of small organisms that decompose dead tissues or otherwise contribute to the soil's ability to support the association, greatly swelling its numbers.

Similar biocompatible associations are found in wetlands, prairies, Arctic tundra, and the oceans but apparently have not been investigated from this point of view. They appear to include fewer collaborators than those of woodlands. In the oceans, where the biomass of animals is very much greater in proportion to that of the chlorophyll-bearing plants that support them, the struggle for survival is fiercer and predation more rife, a truth to which the huge production of eggs of many marine creatures, far exceeding that of any terrestrial animals except possibly queen termites and bees, bears unimpeachable testimony. Nevertheless, in the oceans biocompatible associations do occur, as with cleaner fishes and their clients.

Preferential treatment of biocompatible associates would benefit the indispensable sustainers of terrestrial life but certainly not everything. It would protect neither invertebrate parasites nor parasitic cuckoos and cowbirds, all of which are only a froth (although often a smothering froth) on the surface of the living world. Whenever they seriously threaten human life or economic interests, vigorous, often costly efforts are made to exterminate them. Predatory vertebrates, especially among mammals and birds, present special problems. Mostly solitary, unsocial creatures, they do not fit into any biocompatible association, but on the contrary prey, often heavily, upon the members of such associations. Because many of them are big and powerful, they frequently excite humans' misplaced adulation of bigness and power (a major cause of their misfortunes), and not a few win admiration by their grace or beauty. Contributing little or nothing to the support of the living community (except its scavengers), they make heavy demands upon it. If not deliberately trying to reduce their numbers, a conservation program committed to biocompatibility rather than undefined bio-diversity should at least stop spending all the money and effort now given to their protection and increase.

One of the gravest mistakes of wildlife management in our time is the reintroduction of predatory birds and mammals into areas where they have long been absent, such as the artificial establishment of peregrine falcons in cities. The undesirable, often disastrous, effects of introducing alien animals, even some admirable in themselves, into countries like Australia, New Zealand, and the United States have long been recognized and deplored. Reintroduction of large and dangerous species may become equally deplorable.

Predation is widely viewed as indispensable to prevent populations of animals becoming so numerous that they destroy their habitats, "eating themselves out of house and home." Even those who condemn predation as a major evil, a lamentable miscarriage of evolution, may grudgingly concede that it is a necessary evil. Nevertheless, the role of predation in regulating animal populations has been exaggerated. It is most obviously necessary in the case of large browsing and grazing quadrupeds—deer, antelopes, horned ruminants, elephants, and the like—which may so severely overexploit light woodland or grassland that it may take years to recover after the exploiters' numbers are reduced by widespread starvation. Where elephants are protected, they become too numerous and so damage their range that, despite sentiment, their herds must be culled to avert disaster. Shooting of excess individuals by expert marksmen is kinder than the methods of predators, which too often tear the flesh of still living victims.

When we turn to frugivorous and insectivorous birds, we find a very different situation. It is hardly an exaggeration to say that they are incapable of ruining their habitats. In an unfavorable season, fruits may become so scarce that hungry birds are reduced to eating them before they ripen, when they are harder to digest and less nourishing but may already contain viable seeds. The birds' reproduction may be depressed, and some may starve; but the fruit-bearing trees and shrubs will not be injured by premature removal of their fruits, and next year they can yield abundantly. Similarly, nectar drinkers can hardly injure flowering plants, even if, as sometimes happens, they damage flowers by piercing or tearing corollas to reach the sweet fluid. When nectar is scarce, they may turn to insects, as hummingbirds frequently do. Insectivorous birds can rarely glean so effectively that they exterminate the insects, spiders, and other small invertebrates that nourish them. With their rapid reproduction and reduced pressure upon them, they soon restore their populations and continue to support the insectivores.

Birds can regulate their populations without outside intervention. A widespread method is territoriality, which adjusts the number of breeding pairs to the areas and resources adequate for rearing their broods. The size of broods is correlated with the longevity of adults. At latitudes where the rigors of winter or the hazards of long migrations to escape winter reduce life expectancy, broods are substantially larger than are those of related species at low latitudes, where the average life span of resident birds is considerably longer. In contrast to mammals, which often begin to reproduce before they cease growing, many birds delay breeding for one or more years after they are full-grown. Extreme examples of this are long-lived marine birds, many of which do not breed until they are five to ten years old, and they lay only one egg, as among albatrosses.

"Pest birds," like Red-billed Queleas in Africa and Eared Doves in Argentina, appear to contradict the foregoing statements by building up excessive populations that devour field crops, especially grains. They live in artificial situations. Farmers unintentionally help them multiply, then complain when the birds take advantage of agricultural bounty. Predators fail to reduce the teeming populations of these birds enough to save the crops. Thus, we might say, with reference to birds, that predators are either unnecessary to control populations or are ineffective. The same appears to be true of many other kinds of animals, but to discuss this matter here would lead us too far astray.

As the forces of destruction increase and their weapons become more devastating, conservationists wage a losing war. It is time to reconsider our strategy. The promotion of biodiversity is unselective, supporting both our allies and our enemies in our major endeavor, which is to preserve ecosystems. When we analyze an ecosystem, we find it an association of organisms that by their diverse roles mutually support one another, as in the plant-pollinator-disperser alliance—thereby making and preserving the system, with a large admixture of organisms hostile to these key members of the system. The former support our efforts to preserve forests and other ecosystems, the latter oppose our efforts. Instead of maintaining an essentially neutral attitude toward the protagonists in the internal struggle that afflicts an ecosystem, we should throw our weight on the side of the defenders, giving them preferential treatment and whatever aid we can, perhaps not trying to exterminate all their enemies—in any case an impossible task—but at least not supporting them. If we humans could make ourselves more compatible with the biocompatible associations that are the mainstay of the natural world, we would form an alliance that might preserve it indefinitely.

After this digression, which seemed necessary to counter certain objections to a conservation program that would exclude from protection some of the most predatory vertebrates, let us return to the advantages of biocompatibility over unlimited biodiversity. In the first place, it would help to preserve the maximum sustainable number of individuals (our second alternative) of the protected, nonpredatory, or mildly predatory species, which are nearly always more numerous than the animals that prey upon them. In particular, it would help to retard the widely lamented decline of many species of birds, especially the Neotropical migrants. Predation is only one of several factors in their plight, but it is by no means negligible; raptors take a heavy toll of migrants, especially while they are concentrated at the staging places where they interrupt their journeys to replenish their depleted reserves of energy.

By benefiting the extremely important plant-pollinator-disperser association and its allies, biocompatibility would promote human economic interests (our third alternative). It would make close association with nature more rewarding and pleasant to the growing number of people who enjoy the majesty of trees and the beauty of flowers and birds and are distressed or repelled by the sight of predators striking down and tearing their victims and the hideously mangled remains of what yesterday was a beautiful animal going peaceably about its business and enjoying its life. By no conceivable *effort* could conservationists, however numerous and well funded they become, bring perfect harmony into the living world, but by their united efforts they might bring it a little closer to the realization of this ancient, widespread, and perennially attractive ideal.

NATURE THROUGH TROPICAL WINDOWS

(1983)

Windows of the Mind

I count myself fortunate to have lived most of my life where balmy air and paucity of pestilent insects have made window glass and metallic screens superfluous. When we throw open our wooden shutters before sunrise, nothing separates us from the outer air. Gentle breezes, the fragrance of flowers in the garden or the neighboring forest, butterflies and airborne seeds drift in through the windows unimpeded. Through them the loveliness of plants and the grandeur of distant mountains greet our eyes, unmarred by anything ugly or sordid.

Unless the windows of our minds are also open, the windows of our houses may admit air and daylight but little to nourish the spirit. I often wish that the windows of my mind were as transparent as the glassless window through which I look. Much that enters through the window fails to enter my mind, because my senses, on which I am wholly dependent for verifiable knowledge of the surrounding world, do not report it. In the cases of a wide range of electromagnetic waves and of magnetic fields, I can prove this by turning on a radio or looking at a compass—indeed, even when I close all windows and doors with solid wood, I cannot exclude them. I have little doubt that I am surrounded by other radiations, emanations, or influences whose presence I cannot demonstrate. Our increasingly subtle technology has not yet provided instruments that translate them into signals to which my senses respond, and they do not directly affect my mind in a wholly convincing manner. Moreover, far from being attentive to all the signals that my senses report to me, I am blind and deaf to many of them, as everyone must be to avoid distraction. I do my best to heed those that seem most significant, and regret that they fail to reveal much that I ardently wish to know.

Despite . . . laudable efforts to extend the range of human knowledge, our understanding of the universe is still pathetically limited. We still live in the shade of ignorance about the things nearest to us. That there is a psychic side of Being no one could rationally doubt; our very doubting, a psychic phenomenon, would prove its existence. We are confident that other humans, so similar to ourselves in all observable aspects, have thoughts and feelings more or less similar to our own, but we lack observational proof of this. For positive science, only our senses, directly or with the aid of ever more refined instruments, provide reliable data—all else is conjectural. Nevertheless, that animals, plants, and even minerals have a psychic, no less than a material, aspect is too highly probable to be dogmatically denied. If atoms are wholly devoid of feeling, how does it happen that we, who are made of them, can feel? A whole vast side of reality, indispensable not only for understanding the universe but for the intelligent, compassionate regulation of our relations with the living things that share the Earth with us, remains hidden from us. We must open the windows of our minds still more widely and make them more transparent, perhaps waiting for evolutionary changes that diminish our psychic insulation, before we can hope for full illumination.

Suppose that we could overcome our present distressing limitations and see things as they really are, what would we find? I am convinced that we would discover that we live in a universe that has been striving from its prime foundations to increase the value of its own existence, which includes ours and that of everything around us. For what would be the worth of a universe spread over billions of light years of space, perhaps infinite, if neither the whole nor any of its parts took pleasure in existence? What difference could it make to anybody or anything whether such a universe existed or ceased to be? What would be lost if it were suddenly annihilated? Can we imagine any futility more immense than trillions of atoms vibrating with no trace of feeling, never realizing their ability to create lovely forms and conscious beings; billions of stars dissipating their energy vainly in the void abyss; millions of planets forever barren of vibrant life—a universe thickly interlaced with rays of light that never convey beauty to appreciative eyes or knowledge to eager minds?

Our own unquenchable thirst for a happier, more rewarding and meaningful life, enriched by ever higher
values, is a more developed expression of an urge that
permeates the very foundations of a universe that refuses
to rest in utter barrenness, but tries stubbornly to enhance
its existence. It does this by building up the ultimate par-
ticles into integrated structures—into patterns that tend
to increase in complexity, amplitude, and coherence. This
process of harmonization, which pervades our planet and
probably all others where physical conditions are favorable, advances in several stages, as is necessary to give
existence its highest value. First, it must consolidate its
materials into incandescent stars that provide continuing
sources of energy, surrounded by planets whose milder
temperatures permit the formation of finer structures. A
sun and its planets are an admirable example of a harmoniously integrated pattern on a vast scale, so stable that it
endures for aeons. Next, it covers such planets, of which
Earth is a splendid example, with beautiful forms and
colors, including crystals, sunrises and sunsets, rainbows,
and the infinite variety of lovely vegetable forms. Plants,
and even crystals, may enjoy their existence, but lacking
eyes they can hardly appreciate the beauty of the things
around them—or their own. Lacking olfactory organs,
plants may never sense the fragrance of their flowers.
They can neither produce nor enjoy melodies. Accordingly,
a third stage was indispensable for the realization of
many of the highest values. Animals, often themselves
beautiful, with sense organs and minds to perceive the
beauty around them, with the ability to produce and to
hear harmonious sounds, with the capacity to cooperate,

to love, to know, and to cherish all things beautiful and good, were needed to elevate the value of existence.

Without a guiding Intelligence, such animals could be created only by a painful process of trial and error, with many false starts, blunders, and miscarriages. To equip animals with efficient sense organs and perceptive, appreciative minds required an immensely long time, of which the cosmos has no lack. We are the chief beneficiaries of this prolonged, hazardous process, which has caused so much suffering, and we would be unworthy of the splendid endowments in mind and body that nature has given us, if we were not constantly thankful for this high privilege. The best way to show our gratitude is by caring devotedly for whatever embellishes or elevates our lives. Such cherishing appreciation is needed to fulfill the cosmic striving to make existence ever more precious and desirable. When we appreciate, cherish, and try to understand—and help others to do the same—we fill the role that appears most appropriate for us when we survey the whole course of cosmic evolution and our place in nature. Moreover, when we strive earnestly to make our lives beautiful and satisfying by appreciative enjoyment of the many lovely and benign things that surround us, we live conformably to nature's upward trend and can expect its continued support—provided always that we live intelligently and moderately, making no excessive demands upon Earth's bounty.

To play our proper role in the cosmic order, we must keep our windows open, not only those of our dwellings but, above all, those of our spirits. We must permit no hard dogmas or hoary creeds to narrow our vision or trammel our inquiring minds. The more we look for order and beauty in the natural world, the more we shall find, whether we use our unaided eyes, peer through a microscope, or gaze through a telescope. But to perceive sensuous beauty is not enough. We should spare no effort to see beauty in the patterns of life, the mutual adjustments, of the diverse creatures that surround us, and we should not neglect the noble, kindly acts of humanity. We should remember, too, that, open our eyes and our minds as widely as we can, much will escape us. Except in our individual selves, we have firmly established knowledge of only one aspect of things, the external side, beneath which lurks a psychic aspect to which our windows are still stubbornly opaque. Unless we or our descendants polish them to perfect transparency, the ultimate mysteries of the universe will remain veiled from us.

It would be folly to suppose that while we seek the beautiful and lovable we shall not find much that is hideous and abhorrent. Although to dwell much upon evils and agonies that we can neither remove nor mitigate is to oppress our spirits without benefit to others, it would be fatuous to close our windows tightly to them and pretend they do not exist. The best course is to try to understand how they arose as the inevitable result of a fundamentally beneficent creative process with limitless perseverance, but no evident control by a foresighted Intelligence able to guide and moderate its often excessive intensity. The evil and the ugly may be regarded as by-products, or secondary results, of the cosmic striving to make existence ever more desirable. Nearly everything that exalts and enriches life, and certainly our ability to perceive, to enjoy, and to appreciate, depends upon the existence of harmoniously integrated patterns of atoms, which is what organisms of every kind essentially are. But these patterns arise in such excessive numbers that they compete for the space, materials, and energy they must have to complete and preserve themselves. Clashing together, they thwart, injure, or destroy one another, causing incalculable pain and misery, as is all too evident in the living world.

To view the situation in this light should cause no consternation to us who are endowed with what has been most lacking in the cosmic process—foreseeing minds and the ability to cultivate the high virtue of moderation. If we use these precious gifts wisely and consistently, never losing sight of our proper role in a universe that strives to increase the value of existence, we can bring happiness and fulfillment to our lives by wide-eyed, cherishing appreciation of everything worthy of our love and admiration, with fewer of the sorrows and disgusts that now oppress us. Overcoming the feeling of alienation from the sources of our being that so often dejects modern humans, we can cultivate loyalty to a cosmos that is the source of our yearning for a more satisfying or blessed existence, a cosmos that will not fail to support us if we cooperate intelligently, unitedly, and moderately with it.

In the aeonian striving of the universe to increase the value of its own existence by means of creatures that might be regarded as its organs for enjoyment and appreciation, those who delight in wild nature, and above all dedicated naturalists who try earnestly to disclose its secrets, play a special and most important role. By opening their minds' windows to sights and sounds beyond the narrow human sphere that confines the outlook of...many, they immensely increase the number and variety of realized values. While they rejoice in the beauty widely diffused over Earth's face, they reveal much more that is hidden from casual view. They trace admirable patterns of organization, and of cooperation among organisms. They witness among nonhuman creatures many examples of behavior that, when practiced by ourselves, wins our highest praise. They know the exultation of discovery.

Even our distress and indignation at many things that we behold in nature—predation, parasitism, violent conflicts of all kinds, excessive reproduction that leads to widespread starvation—should be regarded as a value that the world process has brought forth in its forward march, a moral value of the highest order. Since the ethical consciousness is evidently an achievement of evolution at an advanced stage, it is a revelation that nature does not rest complacently in its crudities, but is striving, especially through us, to overcome them. Perhaps this is a presage of future mitigation. To suppress or disparage our moral indignation at nature's harshness is not loyalty to nature, or the cosmos, but repudiation of one of the finest things, one of the highest values, that nature has achieved.

THE GOLDEN CORE OF RELIGION

(1970)

Introduction

We are religious because we love life and cling passionately to our conscious existence. The more we awake spiritually, the more we experience the values of such existence and dimly surmise its still unrealized potentialities, the more precious it becomes to us. The basic postulate of religion is that conscious life is desirable, worth preserving and fulfilling. Jesus understood this well when he declared: "I am come that they might have life, and that they might have it more abundantly."

Religion is life's ceaseless effort to preserve and perfect itself, become at last self-conscious, foreseeing and, in consequence, fearful amid the thousand perils that beset it. It was said of old, and has been reiterated by modern students of religion, that fear made the gods; but this is a half-truth. We fear only when that which we wish to preserve is threatened. Love of life, concern for the things that support and embellish it, is prior to fear. When we pursue our analysis far enough, it becomes clear that it is our attachment to conscious existence, which made the gods. Religion begins at its natural starting point, the instinct of self-preservation, which has been called the first law of nature. Its function has been to deepen and broaden this natural impulse. Increase in depth leads to care for our character and spirit even more than for our organic bodies. Increase in breadth leads finally to concern for the whole of which we are a part.

The maintenance of life involves activities of various sorts, which bring us into relation with a multitude of things of diverse natures. Our first necessity is to feed, clothe, and shelter ourselves; and for these purposes we generally make use of things which we regard as inferior to ourselves, so that we may apply them to our purposes without considering their own feelings and desires, if such they have. Art has from ancient times been the most inclusive term for all those activities whereby we exploit and turn to our use the materials and forces that nature provides. Nowadays we tend to restrict this term to the fine arts, such as painting, sculpture, and music, although we still speak of the culinary art or the art of horticulture. Technology is an advanced form of art that leans heavily upon scientific research. The names that we employ make little difference, so long as we recognize that the most primitive craft and the most advanced technology have this in common, that they transform for our use materials, which make no recognized claim to our consideration.

In addition to things, which we look upon as inferior to ourselves, the world contains beings that we regard as, in some sense, our equals. Even if we surpass them in strength, beauty, intelligence, or wealth, they make a claim to our consideration that we cannot disregard. We cannot treat them merely as instruments or means to our own ends, but must regard them as ends in themselves, and in this sense on a level with ourselves. The regulation of our dealings with beings whose rights or claims we recognize as valid is the province of morality. The scope of the moral community has varied immensely in different ages and cultures. The moral code of the primitive savage commonly failed to govern conduct toward people outside the tribe. To the slaveholder, the slave was a tool to be used, a sort of detached organ of the master's body obedient to the master's will, not a fellow human being whose right to a full and happy life was equal to that of the master. In the West, animals in general have been regarded as objects to be exploited; although from ancient times, and especially in the East, a more exacting morality has demanded better treatment of them. In so far as we recognize in any creature a claim to our consideration which prevents us from exploiting it regardless of its own will or feelings, we admit it to our moral community.

To adapt to our uses, by art or technology, materials, which we regard as inferior to ourselves and feel free to exploit, and to achieve satisfactory moral relationships with beings that we recognize as in some sense our equals, would, it seems, so occupy our intelligence and strength that we would have little time for anything else. Many people, indeed, appear to be satisfied if they can live comfortably and win the respect or good will of their neighbors. But from a remote epoch there have been those who feel that competence in the arts and moral conduct are not enough, because in addition to the things below us and those on the same plane with us in the scale of being, there is also something above us to which we must adjust our lives. To many, this higher order of being has been represented by the gods, or by God; but some thinkers have adopted the pantheistic view and regard the whole universe as divine. The essential point is that to be religious is to recognize something greater than our individual selves, greater even than humanity, and to strive to achieve a satisfactory relationship with it. Whether this greater thing with which religion is or should be concerned is a transcendent God or the whole of which we are parts, is a question that need not detain us now. For the present, it is enough to recognize three classes of activities, or three attitudes, appropriate to our dealings with three grades of being: art, for the exploitation of things that we deem inferior to ourselves; morality, for regulating our relations with things on the same plane as ourselves; and religion, to place us in the proper relationship with whatever we regard as higher than ourselves. Only when we achieve such a relationship do the things most precious to us seem secure.

From our beginning, religion has claimed a major share of our time, thought, energy, and wealth. After the effort to feed, clothe, and shelter ourselves, religion has probably received the greatest amount of human effort. Sometimes, comparing the stupendous constructions which people have, since prehistoric times, raised from religious motives with the hovels in which a majority have always lived, one suspects that more effort has been expended on religion than on the building of homes. In many countries, the priesthood or established church has received a large share of the total revenue; in some, religious institutions have owned a large portion of the arable land. Even today in the most enlightened countries, the churches have in aggregate an enormous income and claim the devoted service of countless people.

Sometimes one wonders what is the value of all this activity and outpouring of wealth. What is it worth to the individual? To society? In an age that is highly conscious of economics and insists upon efficiency, religion largely escapes that close scrutiny to which most other forms of human activity are subjected, probably because it is regarded as too personal, too sacred, or else too controversial, to have its productivity assessed. We do not live by bread alone; the values which religion offers are not of the economic order; and it seems difficult to establish a relationship between an expenditure of wealth or energy and the spiritual benefit it yields. Yet some such relationship must exist. In some cases, no doubt, a spiritual gain is too slight to justify a large material outlay, whereas in other cases the immaterial reward is immeasurably greater than the material outlay.

One bold enough to assess the value of religion might tackle the problem from various angles. In the first place, there is religion's claim to prepare the faithful for a blessed immortal life. Since there is no incontrovertible evidence that even a single person has achieved such an existence, the problem does not invite scientific inquiry. Religion's promise of immortality must be accepted on faith, or not at all. Secondly, one might examine the doctrines of religion, for their objective truth or even their internal consistency. But if, as in the present... we are interested in religion as a whole rather than in some particular religion, the first thing that we notice is the lack of agreement among the various faiths. Judaism, Christianity, and Islam recognize a personal God; Jainism, and Buddhism in its original form, do not. These and other Eastern religions hold that the soul, or at least the personality, migrates from body to body before it is finally released; Judaism and the religions derived from it deny metempsychosis. These religions teach that each soul will finally appear before a divine judge, who will examine its conduct while in the flesh and either admit it to eternal bliss or condemn it to endless torment; the Indian religions see no need of a judge, because karma, operating as impersonally as a natural law, ensures that everyone will finally receive what he or she deserves. Christianity holds that we are saved by Christ's blood; the Buddha, in his final message, warned his disciples that their salvation depended on their own strenuous efforts — he claimed to do no more than to point out the way.

These are only a few of the crucial points on which the various major religions are at odds. There has been no lack of attempts to reconcile their so diverse teachings; they may be regarded as allegorical rather than literal, or, as in theosophy, as more or less garbled accounts of one pure doctrine taught by enlightened sages in the misty past. It is far from my purpose to undertake a critical comparison of religious dogmas; they are too controversial and involved in metaphysical perplexities, which I wish to eschew. Besides, I hope that this book will make friends rather than enemies. Avoiding, so far as possible, the vexed subject of religious dogmas and even the assessment of religious ethics, I wish to examine the innate foundations of religion—of all religions worthy of the name. The method that we shall follow is primarily psychological rather than metaphysical. Why are we religious? What qualities of the human spirit find expression in religion? How adequately do existing religions satisfy those spiritual yearnings, which gave rise to them?

I began this introduction by anticipating one of these questions. We are religious primarily because we love and wish to enhance life, and it is painful to contemplate its extinction. To anticipate still more the argument:... as we mature spiritually, that strong attachment to life in a beautiful world, which we inherit from prehuman ancestors, finds expression in appreciation, devoted care, and aspiration. Appreciation adds to simple enjoyment, such as we experienced as children and do still in our less reflective intervals, such overtones as wonder at our presence in a world that offers so much to delight us, gratitude to whatever we conceive it to be that prepared this boon for us, and a certain respect or tenderness toward the sources of our enjoyment, as though they were too precious or too sacred to be rudely touched or carelessly handled.

This feeling leads naturally to the second element in the religious attitude, devoted care. I use the word *care* in its widest sense, which includes *caring about* and *caring for*. To care about something is to be concerned for it, to wish it well, even if we can do nothing for it. The generous, thoughtful person cares about many things that are quite beyond help; for example, he or she wishes all sentient beings to be spared pain and to enjoy such happiness as their nature permits, although for the vast majority of them nothing can be done. Caring about things would be only a sentiment if there were not certain things, animate and inanimate, that we can care for: shield from perils, nurse toward perfection, build or aid by our own strenuous exertion. It is caring for the few things within our reach that gives substance to our concern for the many things that we can only care about; such active effort is proof of our earnestness.

No matter how lovingly we care for ourselves or the things about us, we seem rarely to succeed in making anything all that we wish it to be. We would not appreciate existence in this world if it did not contain much that is good, yet at the same time we recognize, and suffer from, its vast evils. I doubt if anyone who assays himself truthfully will claim to be free from defects of body or character that one would desire to overcome; and the same may be said of those whom we most love. We hardly pass a single day without some incident, great or small, to mar its perfection. We and all that we cherish are swept relentlessly toward final dissolution. Yet, with an intensity proportional to our capacity for religious feeling, we aspire to become better than we are, to make those we love better, to make a better world. Above all, we aspire to save something from the dissolution which common experience assures us will one day overtake our mortal frame, which astronomers predict will, ages hence, overwhelm our planet with all its living cargo. This aspiration for self-improvement, this hope of saving something from the disaster, which threatens finally to overtake everything, has been persistently encouraged by every religion that has appealed widely to humans.

Of these three basic elements, which form the golden core of the religious life, devoted care occupies the most central position and serves as a link between the other two. Appreciation, when sufficiently strong, leads to it; without it, aspiration has nothing to stand on. Only the fool aspires for more without taking the best possible care of whatever advantages he or she has. By caring faithfully for what we are and have, we lay a solid foundation for what we aspire to become and to possess. Devoted care is the heart of religion.

It has been truly remarked that every person's interpretation of religion is based on an inward experience of it rather than on an observation of what it is for others. Since it is unlikely that any person's religious experience is altogether unique, one will, no doubt, by diligent search succeed in finding in the religious expressions of others much evidence that the interpretation suggested by one's own experience applies widely to the religious experience of humanity. But it is exceedingly difficult to find a definition that will do justice to everything that religion has been to everybody who might, by a liberal interpretation of the word, be called religious. Perhaps the statement that religion is a serious attitude toward the whole of our conscious existence, however far we believe it to extend, is the only one inclusive enough to cover the religious attitude to life in all its shades. Religion, then, is the attitude just the opposite of that expressed in the old, careless adage: "Eat, drink, and be merry, for tomorrow you may die." Even Schleiermacher's much-quoted interpretation of religion, as arising from our feeling of utter dependence on that which does not depend on us, will hardly apply to religion in its whole length and breadth; for in some of the more primitive religions, of which that of the Aztecs is a notable example, humans and gods lived in reciprocal dependence: if humans did not nourish the gods with sacrifices, the gods could not maintain the order of nature on which human life depends.

From this it is evident that to understand the essence of religion, what it has meant to humanity as a whole, one must consider not only those more advanced religions that flourish widely in the modern world but, likewise the primitive religions to which, in their vast and bewildering variety, humanity was attached for a very much longer period. If we limit our attention to religions of the type of Christianity, modern Judaism, Islam, and the more advanced sects of that great *melange* of religions known as Hinduism, we shall have a lamentably one-sided and inadequate view of the role that religion has played in human life.... One who considered only these higher religions, and particularly their more mystical side, might conclude that religion is above all a striving for union with God, when in reality this is only a special, late development. Religion is not even primarily an institution for the worship of God or the gods; its fundamental purpose ... is the protection of things precious to people—their life values—against perils that they could not adequately confront by ordinary, practical means. At a certain stage of intellectual development, people conceived that the mysterious processes that so strongly affected their welfare were controlled by supernatural powers, which were eventually personified as gods; [it seemed] prudent to cultivate the good will of these gods as a means of safeguarding whatever was dear.... Since these supernatural beings were as often envious as benign, it was of the utmost importance to placate them. Only after long ages did they become transformed into the supernal Being who was the personification of the highest values, the supreme object of the religious person's desire.

In the [pages] which follow, we shall consider in detail the basic elements of religion—appreciation, devoted care, and aspiration—examining their various expressions and tracing their development through the ages, from primitive to advanced religions. If in this study we fail to clear up, in definitive fashion, those main problems of religion, God and immortality, perhaps we shall learn something of value about ourselves, of our capacities and the direction our development has taken and may continue to follow. Since we are integral parts of the universe, composed of its substance and molded by its dominant process, insight into our own nature should help us to understand that of which we are parts—and not the least revealing parts. Such knowledge of the grand movement in which we are involved should in turn shed fresh light upon our destiny and give direction to our strivings.

In recent years there has been a growing endeavor to bring the various religions closer together by emphasizing what they have in common and trying to reconcile their divergent doctrines. Along with diverse historical and cultural backgrounds, these doctrinal differences are the great obstacles to union. The more one insists on intellectual honesty, the more capable one is of appreciating metaphysical distinctions, the more serious these obstacles are recognized to be. If reconciliation is our aim, the only promising course appears to be that of digging down to prime foundations to those elements in our human nature, which make us religious and building anew from this solid rock. Appreciation, devoted care, and aspiration are aspects of humanity's age-long effort to relate itself correctly to something greater and more enduring than humanity considered as a biological species. The true function of religion is to adjust us properly to the whole of which we are parts. Its tragedy is that, in the absence of adequate knowledge, it has been compelled to make guesses and assumptions about the things which transcend us, and all these assumptions or, to be liberal, imperfect glimpses of truth, have crystallized into hard dogmas; and the irreconcilability of these dogmas has stirred up fierce conflicts among us who should be united in a common endeavor, that of caring devotedly for the best that is in us and for the world which supports our bodies and enriches our spirits.

LIFE ASCENDING

(1985)

The Appreciative Mind

When we reflect upon the vast stretches of time and the countless generations involved, we may concede that a process which depends upon random mutations and rigorous selection in the struggle for existence might shape the human body to its present efficiency, the mind to its actual sharpness, for these advantages promote survival. The strong passions that so often distress us are what we might expect in an animal that for ages had to confront a fiercely competitive world. But when we ask how a process that resembles a game of chance, with dreadful penalties for the losers could have generated such qualities as love of beauty and truth, compassion, freedom, and, above all, the expansiveness of the human spirit, we are perplexed.

The more we ponder our spiritual resources, the more our wonder deepens. We can hardly avoid the conclusion that, stirring in the fecund depths of the Universe, an impulsion or urge that we can hardly conceive has been striving to lift Being to higher levels of awareness and value. Lacking omnipotence or foresight, this urge operates in the living world by the crude methods of organic evolution, blundering, taking unprofitable directions, but by ceaseless effort driving ever upward. The Universe, for all its immense age, might be compared to a youth with high aspirations, little experience, but indomitable persistence, who makes mistakes, suffers, but never ceases to try until attaining some goals. On this planet, we are the chief beneficiaries of this prolonged striving. The more we reflect upon the long ages, the immense effort, the struggle, and the suffering that were needed to make us what we are on a planet as richly endowed as Earth, the more the thoughtful, generous person appreciates and is grateful for this inestimable heritage. The gratefully appreciative mind stands at the apex of a long ascent from the first stirrings of sentience in living or, probably, lifeless matter.

We can hardly doubt that enjoyment is widely diffused over Earth. Despite occasional pains, sorrows, and frustrations, people enjoy their lives, as is evident from their reluctance to lose them. Animals, like children, seem to enjoy their food, their frolics, the companionship of others of their kind, their intervals of quiet repose. To believe that they do increases our estimate of the worth of Earth and makes us cherish it above such apparently lifeless planets as Venus, Jupiter, and all those more distant from the Sun. If plants find even the slightest satisfaction in their beneficent labor of photosynthesis in the sunshine, the value of our planet is greatly enhanced.

Although the presence of creatures that enjoy raises creation to a higher level and gives to Earth a significance that a lifeless planet could not have, this is not the highest, which, even in our limited experience, it can attain. As we know all too well, people can enjoy without an appreciation of the sources of their pleasures; and such unappreciative enjoyment appears to be widespread among animals less thoughtful than ourselves. Appreciation adds to unreflective enjoyment grateful acknowledgment of the sources of our benefits and a sense of obligation to them. Enjoyment may be purely sensual; appreciation arises in thoughtful minds. The sensual animal, human or otherwise, cares only for the sensation; the appreciative person is concerned for whatever enhances life. To the sensual animal, the sources of enjoyment are expendable; to the appreciative person, they are to be cherished and protected because they are intrinsically valuable. At whatever point in the evolution of life grateful appreciation may have arisen, it was a momentous advance for our planet.

Exploration of the contrasts between the enjoyment of pleasures and an appreciation of their sources should help us understand the nature of appreciation. We may enjoy without appreciation or appreciate without enjoyment. Although many enjoy music, only a few are prepared fully to appreciate an accomplished performance. For this it appears necessary to have studied music enough to recognize the technical excellence of the composition and the competence of the musicians and to reflect upon the long years of training and practice that were needed to develop their skills. To have tried to write well increases one's appreciation of a polished style. To know the plants and animals around us enhances our appreciation no less than our enjoyment of a walk through fields or woods.

To appreciate what we do not enjoy requires finer qualities of mind than to enjoy what we are incapable of appreciating. An unwanted gift from one who desires greatly to please us may stir sincere appreciation without pleasure; and we may be grateful to the hostess or host who, to honor us, has thoughtfully prepared a dish that we do not relish. Appreciation may follow rather than accompany enjoyment; perhaps only in later years do we adequately appreciate all that was done by parents or guardians to make our childhood happy and fruitful. Or we may appreciate experiences that, far from being pleasant, were actually painful. In maturity, we may be grateful for the discipline and punishments, distressing at the time, that have helped us become self-controlled, responsible men and women. The mountaineer and the explorer, all who with great effort and hardship have achieved cherished goals, appreciate experiences that were painful and exhausting.

A most important difference between appreciation and simple enjoyment involves the treatment of their objects. The thoughtless pleasure-seeker is frequently careless of the things that gratify, wastes food, squanders or misuses Earth's bounty, mistreats painstakingly made artifacts, litters the ground with trash, may even impair health and capacity to enjoy the sensations that are most craved. In contrast to the former, the appreciative person cares for whatever delights, is grateful for the land's largess, does not waste food or other resources, cherishes the products of human industry and art, leaves the spot where he or she picnics as lovely and unlittered as it was found or, perhaps, even cleaner, and is careful not to diminish the capacity to enjoy or appreciate by overindulgence. He or she values things for their own sakes, not merely for the pleasant sensations they can yield, always husbands, never squanders.

It is, above all, in relations with living creatures that the appreciative person differs profoundly from the unappreciative. The latter too often treats dependents and those who serve in any way as instruments or tools to administer to comfort, pleasure, or profit. He or she ignores any qualities not useful and discards, like a worn-out garment, the person or animal who is no longer serviceable. To the appreciative mind, animate creatures are an end in itself, with attributes and capacities additional to those directly useful. Their individuality is to be respected and they should never be used as feelingless tools. Not only is the appreciative person grateful for all services, including those that have been paid for, but, as far as possible, helps dependents develop whatever promising traits may be detected in them, even those of no direct value to himself or herself. Those who pursue and kill free animals for pleasure appear incapable of appreciating their beauty, the mystery of the senses that guide them over vast distances, their devotion to nests and young, their unexplored capacity to enjoy and to suffer. One who appreciates the marvelous organization of a living animal could never needlessly deprive it of its life, least of all for the base excitement of killing.

It is evident that, although often closely associated, enjoyment and appreciation are different mental states, the first dependent largely upon sensations, the second upon more advanced psychic qualities. Without pleasure, joy, contentment, satisfaction with existence, and all similar affective states that we may include in the broad category of enjoyment, appreciation could hardly have arisen. Grateful appreciation is a precious addition to unreflective enjoyment, lifting it to higher levels. It appears to be a relatively recent development, and it may be increasing in the more thoughtful moiety of mankind. Indeed, unless appreciation, and all that it implies, grows apace, our sources of enjoyment will dwindle.

Like enjoyment, appreciation is often associated with love, yet it is not quite the same, and it will further clarify the nature of appreciation if we examine its relation to love. Before we do this, it seems necessary to explain the sense in which we use a word that is applied to the most diverse situations, ranging from sensual attachment to spiritual devotion. The outstanding characteristic of love appears to be desire to be near its object, although not necessarily in bodily contact with it. When it is absent, we yearn for its presence; when it is near, our happiness or contentment increases. Even the thought of being long separated from what we deeply love is distressing. Moreover, generous love not only cherishes and protects but strives to enhance its object, to increase its happiness or attainments if a person, to make it more perfect or enduring if a lifeless thing. In its highest expressions, love is simultaneously altruistic and egoistic, for by serving and enhancing what we adore we increase our happiness and self-esteem.

Although love and appreciation often go hand in hand, either may flourish with little of the other, for the former may consist of much feeling and little thought, whereas the latter may arise from much thought and little feeling. Accordingly, in childhood we tend to love more than we appreciate; but, as we grow older, we often appreciate much that we can hardly be said to love. If to be distressed when separated and comforted when reunited is admitted to be the distinguishing feature of love, a little child, even an infant, dearly loves parents and home; but can hardly appreciate their good qualities, or their efforts to keep him or her healthy and happy, or all that is involved in maintaining a well-ordered household. A child may become so strongly attached to pets, dolls, or toy animals as to be inconsolable if they die or are lost, then after a few years may detect little to admire or appreciate in things once dearly loved. Children live in a fairyland where imagination and the affections predominate over the understanding of the sources of our satisfactions and delights that is the foundation of true appreciation.

As a generous mind matures, its love expands and deepens, but its appreciation spreads still more widely. We may appreciate the sterling qualities or good offices of people for whom we have a kindly regard that scarcely amounts to love, for we neither yearn for their presence nor are distressed by their continued absence. We may appreciate the benefits of a society that safeguards our freedom and produces what we need, yet prefer to dwell at a distance rather than in its midst. Although we may love one person, one home, or one animal with the deepest devotion, our love is often generalized instead of being centered upon particular objects or places. Ill at ease if not positively unhappy in a great city, one who loves wild nature yearns intensely to return to it, but many are the localities that can satisfy this longing. The bird lover is not so strongly attached to one individual bird, or even one species, that he or she cannot be happy almost anywhere that birds abound. Deprived of books, one who loves them feels a great void, yet the hunger for good reading may not be for one particular book or the works of one author. This expansion of interests and affections as the mind matures contrasts sharply with the condition of the child who is miserable when separated from the one home, the one mother, or even the one toy or pet that is the focus of love.

The first requisite of appreciation appears to be associative thought. Our thoughts must pass beyond the sensation or situation that brings us pleasure or satisfaction to its source or sources; to the person who gives us a gift or performs a service for us; to the society in which we dwell contentedly; to nature which sustains and enriches our lives. The farther from our actual situation that our thoughts can reach, the more profound our appreciation is likely to be. Where other essential attributes of the appreciative mind are not lacking, knowledge and the studious habit greatly increase appreciation. Thus, one familiar with the history of humanity's prolonged, bitter struggle to win and preserve freedom of thought and other civil liberties will most appreciate the institutions of a free country. One who knows how long it took to develop high-yielding, nutritious plants and agricultural practices that insure continued abundance will most appreciate his or her daily bread. The biologist or paleontologist who has followed the immensely long, hazardous course of life's evolution is best prepared to appreciate the human body and all its high capacities. None better than the astronomer who has widely surveyed the Universe can appreciate the uniqueness of our planet and its generous hospitality to life.

Imagination that can give life and color to dry facts may heighten appreciation. To imagine what it must be like to live under a despotic government or in a police state should sharpen our appreciation of a free society. To imagine the life of a chronic invalid or an incurable cripple should increase our appreciation of unimpaired health. The mind that can visualize, even vaguely, the long ages that were needed to prepare our planet for advanced forms of life, and to create its many vegetable and animal species that serve or delight us, will most appreciate its present benignity. And, even more than imagination, actual experience of poverty, sickness, a depressing environment, or persecution will make us more intensely appreciative of present prosperity, health, pleasant surroundings, and freedom.

Spontaneous sympathy is an important element in appreciation. Often simple, poorly educated people, whose happiness so largely depends upon their relations with those around them, have more of this quality than more cultivated minds, whose thoughts range far from homely, everyday occurrences. These simple people may be more keenly appreciative of what others do for them, for little gifts and attentions, while those with greater amplitude of thought and knowledge are better able to appreciate what nature or human history has contributed to our welfare. Sympathy with the person or animal who toils and sweats in our service increases our appreciation of what is done for us.

Scarcely anything contributes more to appreciation than aesthetic sensibility. One who delights in the majesty of trees, the loveliness of flowers, the song of birds, the grandeur of landscapes, and all the beauty of nature can hardly avoid appreciating them and his or her life amid them. Responsiveness to art, including painting, sculpture, and music, at least in its more complex forms, appears to be less spontaneous and widespread, more dependent upon training and cultural influences, than responsiveness to natural beauty. Appreciation of art may be an acquired rather than an innate capacity, but one that can greatly enhance life, especially of those who live in great cities, far removed from nature. Unfortunately, aesthetic sensibility, one of the greatest spiritual assets of those fortunately situated, can become a severe liability. If forced to dwell amid ugliness and disorder, the aesthetically sensitive person suffers more than one whose sensibilities are duller, so that, instead of appreciating existence, he or she may come to abhor it.

As haughtiness is a great enemy of appreciation and gratitude, so humility increases them. The person who believes that everything done for him or her, every gift, service, or distinction received is no more than what is strictly due to one of such high rank or outstanding merit is unlikely to be appreciative or grateful. Such an attitude may resemble that of a despot of old, who believed that subjects were created to serve the divine person, or that of certain citizens of modern welfare states, who are convinced that society owes them everything they cannot earn for themselves…Truly appreciative, grateful persons believe that they receive more than their due. This attitude of humble thankfulness may extend from life itself to the smallest gift or service; and, at whatever level it appears, it enhances appreciation and enriches life. We may reflect that we have done nothing to earn or deserve a well-endowed body and a perceptive mind but that they were bestowed on us as a free gift. At the other extreme, if we remember that the stranger of whom we ask a direction owes nothing to us, a courteous response will be more appreciated and will lighten our steps if the journey is long. If we never expect anything of anybody, we shall never be disappointed but will be more grateful for everything that is done for us. Even the return of a loan should make us thankful, for many a borrower has defaulted on the debt.

Although in moderation humility increases appreciation and sweetens life, like other virtues, it may be carried to an extreme that becomes a vice. To believe, as certain religious zealots have professed, that one is utterly worthless and deserving of nothing would destroy the appreciation of our splendid natural endowments that is the foundation of a truly religious attitude to life.

To be adequate and sincere, appreciation requires the generosity that recognizes the worth of those who help or serve us, the full value of what they give or do for us, and the excellence of everything in the natural world that supports or enriches our lives. We must not stint praise where it is due or fail to acknowledge merit where it oc-

curs. To undervalue those who are kind to us, the worth
of their services or gifts, or our delight in nature withers
appreciation.

Among the most insidious enemies of appreciation is
sensuality, which might be defined as excessive indulgence
of the contact senses, taste and touch. Sensuality makes
ends of means. It overindulges in eating and sex, which
are means for life's perpetuation, not its ends. Accordingly, sensuality is akin to miserliness, which makes the
possession of money an end rather than a means, and to
fanaticism, which intensifies its means while losing sight
of its ends. Sensuality narrows the range of enjoyment
and appreciation; by concentrating interest upon objects
and situations that yield pleasure by contact, it distracts
us from the far more numerous, varied, and elevating
things accessible to eyes and ears. Although on the whole
the contact senses tend to imprison the spirit in its body,
whereas sight and hearing lead it outward, so great is our
need to reach beyond ourselves that in the blind touch
becomes more acute and compensates in some measure
for the loss of vision—another example of the admirable
adaptability of the human organism.

Acquisitiveness also narrows interests and limits
appreciation. The number of things that we can possess
is only a small fraction of those that we can enjoy without owning them. To admire without coveting greatly
increases contentment. Instead of desiring the beautiful
things that we see, we should be grateful that they exist for our enjoyment without our laborious care. This
is eminently true of all the grand and lovely sights that
nature presents to us and, even, of many of our friends'

and neighbors' possessions—their gardens, the façades of their houses, the pictures on their walls. "The collector," wrote Anne Morrow Lindbergh, "walks with blinders on; he sees nothing but the prize...the acquisitive instinct is incompatible with true appreciation of beauty."

Appreciative persons are restrained, even mildly ascetic, in their enjoyments. Glut of sensual pleasure and luxurious ease are foreign to their nature. They seek experiences that expand their vision of the beauty and wonder of the larger world, rather than sensual delights that confine the mind to its body and may impair its capacity to perceive, understand, and gratefully appreciate. They hesitate to sacrifice to appetites or passions finely organized beings, with which they prefer to coexist harmoniously. They make no unnecessary demands upon the productivity of a planet already overburdened with its excessive progeny. They live simply and wholesomely, in order to remain, as long as they live, a sensitive organ of appreciation, grateful for their blessings, diffusing love and goodwill.

The fine fruit of appreciation is gratitude. We may distinguish between appreciation of the gift and gratitude to the giver, but the distinction is somewhat forced. We appreciate the motives that prompted the gift, the giver's friendship or goodwill for us. When we turn to nature, and all that it contributes to our welfare and delight, it is more difficult to separate gratitude from appreciation. The traditionally devout may thank God for nature's bounty; but one who regards nature as a self-created and self-regulated system, dependent upon nothing beyond itself, may be profoundly grateful for its manifold gifts to body and spirit. Gratitude and appreciation are two aspects of the same mental state. Appreciation is commonly grateful appreciation.

The appreciative mind is concerned for the welfare of whatever it loves or admires; it cherishes and cares. Of caring we may recognize two degrees, caring about and caring for or taking care of. Our ability to care for is limited by our energy and resources and confined to the few things that we can nurture or protect, but no bounds can be set to what we care about. We care for our own persons, our dependents, our homes and gardens, and, if we live close to wild nature, the tiny segment of the natural world over which we exercise some control. One deeply concerned for humanity's future, for the beauty and fruitfulness of the unique planet that bears us, cares about things too big to respond to unaided efforts. But, when enough people who care about great matters band together and make their voices heard, they may persuade nations to care for what they care about. Through caring, their grateful appreciation of nature's beauty may lead to effective measures for its protection. Through caring, appreciation of humanity's undeveloped potentialities may help produce a race more grateful for the privilege of living on so favored a planet and more responsible for its welfare. The most revealing aspect of our characters is what we care for and about, and this, in turn, is determined by what we appreciate. Our greatest claim to dignity, our most godlike attribute is our ability to appreciate and care intensely for or about everything fair and good that earth contains.

The capacity to appreciate, which so enriches our lives, is not without its darker side. As it watches helplessly the erosion and destruction of what it most values in the contemporary world, the appreciative mind can hardly avoid despondency. And even in the most favorable circumstances, as in a peaceful, prosperous world where humans lived contently in harmony with nature, the mutability of all things under the sun, the inevitable decay of what we most cherish, including our own powers, may induce spells of melancholy. Our greatest joys may be haunted by our greatest fears. As Keats perceived,

> *in the very temple of Delight*
> *Veil'd Melancholy has her sovran shrine.*

This brings us to the final outstanding attribute of the appreciative mind: it aspires. Not a world of misery and gloom, not a "vale of tears," is that best fitted to make us yearn for a happier existence. Such a world could hardly develop our most precious capacities or prepare us to imagine an excellent one. On the contrary, a world richly endowed, with much to enjoy and appreciate yet infected with strife, decay, and death, is most apt to foster our aspiration for life more prolonged, exempt from all the circumstances that distress us here.

Thoughtfulness, imagination, sympathy, aesthetic sensibility, humility, generosity, gratitude, freedom from sensuality and acquisitiveness, a great capacity to care for or about whatever it loves or admires, aspiration—these are the outstanding attributes of an appreciative mind. Although they depend in large measure upon innate qualities, they may be fostered by a judicious education. As these attributes grow, living becomes more rewarding and meaningful. Above all, the appreciative mind finds life significant. Boredom and vacuity are strangers to it, for, in a world so richly endowed as ours, it always finds something worthy of its attention, admiration, and devoted care. Born of passive contemplation, appreciation grows into satisfying activity.

An appreciative mind is an instrument on which the cosmos plays its tunes, a canvas on which the Universe paints its pictures. The whole course of cosmic evolution appears to have been directed toward forming such minds, which impart to Being its highest significance, and preparing a stage for their activities. By reverently and humbly acknowledging all that it owes to processes that long antedated its own existence, the appreciative mind becomes the holy or sacred mind. In simple natural piety, without theology or dogma, without making vast unprovable assumptions, it cultivates a truly religious attitude toward life and the cosmos to which it owes so much. Established upon immediate experience rather than upon ancient revelations or esoteric doctrines, its piety is unassailable by skeptic doubts. Grateful appreciation is the foundation of true religion.

HARMONY AND CONFLICT
IN THE LIVING WORLD

(2000)

Epilogue

Whether in the mind's eye we survey the solar system, its nine planets floating majestically around the Sun, satellites orbiting around most of them, every celestial body remaining in its own space in a system so balanced and orderly that it has endured for ages; or through a lens we admire the filigree tracery of a snow crystal; or we reflect how our brains spontaneously integrate in meaningful figures the myriad discrete vibrations that excite the retinas of our eyes—when we contemplate all this, and many similar facts, we become convinced that, from its physical foundations to its highest developments in the realm of mind and spirit, the universe is pervaded by a movement that arranges its constituents in patterns of increasing amplitude, complexity, and coherence: the cosmic process of harmonization. While bringing order out of chaos, harmonization enriches the cosmos with values, raising bare, meaningless existence to full, significant existence.

Most notably, it has covered Earth with graceful forms and bright colors and has equipped certain animals to see and enjoy all this beauty. We owe to this tireless process, the true constructive factor in the evolution of life, all that makes living precious to us. It is the source of our moral nature, the foundation of our felicity.

The growth of an organism of whatever kind is an excellent example of harmonization. By adding molecule to molecule, cell to cell, organ to organ, a plant or animal grows into an organism of great complexity. Its survival from day to day depends upon the integration of all its parts and functions into a coherent system of mutually supporting organs. Even a protozoan hardly visible to the naked eye is a very complex creature, with a nucleus and plastids performing diverse functions and, on the scale of the atoms of which it is composed, an organism of great amplitude. Large animals containing trillions of atoms and billions of cells, a great diversity of organs, all united by circulatory and nervous systems, are marvels of coherent, self-regulated complexity, such as we have not yet achieved in our most intricate machines. When we reflect upon the vast variety of organisms, the multitude of species, and the incalculable billions of individuals that cover our hospitable planet, each a product of harmonization, each a harmoniously integrated system, as it must be to remain alive and active, we recognize that on Earth harmonization has been a highly successful process.

We might expect that organisms made by the same constructive process, alike in so many ways that biologists have recognized, would, whatever their outward shape, form a harmonious community of living creatures; that the relations between all members of the immense assemblage would be as harmonious as the internal organization of each of them. Why does the process that has brought order and stability to the solar system, that aligns atoms and molecules in glittering crystals, that is active in the growth of every least organism, fail so dismally to bring concord into the relations of all these organisms? Why does the world process, instead of continuing steadily onward in the same direction, adding harmony to harmony at an ever-higher level of integration, abruptly falter or reverse its course when it passes beyond the individual organism? Why does a cosmic movement having as its only goal or purpose, as far as we can tell, the enrichment of Being with high values produce so strange a mixture of values and disvalues, of good and evil? When we contemplate all the strife, carnage, and disease that afflict the living world, the fear, hatred, rage, pain, and frustration that distress us and, apparently, other animals, we sometimes suspect that pain and sorrow outweigh joy, that the farther life advances, the more it suffers. Success in covering Earth with myriad living forms fails to bring harmony among these forms, to make the living world what, in view of the process that pervades it, we might expect it to become.

The causes of this failure are not far to seek. The primary cause is the insulation of organisms. The integuments indispensable for the protection of all the delicately balanced physiological processes that preserve life make of each organism an almost closed system, independent of other similar systems. Their insulation is not only physiological but psychic: just as the malfunction or disease of one does not directly affect the health of another, so the joys and sufferings of one creature are not felt by another; one animal can agonize and die without causing the least discomfort to another of the same or a different kind. Even humans with a developed language and other means of communication often feel remote from those closest to them. Difficulty of communication often seems to separate us by interplanetary distances not only from animals of other species, including the domestic mammals and birds most intimately associated with us, but frequently from other humans all without the admirable arrangement that keeps every planet in its course, never clashing with another.

Thus, physiological and psychic insulation makes it possible for one creature to exploit, maim, torture, or kill another without physical or mental consequences distressful to itself. Add to this the excessive abundance of organisms, which throws them into relentless competition for almost everything they need to sustain life and to reproduce, and we have the stage set for all the miseries that creatures inflict upon one another day after day and everywhere, which in aggregate far exceed all that the living world suffers from the intermittent and local excesses of lifeless nature, such as earthquakes, volcanic eruptions, hurricanes, and floods. Life's great misfortune is that evolution, dependent upon random genetic mutations that are more often harmful than beneficial, is a process in which quality too frequently wages a losing battle against quantity. Although the growth of an organism is a mode of harmonization, the organism's form and function are determined by its genetic endowment.

Harmonization arranges the genes in the most coherent pattern they are capable of assuming, but it can operate only with the materials available to it.

The failure of harmonization's success in covering Earth with abundant life is not absolute, as everyone who has experienced happiness and true values should bear witness. In the previous sections, we noticed some of the ways in which animals cooperate to increase the safety or enhance the quality of their lives. Noteworthy are the foraging flocks of mixed species of birds, the relations between cleaner fish and their clients, the adoption of lost or orphaned young by birds and mammals, and the concord that prevails in groups of cooperatively breeding birds. Especially significant are the mutually beneficial interactions of plants and the animals that pollinate their flowers or disperse their seeds in return for food in the form of nectar or fruits. Harmonious associations can arise among individuals of the same species, of different genera or orders, of different zoological classes of animals, and even between animals and plants.

In our more optimistic moods, we may take peaceful associations as indicative of the direction in which the living world is moving, to make them more common in future ages, perhaps, if all goes well, to the virtual elimination of strife. Nevertheless, it remains true that in the present age competition and merciless exploitation are much more frequent in the animal kingdom than is harmonious cooperation. Conflict and predatory violence are so widespread and conspicuous that people have long been familiar with this harsh aspect of nature; many of the cooperative associations were unknown until, in recent times, the patient observations of naturalists disclosed them—which makes it appear probable that many more remain to be discovered.

In many ways, the most successful product of evolution and harmonization is humankind. In an exceptionally well-endowed and enduring body, well equipped with sensory organs, the human being has a large brain and an active mind. These advantages, coupled with hands that are the most versatile executive organs in the animal kingdom, enable us to fill our needs and modify our environment to our own advantage as no other animal can; to spread over every habitable region of Earth and to become by far the most abundant large terrestrial animal. Despite all these advantages, it appears that we are rushing headlong to the failure of our success, which will not be far distant if we do not promptly reverse our course. By our soaring billions, we are overexploiting the planet's productivity, devastating the environment, polluting air and soil and water. And as humans become too abundant, their average quality decreases, as is evident from the mounting crime rate, the increasing addiction to stupefying drugs, and the greater fecundity of the least competent and responsible moiety of the population.

The addition of humans to the long list of extinct animals would be lamentable because people bring to the living world qualities otherwise rare or lacking: ability to appreciate its beauty; to seek knowledge and understanding; to care devotedly and unselfishly for Earth and everything good and lovable that it contains; to feel compassion for fellow creatures of all kinds; and to be grateful for manifold blessings—all of which are attributes very unequally developed among humans.

What is needed to save humankind from self-destruction is common knowledge: population must be stabilized or, preferably, reduced by restricting the birthrate; the environment must be protected. The burning question is whether an organism physiologically and psychically insulated from all others can transcend its limiting integument to feel itself part of an encompassing whole on which its own prosperity depends; to recognize its responsibility to this whole; to feel instinctive or imaginative sympathy for other creatures; to restrain its appetites and dominate its passions in order to live more harmoniously with others. We know that some individuals are capable of cultivating this wider vision and living in its light. If a larger proportion of humanity could attain this spiritual level and the generosity that corresponds to it, success might follow success, directly for humankind, indirectly for a large segment of the living world.

An augury for success is found in the history of human intellectual development. Over the ages, we have learned not only to use our facile hands for ever more complex creative tasks but also to employ our restless minds for deeper understanding of nature. The superstitions that filled, and too often oppressed, the minds of our ancestors have, with the growth of philosophy and science, been largely dispelled from the thoughts of the more enlightened of our contemporaries, although unfortunately they linger stubbornly in a large part of humanity. Our success in clarifying our thoughts and combating many of the diseases that afflicted our progenitors should encourage us to tackle more resolutely the immense and yearly growing problems that confront humanity but are not intrinsically insoluble. What is lacking is the foresight and the will to make Earth a fit abode for the children that we beget in excessive numbers, for their remote descendants, and for the many creatures that might dwell compatibly with them.

OTHER BOOKS BY ALEXANDER SKUTCH

- *LIFE HISTORIES OF CENTRAL AMERICAN HIGHLAND BIRDS*
  (Berkeley: University of California Press, 1954;
  Cambridge, Mass.: Nuttal Ornithological Club, 1967)

- *THE GOLDEN CORE OF RELIGION*
  (Aberdeen, Scotland: Aberdeen University Press, 1970)

- *A NATURALIST IN COSTA RICA*
  (Gainesville: University Press of Florida, 1971)

- *LIFE OF THE HUMMINGBIRD*
  (New York: Crown Publishers, 1973)

- *A BIRD WATCHER'S ADVENTURES IN TROPICAL AMERICA*
  (Austin: University of Texas Press, 1977)

- *THE IMPERATIVE CALL: A NATURALIST'S QUEST IN
  TEMPERATE AND TROPICAL AMERICA*
  (Gainesville: University Press of Florida, 1971)

- *A NATURALIST ON A TROPICAL FARM*
  (Berkeley: University of California Press, 1980)

- *NEW STUDIES OF TROPICAL AMERICAN BIRDS*
  (Cambridge, Mass.: Nuttal Ornithological Club, 1981)

- *BIRDS OF TROPICAL AMERICA*
  (Austin: University of Texas Press, 1983)

❧ *NATURE THROUGH TROPICAL WINDOWS*
(Berkeley: University of California Press, 1983)

❧ *LIFE ASCENDING*
(Austin: University of Texas Press, 1985)

❧ *LIFE OF THE WOODPECKER*
(Ithaca, N.Y.: Cornell University Press, 1985)

❧ *HELPERS AT BIRDS' NESTS: A WORLDWIDE SURVEY OF COOPERATIVE BREEDING AND RELATED BEHAVIOR*
(Iowa City: University of Iowa Press, 1987)

❧ *A NATURALIST AMID TROPICAL SPLENDOR*
(Iowa City: University of Iowa Press, 1987)

❧ *BIRDS ASLEEP*
(Austin: University of Texas Press, 1989)

❧ *LIFE OF THE TANAGER*
(Ithaca, N.Y.: Comstock Publishing Associates, 1989)

❧ *A GUIDE TO THE BIRDS OF COSTA RICA* [with F. Gary Stiles]
(Ithaca, N.Y.: Cornell University Press, 1991)

❧ *LIFE OF THE PIGEON*
(Ithaca, N.Y.: Comstock Publishing Associates, 1991)

❧ *ORIGINS OF NATURE'S BEAUTY*
(Austin: University of Texas Press, 1992)

❧ *THE MINDS OF BIRDS*
(College Station: Texas A&M University Press, 1996)

❧ *ORIOLES, BLACKBIRDS, AND THEIR KIN*
(Tucson: University of Arizona Press, 1996)

❧ *ANTBIRDS AND OVENBIRDS: THEIR LIVES AND HOMES*
(Austin: University of Texas Press, 1996)

❧ *LIFE OF THE FLYCATCHER*
(Norman: University of Oklahoma Press, 1997)

❧ *TROGONS, LAUGHING FALCONS, AND OTHER NEOTROPICAL BIRDS*
(College Station: Texas A&M University Press, 1999)

❧ *HARMONY AND CONFLICT IN THE LIVING WORLD*
(Norman: University of Oklahoma Press, 2000)

06.018

ALEXANDER SKUTCH:
AN APPRECIATION